The Night of the Old South Ball

The Night of the Old South Ball

And Other Essays and Fables

by

Edwin M. Yoder, Jr.

Yoknapatawpha Press
Oxford, Mississippi

Published by Yoknapatawpha Press,
P.O. Box 248, Oxford, MS 38655

ISBN 0-916242-53-6   LC Catalog Card Number 84-50851

Printed in the United States of America
Book design by Lawrence Wells

For My Parents

Contents

II. AMERICAN PORTRAITS

III. MYTH AND PERSPECTIVE

IV. LITERARY FOOTNOTES

Foreword

IT MAY BE good form—certainly it is standard—to apologize for reprinting one's old pieces. I blush to say, however, that I am rather fond of some of the fugitives from wastebasket and fish market that follow. Flawed as they are, often wearing telltale marks of the speed with which I wrote them, they remain as hard to dislike as one's own children.

All but the most impersonal writing is in some ways an act of vanity anyway; it might as well be admitted. Unless he writes for himself as an audience of one—and most writers surely begin with that audience—an essayist assumes that what he says and how he says it will interest somebody, somewhere.

I have resisted the temptation to compound vanity by making fussy revisions. Late in life the novelist Henry James, one of my literary heroes, undertook a monumental and exhaustive revision of all his novels for the famous New York Edition. But he was James and I am not. He was a great artist and I am only a newspaperman and very amateur historian. Among the modest virtues of journalism, moreover, is that it carries the flavor of a time, an issue or a mood.

Some turns of language or phrase—"Negro," for instance, where "black" is now usual—sound a bit awkward and might have been updated—but weren't. Some old castings of thought, or argument, cry aloud for what Lillian Hellman, borrowing from the Renaissance painters, calls "pentimento." It is a wonderful word, literally meaning "repentence"; and as applied to painting it was the act of reconsidering, by painting over, an earlier image.

But once begun where might pentimento end, and what indeed would be the point of it? I have quietly corrected some errors of fact, though some probably remain; and I have brushed up a few glaring inelegances. But 99 per cent of these children are called in from the street as they first were sent out to play, a bit the worse for time's wear but dressed as they were.

I have been in one or another form of commentary journalism, now, for quite a long time: Since those rollicking student days in Chapel Hill in the 1950s which are described, I hope not too flippantly, in my piece "Unquiet Olympus." All along, I have tried to learn from the masters of the essay form, from Mencken to Orwell, from Bertrand Russell to G. K. Chesterton. If their example has misfired they are not to blame, but I cannot fail to acknowledge the debt.

Essay journalism, I believe, earns its keep by imparting interesting information, or a fresh view, or some amiable blend of both. My own magpie's relish for facts may be hereditary in one who comes from a long line of schoolmasters. In excess it can be a vice, and I often find myself battling against the pendantic urge. For the scattered signs of some lost battles, I apologize.

Finally, I have been lucky in friends, editors and associates. My wife Jane Warwick Yoder is the only critical genius I know well. Eve Auchincloss, as an editor of Book World, was a generous editor and correspondent for a decade or more. William Snider in Greensboro and James Bellows in Washington knew how to edit without pencils. My colleagues James Ross, Jonathan Yardley, Perry Morgan, Woody West and Jeffrey Frank, in North Carolina and in Washington, did me many favors. I am grateful to Larry and Dean Faulkner Wells for inviting me to make this collection, and to my dear friend Willie Morris for writing the introduction. To them and to many other friends and colleagues who have written or spoken in kindly ways about my work over the years I owe more than I can repay.

E.M.Y.
Alexandria, Va.
May 23, 1984.

Introduction
by
Willie Morris

I FIRST LEARNED of Edwin M. Yoder, Jr. in the fall of
'55, when we were twenty-one. He was the editor of *The Daily
Tar Heel* at the University of North Carolina, I of *The Daily
Texan* at the University of Texas. I began to notice his brilliant,
incisive pieces, the best in college journalism of that era. We
started a correspondence which intensified when each of us got
into considerable trouble as student editors. I could not have
known then that this was the inception of a lifelong friendship,
and in a sense collaboration, which would deepen from boyhood
into middle-age.

We both won scholarships that would take us to Oxford
University. We met in the lobby of the Taft Hotel in New York
City the day before we were to sail with the rest of our contem-
poraries to England, and this marked the beginning of an un-
hurried, continuing conversation only temporarily interrupted
over the years, one which would resume after the absences
wherever it happened to have left off, often in the middle of a
sentence. The next morning a handsome Texas girl in a fur coat
came on board *The Flandre* and left Ed Yoder and me two bottles
of Jack Daniels'. "Save them for the foggy days in London at
Christmas," she said. With assistance from Ooms of Amherst,
Selig of Yale, and Schwartz of South Dakota, the sour mash was
gone before we reached the Statue of Liberty.

Yoder read Philosophy-Politics-and-Economics at Jesus
College. ("I have a friend in Jesus" naturally became our iden-
tification of his indwelling whereabouts.) He was a brilliant student, a loyal comrade, a sensitive and observant young man with
an eye and an ear cocked to the nuance and resonance of the
haunted European culture. As one's friend he was remarkably
kind, whimsical, and supportive, and never for a moment mundane or predictable. It did not take one long to appreciate his
intellectual and emotional honesty, his catholicity of interests
and education, his irreverence before the icons, his pristine Old
Catawba fun.

Many were the evenings we shared brandy and cigars with

xii

the intrepid Warden of Rhodes House, who had been General Montgomery's chief-of-intelligence during World War II and who once told Ed Yoder and me when we inquired of his politics: "I'm a right-wing Tory, which I understand is considerably farther to the left than anything you have in the United States." In London on the term breaks we were inexorably drawn to the Strangers' Gallery of the House of Commons, overlooking the benches where Winston Churchill in his dotage sometimes dozed on a back row. There was Paris in April (the author describes with vivid accuracy and pathos in these pages the doomed odyssey of a 1927 Buick which a cadre of us christened "The John Foster Dulles"), Scandinavia and Germany in the summer, and the following year a large Victorian manse in north Oxford across the street from T. E. Lawrence's boyhood home. Here Yoder lived in the minuscule garret surrounded by mountains of books and swirls of pipe smoke, into which he solicitously welcomed his fiancee, the ineffable Jane Warwick of Knoxville and Chapel Hill, who brought us care packages and the news from Eisenhower's America and the clean, bittersweet remembrance of all the girls we had left behind.

We learned early of Ed Yoder's abiding affection for his beloved North Carolina. His hometown was Mebane in the rolling piedmont hills; some of the most poignant and affecting words in this volume are of that hamlet and that state, and of his returning there from across time and the distances. There was his native Presbyterian church—"microcosm of a tight-knit society from which no secrets could be, or were, hid"—and the hideaway vacation spot on the Carolina shore at Wrightsville, where village fathers "took a squinty view of innovation." And in the memorable essay " 'Toiling on the Mound' at Mill Creek," dare I reveal that the indefatigable Ripley, who walked twelve men in a row and whose history teacher-coach lectured on the benevolent *depots,* may have been Yoder himself, who once confessed to us at a sidewalk cafe on the Ile St. Louis that he threw his arm away in one inning's work against Haw River? The autobiographical strain, though adroitly disguised, seems obvious here.

Yet everything for Yoder in those European years seemed to come back to Chapel Hill—his "Unquiet Olympus"—and his memories of "this enduringly lovely and beguiling place" are a skein which run through his pages. There is the palpable presence of Thomas Wolfe, the example of brave and intriguing figures like Frank Graham and Phillips Russell, the nocturnal revelries and the eccentricities of noble professors, the evocation of his friend Altgeld—the sartorial Confederate general who returns naked from the Old South Ball—as well as the indelible experiences on *The Daily Tar Heel*. Just as Chapel Hill was the matrix of Yoder's past, I remember, too, from Oxford the individuals he admired, and does now with rare eloquence and insight in these essays: Shakespeare, Macaulay, John Stuart Mill, Thomas Jefferson, H. L. Mencken, Jonathan Daniels, Ralph McGill, William Faulkner, C. Vann Woodward, William Styron, not to mention the anonymous and self-effacing stylists who translated the King James *Bible*.

After his European years, there was a stint in the Air Force, which provided him with his affectionate essay on his harassed country-boy sergeant, his time with *The Charlotte News* and the *Greensboro Daily News,* his tenure on the *Washington Star* where in 1979 he won a long-overdue Pulitzer, and now his position as a national columnist for the *Washington Post* syndicate.

In *The Night of the Old South Ball* Yoder takes his superlative talents among the ebb and flow of the human events of his lifetime. He has achieved here a mastery over an extraordinarily wide range of topics which to me demonstrates one of the most eclectic minds in contemporary America. His commentary and satire on people and places, his portraits of politicians, statesmen, novelists, poets, journalists, teachers, his elegant and candid historical pieces, his reverence for the past and for the memory of youth—all these are suffused with his own exacting values and ironic wit and place him indisputably in the front rank of our essayists.

To read Yoder in these pages is to derive a sense of the great variety of American life and landscape, of the achievements and foibles of its citizenry, and of the strengths and failings which emanate from the union of such disparateness and complexity. He handles all of it with equal felicity and with a voice of exceeding good humor and common sense—the clear, unintimidated voice of the scholar-turned-journalist. "The world of sensibility," he writes, "far from being the esoteric playground of the happy few, is actually a democracy, accessible to anyone of reasonable intelligence and feeling with the will to train and use them." The words in this book suggest him to be a devotee of the Enlightenment; he loves the reasonableness of the Eighteenth Century. Yoder in the Twentieth Century could be likened to a lone and intrepid marathon athlete of old strolling observantly through the maelstrom of a Super Bowl goal-line stand.

Invariably one of his favorite subjects is the decline and fall of the English language, particularly in the era of television— "silencer of conversation," he has written elsewhere—"brutal processor of mass-minded sensibilities." His gift and passion for clean, flexible language are everywhere evident in this collection, and the reader may inevitably put these in counterpoise to, let us say, the unfortunate Spiro Agnew's prose indulgences as described in "Spiro's Chocolate Factory": "He is nearly always off-key by a half to a quarter tone...like a monotone with a passion for singing Bach arias."

He is profoundly involved, too, in defining his native South in its turbulent generation of change. "I was more comfortable," he writes, "with 'the South,' for all its faults, than I am with 'the Sunbelt,' with all its vulgar energy." His essay on W. J. Cash, for instance, written in the fateful year 1964, is nothing less than prophetic. Never one for myth, including the accumulated myths of his region, he cuts through the sham and the placid exteriors of the historic South to reveal the wastes and hypocrisies—and also the distinctions and nobilities. His own complex love and ambivalence about being a Southern-American in the modern day give this book much of its force and pathos.

Having dwelled and labored for some years in Washington, D.C., Ed Yoder views his "Imperial City on the Potomac" with trenchant realism, yet also with an ironic and bemused affection. "There are layers of governmental specialization here," he writes, "rivalling medieval refinements of speculative theology." Nowhere are his rapier thrusts more efficacious (his preference forever being for the humiliating trickle of blood over the fatal axe or sword) than in his treatment of the persistent rivalries and hostilities between our political capital and our cultural capital—Washington vs. New York City—and he leaves scant doubt that he chooses the ebulliently byzantine and peculiarly American Potomac mind to certain intellectualized and case-hardened aspects of the Manhattan one. I wish to take him seriously when he proposes a New York embassy on Massachusetts Avenue.

On political writing he asks for precision and economy: " 'Populist,' I surmise, can mean not only any political insurgent of popular appeal, but racist, anti-Semite, xenophobe, rabble-rouser, demagogue, utility-baiter, or rustic." He applauds Jimmy Carter's insistence on probing the serious question of America's self-indulgence, and sees his Presidency as "an interval, a pause, between the disintegrating hopes of the 1950s and 1960s and the stark reaction that came with Reagan." Yet Carter lacked "the epic sense and the streak of naughtiness that may be essential to great public men." Does the author's ambivalence toward Carter derive from a Southerner's pride and protectiveness but also disappointment at a lost chance?

Of all Yoder's gifts, perhaps the most distinctive is his unwavering sense of the humanistic tradition and of the complexity of the past. To understand him, I learned years ago, one must perceive the ineluctible hold which history has on him—history in its majesty and sweep, its responsibility and thrall. "Most of the best narrative history in English," he writes, "has been the work of amateurs." History is part of him.

The Night of the Old South Ball is, like all writing that comes from the soul, a reflection of a man. Edwin M. Yoder, Jr. reveals himself as a man passionately involved in the events of his day, but who eternally sees them from the deeper perspective of time passing. "Ours is an age," he once wrote, "given to formulas, jargons, ideologies, systems, attitudes, stereotypes, all of them ways of evading human experience and guarding one against the task of coming to terms with it." His courageous eye, civilized wit, and compassionate heart are part of our common good. My old friend has not changed much since the distant Oxford days—merely deepened.

I. People, Language, Places

The Night of the Old South Ball

ON THESE CRISP September days I find myself recalling the misadventures of my freshman roommate—Altgeld, let us call him—who in the autumn of 1952 entered into the mystic bonds of the Kappa Alpha Order.

I am told that Greek letter societies no longer flourish as they did, which from the academic or democratic point of view may not be amiss. But that is no gain for color or plumage. Having recently packed a freshman daughter off to college with a dozen pairs of faded blue jeans and shirts to match, I surmise that their decline has something to do with the gypsy style affected by the studentry. It leaves little room for the sartorial rivalries that once absorbed fraternity row.

My friend Altgeld, as we have agreed to call him, was above all a fastidious dresser, a clothes horse, whose wardrobe was *comme il faut* for every fraternal occasion. There were well-fitted tweed jackets (single vent), three-button collars frayed just so, striped ties, pleatless flannel or khaki trousers neatly (and pointlessly) belted in the rear. His lengthier toilets signaled very special events at the KA house.

KA, mind you, had not seemed Altgeld's inevitable berth. At the seat of higher learning of which I write, there was a niche for every seeker of brotherhood. But not all niches were equal. There were subtle gradations of tone and splendor, the whole was distinctly hierarchical. One lodge abounded in lacrosse-playing Marylanders, whose long Sabbath slumbers after festive evenings even the strains of the processional hymn at the Episcopal church across the street could not disturb. Another attracted native sons of good old families, others either Southern lads from Northern prep schools, or Northern lads from Southern ones.

KA, for its part, was self-consciously Southern. From above the chimney piece, General Lee's portrait looked benignly down, as did the crest with its chivalric legend: *Dieu et les dames*. Since

Altgeld was of Pennsylvania ancestry, his reception there was a minor mystery. Perhaps there was an obscure Copperhead in the family tree.

Certainly Altgeld's tailoring added a Solomonic glory to the Order's affairs—or would have, but for what I must call his sartorial nemesis.

I swear, if Altgeld had put on a suit of armor, a hole would have appeared in it spontaneously. One Saturday before a football game, a resident of the hall, after some early celebration, took a switch-blade knife to Altgeld's splendid porkpie hat (in school colors) and left little of it but a tattered sun-visor. Another evening, before a big mixer with the best campus sorority, Altgeld fell to an exultant bout of Indian-wrestling in a nearby room and popped most of the front buttons off a new shirt. Attempting a preliminary drink of wine from a goatskin one night before a formal dance, Altgeld sprayed himself deep purple.

Now the great event of the year for the KAs was the Old South Ball, a grand affair much resembling a pre-war scene at Tara. The girls dressed like Scarlett O'Hara, while all the brothers, in rented Confederate gray, played variations on Ashley Wilkes. The approach of this affair was heralded for weeks by sprouting whiskers, which then—this was before campuses had so many "tomentose individuals," in Mr. Agnew's memorable phrase—was quite noticeable.

On the appointed evening Altgeld looked splendid indeed in his scraggly goatee and rented general's uniform, complete with epaulettes and ceremonial sword. The ball was to be held safely distant from the prying eye of authority, at a hotel in a neighboring city 10 miles away, and as the hour approached everyone wondered what awful things would happen to the general's uniform before Altgeld left. Would he tumble down the dormitory stairwell and break the sword? Would he rip the tunic *en passant* upon an unseen nail? Perhaps not; it seemed his lucky night. At exactly 7 p.m., the general left triumphantly for the ball, every button in place, his braided hat in one hand and an imposing jug of bourbon in the other.

It was the slamming of a taxicab door, attended by loud oaths, that rather startlingly heralded the general's return at 4 a.m. Beneath the window, the streetlight dimly disclosed a now swordless figure clad only in undershorts, paying $12 for the ride and rather the worse for the jug of bourbon.

But where was the uniform? The ballroom, as we later pieced the story together, had been too hot and the sword awkward for dancing. At some early hour of the morning, the make-believe warriors and their ladies had made their way to the hotel's indoor pool. Only, after this refreshing interlude General Altgeld's Civil War finery was not to be found—nor has it been, so far as I know, to this day. Nor was his date or his ride home. This ultimate sartorial disaster cost Altgeld $12 for the cab ride, and $75 to the rental shop.

When I left the room at 10 the next morning, the general lay abed in deep sleep, snoring heavily, and looking altogether peaceful even in ultimate defeat. But there was no doubt about it. The general had been failed by both God and women.

—*September 29, 1977*

Closet Loyalist

I am perhaps the only American of my acquaintance who is not altogether sure he would have rebelled againt George III in 1776—or at least the only one who admits it. As I reflect on this confession, so inopportune in the Bicentennial year, I think my doubts can be traced to several factors, personal and historical.

My paternal ancestors, who settled peacefully in central North Carolina about a quarter century before the Edenton Tea Party—that state's outstanding gesture of impudence against King George III—were stolid Palatine and Swiss Germans who relished freedom of worship and, so far as I know, took no active interest in imperial British disputes.

Had it occurred to any of them to disturb the king's peace as it then prevailed? I doubt it. I suspect that those who enlisted to fight Banastre Tarleton's red-coated cavalry (as some later did) were unangered by crown policy, and took arms against the king for personal reasons having little to do with the high-flown slogans of Jefferson and Thomas Paine.

Loyalism was not lacking in the Southern colonies. A dear friend of mine had a trip to Williamsburg utterly spoiled, some years ago, when he discovered a unit in Cornwallis's order of battle at Yorktown labeled "North Carolina volunteers." The discovery humiliated him. It shouldn't have.

One sign that this country is coming of age, in the Bicentennial year, is that the American loyalists, in their variety, are getting a sympathetic look from historians. Bernard Baylin's

4

study of Gov. Thomas Hutchinson of Massachusetts, one of the best of American biographies,won a National Book Award last year. Prof. Robert McC. Calhoon's detailed and readable inquiry, *The Loyalists in Revolutionary America,* demolished the simplistic notion that there was a prototype "loyalist," an elitist scoundrel who preferred royalism to republicanism.

Which brings me, belatedly, to the cause of this reflection: a recent London dispatch from Lloyd Timberlake of Reuters, the British news agency, about the so-called Loyalist Papers project. This is a collaborative transatlantic project to learn more of those historic losers, the American loyalists. Mr. Timberlake's far-fetched claim is that the loyalist story goes "untold in America mainly because Americans are slightly embarrassed by the large numbers of colonists who backed the 'wrong side.'" Mr. Timberlake compounds this silliness by suggesting that, as to the loyalists, "there is little money available for research" because "most people feel…that the subject is best forgotten."

Mr. Timberlake may just be plucking a few eagle feathers for the fun of it, but if he's serious, this much should be said: It is more accurate to say that Americans, taken in the mass, are a peculiarly unhistorical people. They forget easily and indiscriminately not only about loyalists but about most figures now dead and gone. Embarrassment of the sort felt by my friend as he beheld the cyclorama at Yorktown figures only marginally.

It is entirely healthy, in any case, that the losers as well as the winners of the American Revolution be studied, their stories contemplated, in the Bicentennial year. Those of us who aren't historians can profit from the study of loyalists as well as of "patriots."

We stand to gain two qualities of mind that seem especially lacking in us—a sense of the complexity of the past and of how hard it is to pass easy moral judgment on the characters and motives that shaped it. And we might gain a greater appreciation of principled devotion to a losing cause. It is much needed.

The pop-gurus of American life saturate us with victor-worship. They tell us that it is disgraceful to lose, never so much as reaching the question of whether causes are ever worth losing in. This is a subtlety well beyond the ken of the Lombardian ethic.

Of course, victors usually write the history books, so that given our conditioning in the victor's frame of mind, it requires an effort of will to imagine how so many could have been of contrary mind.

The history of the American loyalists—the kind of history

we are getting from Bernard Baylin and Robert Calhoon anyway—teaches the value of the tragic sense in understanding the
past: How it was, for instance, that the upright and conscien-
tious Thomas Hutchinson of Massachusetts failed, despite desperate efforts, to mediate the feud between his fellow Bostonians
and Lord North's government. Of course there were heroes and
rascals aplenty, in both camps. But to be embarrassed by the
recollection of loyalism?

Rubbish, Mr. Timberlake of Reuters.

—January 22, 1976

My Own Peanut Patch

There was a picture in the papers the other day that
caught, as weightier items could not, the eye of a returning
vacationer.

It showed President Carter and his brother Billy in a field
in Plains, examining most intently the health of their growing
peanuts. The President, clad in his country attire and bent nearly double, has his fingers well out of sight in the nourishing
Georgia soil. The glare intimates that the day was not cool. The
President, we are told, is on a "brief vacation."

It is the lot of presidents to be lured into poses for lurking
photographers. Perhaps one had just shouted, "Mr. President,
how about bending over to look at the peanut roots?" Perhaps.
I prefer to think not. The scene has a look of spontaneity and
repose. Here, one assures oneself, is a man doing something he
likes, something he does well, something that puts captains and
kings far from his mind, something familiar and restorative. If
it's also good for the peanut crop, so much the better.

We are all, I think, defined by our vacations. They disclose
a corner of the soul. They do not choose us, as work often does.
We choose them.

My own peanut patch, so to say, is the coast of my beloved
North Carolina. There, mere hours and a few hundred miles
ago, a photographer would have caught me in a posture far less
edifying than the President's, sprawled on the sand with a con-
soling drink and staring vaguely off in the direction of Africa.

6

At intervals, someone goes on what we call "a mission of mercy," that is, back to the cottage for cold beer.

In the middle distance, under a brilliant noonday sun, there is from time to time the loud thud of a starter's gun. It scatters into liquid motion—the most graceful, I think, on earth—a lazily circling crowd of sailboats. They race, close hauled, for a certain bobbing buoy.

Beside me, cast aside in the clutter of oils and lotions and towels that mark our changeless little outpost, is a new book on a great poet. Its complexities simply won't go down on top of the witty delicacies of Nancy Mitford's novels, which all of us have been reading with roars of laughter. What is *The Waste Land,* on such a day, after the eccentricities of Uncle Matthew Radlett?

If one tires of watching the sailboats at sea, there are the promenading walkers and joggers along the edge of the surf to watch and discuss. Some are sleek and beautiful, and carry themselves like a Botticelli painting suddenly animated. Others are mauled and thickened by devouring time. It is the least predictable of parades.

After hours of broiling here, in defiance of the best medical advice, one may sail a bit in the sound, or run a few miles to watch the tidal currents in the inlet, or play a few sets of tennis, or simply retire to shelter for corned-beef sandwiches that would be edible nowhere else. Or one may do nothing—one may merely lie still. There are no surprises, no new scenes or faces or names, no new sensations, and best of all, by an ancient and rigidly enforced rule, no newspapers or newscasts.

One enters deeply upon that spell so eloquently described, a few years ago, by my distinguished colleague, Mr. Eric Sevareid. "We shall sit quietly in a rocking chair," he said of an impending vacation, "and then after a week we shall slowly begin to rock."

Those whose notions of vacation involve the scaling of mountains, or the exploration of exciting new scenes, not to mention pilgrimages to "ferne halwes, couthe in sondry londes," scorn the scene I describe. They do not approve it. I am not sure that I entirely approve it either. But approval and disapproval are functions of the super-ego, and the aim of this yearly retreat is to gag its hectoring voice and extinguish all volition.

Of course, it is an insidious business to retreat so far from all that is alleged to be important, significant, dutiful, newsworthy, historic, diligent and dull. After a few days one begins to hear, indeed, the siren songs against whose lure the sailors in *The Odyssey* were bound to their masts. After a fortnight or

7

so, one wonders if the way back to work will be found or, if found, worth taking. Somehow it usually is.

But there is no peanut crop to show for the time away.

—August 11, 1977

Mr. Carter in Washington

More than once I have advised British officials going out to Washington not to waste time on Bryce or other authorities but to read Saint-Simon or Proust. For they are going out to a court, the court of the White House and the other rival lesser courts.—D. W. Brogan, "The Unfinished City."

It is often said that Washington is out of touch with the country. But as Eric Sevareid has observed, the country is sometimes out of touch with Washington, too. Both misapprehensions have interesting, sometimes painful, consequences.

Jimmy Carter's miscalculation, looking back now on his sudden rise and fall, was probably of the second sort. He keyed his 1976 campaign to the country's outrage with Washington—or the Washington it imagined: a city remote, self-serving and sometimes cruel. His would be, he said, a government as "loving and compassionate" as the people. Thinking, no doubt, of the Watergate scandal and the furtiveness that sometimes marked the Vietnam misadventure, he promised never to lie, forgetting that an occasional deception, while never desirable, may become a necessary way of avoiding larger evils. He drew a bead on the conventional storybook problems of Washington, from the fable of a bloated defense budget to the fable of a lazy and obtuse bureaucracy. And he vowed to do without the help of all the old Washington hands.

Now, Washington suffers from every vice that has afflicted centers of imperial power since Rome—with a few novelties thrown in. No one transplanted here from less intense political cultures can fail to detect these foibles, the chief of which is a crazed absorption in the exercise of power. The gleaming late-night windows of its official buildings are a constant reminder that government is to Washington what steel is to Pittsburgh, autos to Detroit, and film to Hollywood. This is its glory and may someday be its ruin. There are layers of governmental special-

8

ization here rivaling medieval refinements of speculative theology.

The old catechisms used to say that man's chief end is to glorify and enjoy God, but Washington is as bored by issues of ultimate purpose as Detroit or Pittsburgh. What the country did not clearly perceive—and this was perhaps the source of Jimmy Carters' miscalculation—is that there is no uncommon venality or mischief in these Washington habits, only a special kind of myopia.

Washington might be a better place if a major non-political culture had preceded its selection as a seat of government: one of the saving graces of London, Paris and Rome. But since the republic pitched its tent in a barren river bottom, it is probably vain to fret over its singleness of purpose or its deplorable tendency to breed political technicians who as seldom ponder the ultimate ends of human society as Detroit engineers ponder the ultimate purpose of the internal combustion engine or the superhighway.

Certainly it was quixotic for a defiant "outsider," setting himself up as the tribune of a disapproving country, to tackle its entrenched habits head-on, as Mr. Carter proposed to do. If Washington ever is radically overhauled it will be, I suspect, by internal *coup de main*; and the men on horseback will probably be old Washington hands—more a blend of Clark Clifford and Abe Fortas than a Bible-quoting former naval person from the rural South.

As well as misjudging the nature of Washington, Jimmy Carter underestimated the fickleness of the populist distaste for the capital which he gratified in 1976. He learned, at some personal cost, that if there is anything the great American public dislikes more than Washington functioning well it is Washington functioning poorly. An apologetic and mincing imperialism is not more amiable than a brash imperialism; it is merely contemptible. A president eschewing the formalities and calling everyone by his first name is not more lovable than a chief magistrate in cutaway and white tie with trumpets heralding his every footstep; he is simply a fellow citizen playing president from the wrong script.

It will shortly be seen what mistakes Ronald Reagan will make, but it is a safe bet that they won't be Mr. Carter's. On the fringes of his entourage, there are firebrands smoldering with the right-wing equivalent of the liberal populism that played Mr. Carter false. They will tempt him, also, to simplify politics and to mistake government for a morality play. But Mr. Reagan

9

will see soon enough that a little preaching goes a long way in Washington.

The Carter experience—his with Washington, Washington's with him—has not, I suspect, cured the country's distaste for the imperial city on the Potomac, although it has sharply reminded us of the difference between preaching and governing. Washington has thoroughly chewed up Mr. Carter. Yet there remains a great longing to see the beast on the Potomac tamed and bridled. The irony so vividly pointed by Mr. Carter's sojourn is that the beast will be bridled, if at all, only by masters of those arts and techniques perfected, these last 50 years or so, in the shadow of the Capitol.

Maybe the 1980 election was a vote for the re-professionalization of government, but with the proviso, less easily discerned, that this re-professionalization lead to a sharp reduction of the capital's pretensions, and refocus its gaze upon a few ultimate questions.

—November 27, 1980

Facing the Ethos of Affluence

Jimmy Carter continues to surprise us. According to last week's conventional wisdom he had retreated to camp David to recast his energy policy, his staff or his presidential style. In fact, he was brooding, in the peace of the Catoctins, about the state of our souls.

This is not a usual preoccupation for political executives. Mr. Harold Macmillan, the former British prime minister, once told William F. Buckley that "national morality" is for bishops to worry about. That view is widely shared among the political cognoscenti, especially in Washington.

But Mr. Carter thinks differently. The journalists who visited Camp David last Friday found there a president fretting over national values. He was not, he reminded us, a sociologist or a psychologist. But why, he wondered, do Americans no longer believe that their children will live in a better world than theirs? Why do we save so much less of what we earn than, say, the Germans or Japanese? Why do we seem to set inordinate store

10

by possessions? Why had quantity become more important than quality? Did American values need reorienting?

Most of those who sat around the big conference-room table at Camp David probably supposed, as I did, that Mr. Carter would fight down any urge to address the nation on such imponderables. But he didn't; and in some ways the most significant thing he said Sunday night was this: "In a nation that was proud of hard work, strong families, close-knit communities and our faith in God, too many of us now tend to worship self-indulgence and consumption. Human identity is no longer defined by what one does, but what one owns. But…owning and consuming things does not satisfy our longing for meaning…Material goods cannot fill the emptiness of lives that have no confidence or purpose."

While I tend to agree with Mr. Macmillan that morals are more properly the worry of bishops, it was bold of Mr. Carter to court the inevitable sneers of sophisticates by preaching on this text. His speech fell short of Lincolnesque profundity; but in directing serious presidential attention to the drift of American values, he may have struck a note of some historical importance.

Mr. Carter is unmistakably a puritan, and his concerns are not strange to those who remember the self-critical books that flooded in on the crest of American affluence: David Riesman's *The Lonely Crowd,* Vance Packard's *The Status-Seekers,* William H. Whyte's *The Organization Man,* Thomas Griffith's *The Waist-High Culture,* and above all, John Kenneth Galbraith's *The Affluent Society.* Varying as they did in quality and originality, all condemned self-indulgence, the loss of community, social conformity (the loss of what Riesman called "inner-directedness"), the inordinate attachment to consumer goods, the decay of habits of thrift, craftsmanship, self-reliance and public-spiritedness.

These influential treatises coincided with, and in some ways expressed a reaction against, the ethos of the Eisenhower years: an era, as neo-puritans viewed it, which Mr. Eisenhower himself brought to self-parody by suggesting that every consumer buy a new refrigerator to fight the 1957 recession.

Consumption was not the universal norm of Western civilization, of course. Charles De Gaulle had the feudalistic composure to warn the French (in vain, it now appears) that a consumer society would be a society of "sterile satisfactions"— foreshadowing what Mr. Carter said the other evening. But this was not the tune of American presidents. Whatever their own private tastes, they typically fell into step with the ethos of affluence and shrank from criticizing an economy geared to mass

11

production, planned obsolescence, and the manipulation of taste and consent by advertising.

In some ways—Mr. Carter's instinct is surely right on this—the energy crisis is merely the ultimate symptom of the consumption-oriented society. For what is the energy crisis but a gasoline crisis? And why a gasoline crisis, except that it has pleased us for decades to build our Babylon around the automobile, the most sacred of consumer goods, and its satellites, the superhighway and the suburb?

Was Mr. Carter's presidential frown upon "self-indulgence and consumption" the overture to a crusade, or just a potshot at habits that everyone occasionally deplores but no one knows how to throw off without risking economic collapse? Should it prove the former, July 15th may be noted as the evening a president first used his office—the presidency's bully pulpit—to persuade us that we're caught up in a careening consumer economy that has made a husk of the cities, a miasma of the air, and a deity of the gasoline pump.

Many years ago, Aldous Huxley imagined that the brave new world would bow down to "Our Ford," but would find little satisfaction in this latest of golden calves. Perhaps Mr. Carter agrees.

—July 18, 1979

Grits, Comme Il Faut

My friend George Will, pundit nonpareil, is also a gentleman, a scholar and a judge of fine foods. Of him, as of the model major general, the Savoyard would say that he's information vegetable, animal and mineral/and quotes the fights historical/From Marathon to Waterloo in order categorical. For all I know, Mr. Will can even write a washing bill in Babylonic cuneiform.

But as a Midwesterner schooled in the old and new Englands, Mr. Will is in one crucial respect culturally deprived: He is ignorant of Southern cooking. He is so ignorant of it that—I have this on the best authority—he once seated himself at a breakfast table in the South and was heard to ask: "What is a grit?"

12

What is a grit? When he asked it, the question was not dangerous. He asked it in North Carolina, of gentle people who have a take-it-or-leave-it attitude to grits. William T. Polk, to whose lyrical discussions of Southern cuisine I shall presently return, recalls a hungry soldier—presumably back from long campaigning in Georgia—telling his Aunt Lina in 1864: "All I've had to eat for years, lady, is grits, grits, grits. I'd just as soon lie down and let the moon shine in my mouth." That sums up the Carolinian attitude.

But in Georgia, as I have warned Mr. Will, grits (plural if you please) are not moonshine. It was one thing to ask what a grit was before it began to seem conceivable that Georgians might take over the White House in 1977. Should that happen, "What is a grit?" will be a question to be asked only by a man courting preventive detention. Indeed, it is rumored that Governor Carter might reopen Andersonville for those who do not eat their grits for breakfast and their rice for dinner.

Not, I hasten to say, that Georgians are bigots about food. The catholicity of Georgia cooking runs from the delicate sherry-flavored shrimp and crabmeat newburgs of Savannah to the pit-cooked barbecue of Governor Carter's Americus, with variations between.

I once asked my colleague Perry Morgan, a native Georgian, to describe a country menu likely to be set before a campaigning politician before he addressed the electors. His reply was unforgettable:

"For a draught to whet the appetite," he declared, "there would be a slug of straight corn or bourbon whiskey, drawn from the jug or swished in the glass without the dulling effect of ice cubes. This would be followed by tripe, chitlins, hogmaw, hogshead stew, fried or stewed catfish, possum and sweet taters, fried (or pickled) pig feet, pigtail stew, fried rabbit and peckerwood stew, brains and eggs, blood pudding, squirrel stew, fricaseed raccoon, crow, or sowbelly and thickening gravy. Along with this there would be collards or turnip greens or blackeyed peas, preferably, but most any vegetable boiled with plenty of fatback would do." Wines, he indicated, would be supererogatory.

But to return to grits: A Georgian cannot envision breakfast without grits—nor dinner without rice. The soldier who protested his weariness of grits to Mr. Polk's Aunt Lina could not have been a native grits-eater. The clue is not the weariness but the uncouth belief that grits is a sustaining dish. It is not. It is an embellishment, playing the culinary obligato to eggs and ham (or bacon or sausage) that Yorkshire pudding plays

13

to roast beef. An ignorant fellow who tried to make a solo dish of it would indeed feel himself as slighted as by a mouthful of moonshine.

Grits, *comme il faut,* demand accompaniment—butter at least, and ideally both butter and red-eye gravy. Some connoisseurs prefer grits au gratin—that is, a pie-plate of prepared grits coated with a layer of cheese and briefly baked. Still others like grit cakes, which are made with day-old grits congealed overnight in a glass, then sliced, dipped in egg and fried.

But let there be no doubt of it—grits are a homely dish, nothing fancy, and there are no annals of grits comparable to the annals of certain country hams. Of such a ham, Mr. Polk rhapsodized: "One whose palate had once appreciated this ham would no more eat a midwestern American commercial ham than he would pull a shingle off the roof and devour it. It has the combination of strength and sweetness hardly to be found outside the verses of Lucretius and Chaucer, the paintings of Rubens and Michelangelo, the music of Mozart and Beethoven." Grits, to extend the metaphor, is prose and ballad; it is Mark Twain and Stephen Collins Foster, not Lucretius and Mozart.

It is almost to weep, to think of Mr. Will's boyhood on the plains of Illinois—to imagine all the paltry plates of porridge he ate, innocent of grits. Only Willa Cather could do justice to the pathos of it. I offer the foregoing primer in the hope that if the new regime brings Georgia cuisine to the capital my friend George will not embarrass his hostesses with that perilous question, "What is a grit?" The official directors of nutrition might be listening, and he needn't look for answer to Julia Child.

—June 24, 1976

The Labyrinths of John Knox

In my town, which lies in the rolling piedmont hills of central North Carolina, the oldest church was Presbyterian—naturally. I say naturally because it occurs to me, after all these years, that the flinty severity of that red-clay landscape recalled, to highlanders in exile, the austerities of home.

After many years of neglect, the old church is being restored. We went to view the restoration on a gray Christmas

14

afternoon and at the sight of it memory stirred. The old floors that once sloped, in the fashion of the period, to the pulpit steps are level now and crowded with tables. A kitchen has replaced the choir and the organ. Only the stained glass windows in their highpointed Gothic arches, with their memorials to the town gentry, remain as they were. Only they and the ambience of the place—when the Romans spoke of an imperishable *genius loci* they were right.

As I gazed at the old surroundings, I found myself silently thankful that in Dante's horrific pages no circle of torment is reserved for those distracted in church. Were there such, the hours I passed in the old church, carpeted in red and bathed in the light of sanctity, would have stored up ages and ages of durance there.

It was not merely that the place was, on a Sunday morning, the microcosm of a tight-knit society from which no secrets were, or could be, hid. Seating arrangements were controlled by an unspoken but unshakeable territorial imperative. A family was no more likely to be out of place, if present, than the European colonies of those days, depicted in their splotches of pink and yellow, were likely to be scrambled on a school map of Africa. One knew the faces; one even knew the backs of necks. When Norman Mailer visited the First Baptist Church of Plains several months ago, observing the wrinkles in necks neither more nor less than three-sixteenths of an inch deep, he observed a telling detail of small-town Southern churches.

Nor was it, this distraction, the fault of the appointed and unvarying ritual, from the doxology to the threefold amen, unfolding to the stentorian chords of an organ outsized for the place. Nor was it, in fact, though this was a source of boyish bemusement, that the choir's leading soprano sang, as she played the organ, at Wagnerian levels of volume or that the leading bass was an undaunted monotone.

Nor was it, I suppose, those dread sabbaths when, once a month, the solemn rite of communion unfolded—the church elders sitting *en banc* on the front pew, heads bowed, while trays of discreet vials of grape juice and neatly diced white bread passed down the rows tinkling like Oriental windchimes but never so merrily. It was, indeed, an occasion to strike terror into the carefree heart, at the intonation of those awful words from the Book of Church Order: "Whosoever shall eat the bread, or drink the cup, *unworthily* eateth and drinketh *damnation* to himself." *Unworthily?* How was one to know?

No. All these were, in their way, distractions from the doc-

15

trines to which unregenerate hearts were beckoned in this place, 30-odd years ago. But the true source of the wandering thoughts, O shameful irony, was the utter impenetrability of the sermons. Mr. B, the shepherd of the flock, was a Virginian; indeed he was, like that famous Calvinist Woodrow Wilson, a son of the Valley of Virginia, where Presbyterian truths thrive uncontaminated by worldly adulteration.

There was, in Mr. B's doctrine, no tincture of worldly fashion, no such nonsense as the "social gospel" (dread words, the Almighty being presumed indifferent to the temporal affectations of sinful man). How often, though, did one's mind wander dangerously afield as on a long midsummer day, with the heat at 90 and the funeral-home fans aflutter in every pew, Mr. B threaded his intricate and learned way from page to page of the sermon, from subtlety to subtlety through the labyrinths of Knoxian theology. It was many years ago. But I can still see the pages now, counted as Mr. B turned them, with excruciating slowness it seemed, a great thickness of them plucked from the binders of a loose-leaf notebook to which they would be neatly restored, scrawled in blue ink. Mr. B's sermons lasted for precisely 15 minutes, more or less, as a sermon should—20 minutes at the outside, though the apparent time added a dimension to the word "eternity." They began with a Bible text, clearly enough. Sometimes it would be four minutes, sometimes five, before his rhetorical footsteps vanished into the gloom of words, eluding the strictest attention, like footsteps in a deepening blizzard.

I cannot pretend that I was guilt-stricken at this, as a lad. The sure disappearance of Mr. B's homiletic footprints into obscurity was, at a certain age, one of life's certainties. No, I can't pretend that I felt the bite of guilt as I stood Christmas afternoon surveying the scene in the old church and thinking of the learned obscurity of Mr. B, who was a kind of saint. I was aware only of the residue of it that I carry to this day. Small wonder that Col. Tasker Polk, late of Warrenton, N.C. and of the easy Episcopal persuasion, withdrew his children so abruptly from a Presbyterian Sunday school lest they begin to take religion too seriously. How well he understood! One might go on from such a place to whore after strange gods, or lax doctrines. But on the most basic matters ("Sin," said the Westminster catechism, "is any want of conformity to, or transgression of, the law of God") one was indelibly schooled, distractions notwithstanding. One might not believe it—or believe it all—but one had known the real thing even so.

—December 30, 1976

16

On a Gilbert and Sullivan Toot

Until the D'Oyly Carte Opera Company's bicentennial visit was announced, I had been off Gilbert and Sullivan—cold turkey—for more than 15 years. I thought I'd kicked the habit.

Then I read Joy Billington's piece about the case of poor Harold Wilson—Sir Harold Wilson, K.G., as he now is. Sir Harold, it seems, has been mainlining Gibert and Sullivan since the tender age of six and considers himself incurable. I soon understood—I dug out the scratched old pre-stereo recordings, and even in that watered-down form the Savoy operettas are dangerous. I was soon on a toot. First Gilbert's lyrics begin to creep into your sentences, then your head becomes a calliope of garbled tunes from Sullivan. What a princely waste of time!

Now, the interesting thing about Gilbert and Sullivan operettas is that their authors had the same feeling about them—the feeling that Sir Arthur Conan Doyle had about his Sherlock Holmes stories. During their troubled collaboration, Gilbert and Sullivan thought they should be doing something better with their time. Doyle, you recall, nursed a passion to be a "serious" novelist. He was mortified to suspect that he would be remembered for such frivolities as the Holmes stories, not for his "serious" historical romances. His suspicion was warranted. Who today reads—or wants to read—*Micah Clarke* or *The White Company?* And who today cares a rip about the "serious" dramas of William Schenck Gilbert?

To be sure, his collaborator Sir Arthur S. Sullivan lives on not only at the Savoy theater, but in that most improbable place, the English hymnal—not only in "Onward, Christian Soldiers," but in that appealing Easter hymn, "Come Ye Faithful, Raise The Strain." Sherlock Holmes might have called it "the hymnal mystery": The notations ascribe the melody to Sullivan and the words to St. John of Damascus, 8th Century. But who could sing that very Gilbertesque first verse without a smile of recognition:

> *...God hath brought his Israel*
> *Into joy from sadness;*
> *Loosed from Pharoah's bitter yoke*
> *Jacob's sons and daughters;*
> *Led them with unmoistened foot*
> *Through the Red Sea waters.*

17

The "unmoistened foot" of Jacob's sons and daughters in the Red Sea has an impish touch of genius about it. Is it a literal translation of St. John of Damascus or a suggestion from Gilbert?

I have written, so far, as if I really believed that Gilbert and Sullivan is a frivolous indulgence, if not exactly a vice. Do I believe it? Well, there is a case to be made. In plot, the operettas are tissues of zany implausibility—"rational lunacy," as Felicia Lamport has written, "compendia of incongruities, defying gravity by making steely shafts of satire rest on fluffballs of fantasy."

In so saying, Ms. Lamport was borne up on pinions of Gilbertian rhetoric, reminiscent of the stilted Ralph Rackstraw, sailorboy hero of "H.M.S. Pinafore." But she's right.

Consider "Pinafore," whose denouement takes the classic form of a reversal of roles: The "well-bred captain" turns out to have been inexplicably swapped as a baby for the ordinary tar Rackstraw when both infants were "baby-farmed" by the mysterious Little Buttercup. Rackstraw, now elevated to the solid middle class, becomes eligible to marry the daughter of the now declassé captain; while the captain himself, now abruptly demoted, may marry his one-time "nuss" Buttercup. Ridiculous? Ridiculous. But for a really madcap plot, see "The Mikado."

But we do not go to Gilbert and Sullivan for plots. Apart from the magnificent music, we go to enjoy the best musical satire in the English language—or as Pooh-Bah might put it, "corroborative detail, intended to give artistic verisimilitude to an otherwise bald and unconvincing narrative."

Gilbert spoofs every English fetish and institution, especially those political, in a way not calculated to upset them but to generate detachment and good humor.

The result is actually a sort of institutional affirmation, as in "Pinafore," where fetishes of class are sharply needled from every angle, only to emerge intact at the end. Only the characters have exchanged appointed niches—a salutary lesson in the unpredictability of the human condition.

In Gilbert and Sullivan there is also the material of impenitent Anglophilia. Who cannot admire a society that laughs at itself so elegantly? It is amusing to reflect that while the original D'Oyly Carte company was staging these gentle confections, Wagner was incubating his exhausting German vision of gods and heroes, while in France Offenbach was writing naughty can-cans.

All wear well. But who has the strength of character to cope with Siegfried or Parsifal at the end of a weary day—let alone

18

the energy to can-can—when he can settle back in the easy chair as Sir Joseph Porter sings his immortal song about rising to the top of the tree and becoming Ruler of the Queen's Navee? Not I, not since this addiction returned.

—July 1, 1976

"Toiling on the Mound" at Mill Creek

I don't know whether sportscasters still speak of baseball pitchers as "toiling on the mound," but for me the phrase is forever associated with my old friend Ripley. When the crocuses spring up and the crack of the fungo bat is heard in the land, I think of Ripley and the day he threw his arm away against Mill Creek.

It happened on a blistering Carolina summer day 28 years ago. The turn of events did not amuse Ripley then, but time and philosophy have annealed the wound. "Ripley, tell us about the day you threw your arm away against Mill Creek," I sometimes say. "Well," he begins, "it was 98 degrees in shade and I was *toiling on the mound,"*and soon we're both laughing too hard to go on.

You must understand that at the time of which I write North Carolina was to minor-league baseball what Kentucky was, and is, to horse-racing. It was a mania promising glory. An able-bodied youth might go on from the sandlots to immortality with Selma or Fuquay-Varina of the class-C Coastal Plain League. The most famous living native of our town was a man who kept third base for the Brooklyn Dodgers. In a photograph known to us all, he could be seen watching Babe Ruth pass third on his last round trip for the Yankees.

My friend Ripley—not his real name, of course, though the story itself is altogether true—was able bodied though not agile. Adolescence had so abruptly stretched his arms and legs that his father, remembering the fit of Crane's clothing in Washington Irving's story, was in the habit of calling him "Ichabod." Ripley was lefthanded, too, and it was this fact—and, I might add, the distant ascendancy of Hal Newhouser of the Detroit

19

Tigers—more than striking talent that fired his aspiration to be a great southpaw pitcher.

Indeed—it was the one asset that lent the ambition plausibility—my friend Ripley could throw a baseball very, very hard. His pitches had so much natural stuff on them that it was beyond the wit of a catcher to guess what they would do next. Sometimes they broke left, sometimes right, sometimes up and sometimes down; but none went straight. This was the secret of his brief celebrity as an American Legion Junior baseball pitcher. No one could hit Ripley and few enough, in these pre-hard hat years, ventured close enough to the plate to try. He had a single liability as a pitcher: the base on balls.

The sly patron of Ripley's pitching ambition was Mr. Weems, as we shall call him, who coached football and taught world history at the town high school and coached the Legion juniors every summer. Coach Weems approached life's problems by leisurely indirection, and Ripley was a minor problem because Ripley's father ran the school. As Ripley later came to realize, it was a situation of unsuspected complexity. For instance, the elder Ripley during tight football games would sometimes go down to the bench and make pointed suggestions to Coach Weems. The astuteness of these suggestions did not diminish their awkwardness for Coach Weems in other respects. All Mr. Weems taught the high school boys in "world history," moreover, was some cracker-barrel hygiene and the chapter on the "benevolent despots," a term that amused him since he confounded the second word with train depots. This was known to the elder Ripley as well, who once prompted him: "It's *despots,* Weems," he said. "Nothing to do with trains."

Who, in that innocent era, might have suspected the play of these subtle cross-currents when Coach Weems announced, to our astonishment, that young Ripley would pitch the season opener against Mill Creek? Mill Creek, you see, was a bitter rival; it was a dusty, disreputable community six miles away where modern improvements had a most tentative foothold. Mill Creek's baseball diamond lay on a windy bluff between the railroad tracks and the broad, lazy stream from which the town drew its name. A ball hit long would often bounce across the tracks, greatly complicating the outfielder's work; a wild pitch or throw to home plate often passed through a large hole in the chickenwire backstop and rolled into the creek.

When Ripley, with his uncertain control, walked the first four Mill Creek batters in a row all eyes turned to Coach Weems, who contentedly kept his counsel on the dugout bench, the bill

20

of his blue cap shading the bland expression on his face. No signal came; Ripley toiled on. After four more walks all expected a move from Coach Weems. None came. The humiliating chatter from the Mill Creek dugout intensified. Ripley, still toiling on the mound, walked another four, making the score 9-0. Still no sign of relief. By now Ripley was throwing an occasional ball into the creek. Finally, Coach Weems was seen to ease himself from the bench and advance in a stately amble to the mound, confer with Ripley, and beckon the first-baseman to pitch. "A shame to spoil a no-hitter, Ripley" was his droll comment.

So far as I know my friend Ripley never again pitched a baseball in competition, although it was some years before he became flippant enough to speak of "the day I threw my arm away against Mill Creek." Ripley's interest in baseball entered a slow decline from which, though he is and was an over-achiever in other sports, it never recovered. All he says now, when prodded to tell the story, is: "Well, it was 98 degrees in the shade and I was *toiling on the mound.*" No one had learned the meaning of the old phrase as well as my friend Ripley. He had indeed toiled on the mound.

—March 31, 1977

The Passive Vacation

Some people divide the world into tall and short, fat and skinny, even (so it is said) quiche-eating and quiche-abstaining. These distinctions are trivial. There are two great classes: the active and the passive vacationers.

I have friends whose vacation ideal is strenuous self-improvement—the long-distance cruise, mountain-climbing, listening to music or even, heaven help them, camping.

I prefer the surpriseless vacation, as void of novelty as a fictional best-seller. So for years past numbering, we have come to Wrightsville, N.C., a lovely, sun-drenched place where the village fathers take a squinty view of innovation and where the only new sound is the faint repetitive melody of the Ms. Pac-Man machines at the Yacht Club down the street.

We come at the same time, with the same friends, stay at the same cottage, see the same people and do—or, more importantly, decline to do—the same things, year after year.

21

The menu, depending on the strength of the bluefish run, is 98 percent predictable, down to the triviality of the midday corned-beef sandwich. This wretched substance would give dyspepsia to a robot if ingested more than 500 yards from the sea. With salt air and beer, and a dill pickle or two, it is ambrosia. But the real point is that we have eaten corned beef for lunch for 20 years.

There are, for all we do to avoid them, occasional surprises. Last year's, now embedded in the annals, was the great nor'easter, a nasty storm that strayed from its usual anchorage on Hatteras, or Nantucket, and blew chill winds and rain at us for five days. Usually, St. Petersburg, Fla., where a local paper gives itself away on rainy days, has nothing on Wrightsville. Nor'easters, the natives say, come about every 30 years.

This year's major surprise was a discovery: the delights of not sailing. We had left one sailboat behind. Our son would bring it, we told ourselves, when he finished a summer job and joined us. The other boat, which our friends had brought well over 400 miles, lay unlaunched. It lay unlaunched for days. Then we leveled with ourselves. How pleasant it was to miss the traditional mid-afternoon pleasures of sailing!

For novelty, there were the gravity-inversion boots. Yes! Our friends had bought them—so they claimed—to treat Aunt Martha's back, whose suppleness is not what it used to be. So, as you might imagine, one or another member of the household was often to be seen, at odd hours, absurdly dangling like a weary bar from a door-frame. But this dreadful Hollywood-bred innovation will pass.

We are not quite so torpid as this may suggest. Among creatures of habit, however, mellowed out, the grueling runs in the late-afternoon sun could not be avoided. Otherwise, the pre-dinner rum and tonic would lie less easy on the middle-age conscience.

But to those who go on exciting, adventurous and instructive vacations, this portrait of indolence must be appalling. What could be the point of it?

One point is to extinguish volition, to silence that little nagging voice advocating activity, to flirt briefly with the oriental lure of Nirvana, to consider the sea oats, the tides, the hues of sea and sky.

Another point, surely the greater, is the perfection of a friendship that grows year after year with the inexhaustible conversations among friends that need have no secrets. The usual concealments are not practiced; everyone's quirks are known. Sometimes even the best of friends, or those who think they are, find common vacations disastrous, giving way to restless silences.

With us, it has been blessedly different. On this annual retreat, with the affairs of alleged moment far away, we watch children and godchildren grow from stage to stage and muse endlessly on books, parents, friends, fortunes and the curious twists and turns of self-recognition.

There, we find change enough. That is one reason for giving thanks that this time of year, at this well-beloved corner of the great sea, changes not at all.

—August 29, 1982

"Plain English"

There has been, of late, a certain consciousness-raising—in the dreadful term—about our slovenly abuse of the mother tongue.

Evidence abounds. Woe, in the form of a ton of reproving mail, betides the columnist who writes "who" when he meant "whom." Churchmen in their thousands rise up against clumsy revisionists who untune the ageless idiom of prayer books and Bibles. Consultants flock to Washington to help government agencies translate regulations into plain English "for a change." The therapeutic books of Edwin Newman and Theodore Bernstein sell briskly.

The trend should not be undermined by those modern linguists who pop up here and there to tell us that schoolmarmish rigidity can be bad for good English. Linguists like Mr. Jim Quinn.

No defender of free trade in ideas would think of compiling an index of forbidden writings, but if I were compiling one I would include Mr. Quinn's article in Sunday's *Washington Post Magazine*, entitled "Plain English."

Mr. Quinn's is a siren song for unwary readers, a message of emancipation from worry over English usage. It is, to be sure, warmed-over linguistic modernism, with a pinch of mischief. His message, *"Don't worry; it doesn't matter how you write or talk; no matter how 'ungrammatical' your usage, you can find precedents for it in the long history of the English language."*

And so you may. Mr. Quinn's article poses all the dangers of ill-digested truth; and to rub in his point Mr. Quinn writes in the "Look, ma, no hands" style of the gamin in the back row of English I, sticking out his tongue at Teacher. He flouts all the grammar rules our English teachers laid down, using "Hopefully" to mean "I hope that"; "like" as a conjuction where nice grammarians prefer "as"; and "bad" as an adverb ("how bad we talk"). I think of a naughty schoolgirl in her first topless bathing suit.

Before you join Mr. Quinn and the naughty boys in the back row of the grammar class, however, please understand certain things about the "scientific" linguists whose view he echoes.

Grammar, as they conceive it, is not "prescriptive" but "descriptive"—not a set of dos and don'ts but a list of dids and doeses. Its history shows, indeed, that language is a volatile thing, and that changes thrown up by random majority preferences are not always favored by purists. You can go, as Mr. Quinn does, to the great *Oxford English Dictionary on Historical Principles* and discover distinguished grammatical outlaws, from Shakespeare down. Quinn is not the first to list for us all the innovations Swift tried vainly to head off; he does not list Swift's successes.

Mr. Quinn doesn't disclose all there is to disclose about modern linguistics or about its favorite maxim, which is that native speakers of a language cannot make a "mistake." He doesn't tell us, for instance, that "scientific" (i.e., historical) study of language arose, not coincidentally, in the late 19th Century—along with a companion science, Darwinian biology. The fallacies of linguistic Darwinism—as of its forerunner, "social" Darwinism—are many.

Not even the most diligent efforts of ecologists can significantly alter the verdicts of natural selection in the plant and animal kingdoms, however grotesque or unaesthetic the result. Nature, Darwin taught us, is loftily indifferent to the way in which bird beaks or fruit-fly wings evolve, governed (as we know but Darwin could only guess) by genetic mutation.

The historical study of language may be comparably "scientific" in method; but the shaping of language as a human instrument of precision and art is not ordained by DNA but open to human volition.

A society careless of the precision of the written or spoken word will soon have the language it deserves. If it becomes collectively indifferent about whether "bad" is an adjective and "badly" an adverb; whether "presently" means "now" or "in a short while"; then words will indeed cease to have precise or reliable meaning.

The order of nature which the scientific linguists take as their model is, as far as we know, highly deterministic. The good order of language is, however, governed to a measurable degree by our aspirations and by the standards we affirm.

A national effort to improve our use of language is not quite the fool's errand that Mr. Quinn and other scoffers would have us believe: not quite as ludicrous—as "unscientific"—as a comparable attempt to arrest the evolutionary process of nature.

The history of the language is a fascinating and valuable study, capable of teaching us surprising and often paradoxical lessons about words and their shadings. But having understood its elementary lessons, we need not quail before the odds of history.

—December 15, 1977

Scarlett With Toothpaste

Even with great-grandfathers who were active Rebels—one, a Georgian, was shot from his saddle in Virginia—I don't recall that "Gone With The Wind" was much of a cult at our house.

My father, a historical realist if ever there was one, probably viewed the film as twaddle. My mother, a card-carrying Georgian, grew up in a part of the state that had been in the way of Sherman's March, and perhaps a romantic treatment of the War was too reminiscent of actual pain and deprivation to be entertaining.

So it was strange to grow up hearing people boast of how often they'd seen "the picture." Fifteen times, some had. Everybody saw it often—often enough, at least, to remember the best lines. Years later Willie Morris and I would tease our "little Yankee friends," as his grandmother called them, by doing the heartthrob scenes between Scarlett O'Hara and Ashley Wilkes, on the all-too-stagy grounds of Twelve Oaks, or reciting Prissy's lines *(Lawdy, Miz Scarlett, I ain't never birthed no baby!)*.

But at this late date the thought of watching it on television the other night (infringed, as it would be, by ads for toothpaste and radial tires) seemed repellent. Atlanta would burn without

25

us this time. We would peek, just for curiosity, then turn it off after the first commercial. But as you may suspect, it never got turned off.

Someone—perhaps George Orwell—speaks of "good bad books"—books whose vitality threadbare artifice and outrageous stereotype can't quite hide. "Gone With The Wind" is that kind of film: good bad. If you care about historical plausibility, complexity of characterization, or realism in a plot, it is quite impossible, an outrage. It pictures a storybook South, suffering a doom as capricious as a lightning bolt. Not without a sly smile, I suspect, did William Rose Benet in his *Reader's Encyclopedia* observe that Margaret Mitchell wrote her novel "during a long period of hospitalization." It embodies a sentimentality that W.J. Cash called "one of the least *reconstructible* ever developed."

Every major character, allowing for realistic lapses in the roles of Scarlett and Rhett Butler, is a waxen puppet, as clearly identified as if by a sign labeled Avarice, Pride or Envy in some medieval allegory. Was there ever such a simpering fool as Charles Hamilton? Such a monster of scruple as Ashley Wilkes? Such a saint as Mrs. O'Hara? Such a madamic Madam as Belle Watkins, or mammified Mammy as Mammy, such a silly old bag as Aunt Pitty-Pat with her smelling salts? Of course not.

But wooden characterization perfectly fits the adamant class stratification assumed in "Gone With The Wind," with its rigid hierarchy of planters, field hands, house servants, and "white trash"—always so called, in case you miss the point about Miss Slattery, for instance. It is from bad sociology, not history or instructed imagination.

Nor does the tale unfold, as plausible tales must, from what characters do or don't do. It visits them as casually as a Fate, sometimes distantly and wickedly personified by the Yankees or General Sherman or carpetbaggers, manipulating their little universe. Maybe this is how war sometimes seems to its victims. But it is not the stuff of a convincing tale.

Why, then, do we watch it? Well, here is one man's theory: "Gone With The Wind" snatches entertainment from the jaws of bathos because of Scarlett and Rhett, two misplaced rogues who unaccountably invade this gallery of silly, waxen marionettes with their sins on display—duplicitous, resourceful, self-seeking, grasping, with perhaps a dozen great exchanges which, I have long suspected, F. Scott Fitzgerald added when he reworked the script.

After Scarlett has thrown herself at Rhett for the money to pay the taxes on Tara, he tells her she isn't worth $300, an arguable point, but in any case it's refreshing to have a phony belle so satisfyingly insulted. And when she complains he's no gentleman while the world is crashing about them, he wonderfully says, "It seems a minor point at a time like this." In the old days audiences applauded when the two-timing Scarlett, about to be abandoned by Rhett for good, cries "What shall I do? Where will I go?" and Rhett, pausing at the door, answers, "Frankly, my dear, I don't give a damn." (Believe it or not, children, that "damn" was once thought to be sensationally racy.)

There is something to be learned from these two survivors. But for the rest I trust that the latest generation in the South is safely immune to the film's romantic blandishments. But you never know. All stories are dangerous, and romantic stories are the most dangerous of all. They tell us what we want to believe, not what we need to know.

But enough. The pledge has again been taken. Good-bye, GWTW! It is the pledge I took the other evening, shortly before 8 p.m., when we sat down to hoot at the preposterous opening scene at Tara where the absurd Hamilton boys are courting Scarlett, and she is coquetting it in her crinolines and the slaves are no doubt humming softly in the cotton fields and the war fever is mounting and you can practically see the seams in the painted backdrops. We were going to turn it off after the first commercial.

—March 26, 1981

Saying No to Natural Selection

When an obscure "endangered" clam, the Higgins Eye, halted an Army Corps of Engineers dredging project in Minnesota, *The Washington Star* suggested in a burst of editorial badinage that Charles Darwin should return "to remind the friends of snaildarters and Higgins Eye clams that most species through time are 'endangered' and that most have disappeared...A generous but biologically naive instinct underlies this halting of dams and dredging to prevent the doing of the unspeakable to be inedible."

This was, I say, badinage. No one here imagined that the sponsors of the Endangered and Threatened Species Protection Act of 1973 aspired to stop natural selection.

We were soon corrected. Our attention has been called to Section 4(a) of the act, listing factors which the secretaries of Commerce or Interior must consider in determining whether a species is "endangered" or "threatened." Among them, expectedly, are threats to habitat, overuse for "commercial, sporting, scientific, or educational purposes"; "disease or predation"; and also—most unexpectedly—"other *natural*...factors affecting its continued existence."

It may be beyond the power but not beyond the aspiration of Congress, then, to restrain nature. What we treated as a joke is no joke.

One never knows, in such cases, where legislative design ends and Solon merely nods. The Endangered and Threatened Species Protection Act was passed by Congress in the summer and autumn of 1973, with no dissenting votes in the Senate and a handful in the House. No voices were raised against it, understandably.

A close reading of the floor debate discloses that no deep philosophical or biological questions were plumbed or even raised, although a few bread-and-butter reservations were heard. Senator Eastland sought to be sure that the act did not envisage the protection of the boll weevil, whose extinction his cotton-growing state would welcome; Sen. Ted Stevens of Alaska saw to it that native Alaskans could kill and skin animals for their own traditional purposes.

But the legislative philosophy of the measure was, it seems, as stated by Sen. John Tunney, the Senate floor manager: to add a new protection category for plants and animals not immediately in danger but "likely within the foreseeable future to be so endangered." One species, said Senator Tunney, was vanishing every year on the average; and "each species (the boll weevil and other pests presumably excepted) provides a service to its environment." Casual destruction deprived us of "a diversity of genetic types" and, often, of "esthetic pleasure."

These sterling ecological sentiments were echoed on the House side, one member mentioning the danger to the blue whale, "the most efficient harvester of tiny marine life that exists today...in a protein-hungry world." (The apparent contradiction—that the blue whale could not be at once protected and harvested for its protein—was not explained).

At any rate, Congress in its noble impulse to rescue endangered and threatened animals and plants apparently did not foresee the trivialization of its effort in Tennessee. It did not, it seems, imagine that a $116 million hydroelectric project on the

28

Little Tennessee River would be stopped cold, 90 per cent complete, to allow the 3-inch snail-darter to bounce back from extinction.

But what happens when an endangered minnow and an endangered dam collide? The outcry over President Carter's cruelty to water projects suggests that senators and congressmen view dams as essential protection against the endangerment of their own species, *homo politicus*.

As for the ambitions of the act, it is ironic that the intervention of Congress in natural selection, now construed in favor of the insignificant and inedible snail-darter, should lead to a showdown in Tennessee. That state is now, I believe, rid of the anti-evolution "monkey law" under which it tried John Scopes at Dayton in 1925 for teaching biology incompatible with the book of *Genesis*. And one would hardly equate a measure so enlightened as The Endangered and Threatened Species Act of 1973 with the monkey law.

Still, both measures involve legislative interposition in the realm of biological change; and which will have involved the greater *hubris* is yet to be seen. Tennessee's ambitions were comparatively modest. It sought only to conceal the disturbing evidence of natural selection from impressionable school children. The Congress of the United States, one is intrigued to learn, intends to stop the nasty business in its tracks.

—April 7, 1977

Darwin Without the "ism"

The wife of the bishop of Worcester spoke for many, then and now, when she said of Darwinism: "Descended from the apes! My dear, let us hope that is not true, but if it is, let us pray that it will not become generally known."

A century after his death, and in the anniversary week of "Origin of Species," Charles Darwin, the man, still needs rescuing from the terrors of his "ism." Every year, this week should be designated Darwin Week—a time for appreciating one who would rank among the greatest naturalists even if he had never thought of evolution by "natural selection."

29

To be sure, imagining Darwin without Darwinism is as hard as imagining Newton without gravitation or Einstein with relativity. But let us try.

How would Darwin be remembered today if his theory of natural selection had merely fallen through the cracks, as did Mendel's exactly contemporaneous work on genetics? That could have happened. The president of the Linnean Society, after hearing Darwin's preliminary explanation, remarked that the year "has not, indeed, been marked by any of those striking discoveries which…revolutionize…the department of science on which they bear."

Darwin would, for one thing, be remembered—charmingly—as an assiduous patron of pigeon fanciers and dog-breeding clubs. Breeders of domestic livestock had been shaping animals selectively for centuries if not millennia, though without seeing momentous implications in their breeding techniques. One preliminary reader of "Origin of Species" wished Darwin had stuck to pigeons. "Everyone," he commented to Darwin's publisher, "is interested in pigeons."

But Darwin suffered from scientific genius—the ordinary power of observation vastly magnified and disciplined by powerful theory. All pigeon breeders knew that hybrids often looked like rock pigeons, the ancestral breed. Darwin would not let that curiosity pass without speculating on its meaning for all life forms.

Darwin, ingenious observer, was also our first ecological storyteller, the great-grandfather of our still imperfect grasp of the economy of nature.

Thus he noted the curiosity that bumblebees ("humble-bees," as he called them) alone visited certain wild pansies and red clover. Other bees could not reach their nectar.

"The number of humble-bees," he writes, "depends in a great measure on the number of field mice, which destroy their combs and nests. Now the the number of mice is largely dependent, as everyone knows, on the number of cats…Hence it is quite credible that the presence of feline animals in large numbers might determine…the frequency of certain flowers."

The interdependence of cats and certain flowers is far from obvious, but this is the prototype of the ecological story we hear now—for instance, about the link between the impact of man-made dams on the breeding habits of West Coast salmon and the girth of redwood trees.

Other naturalists had observed the complexity of the "web" of life. For Darwin it was a principle of understanding. A year

30

before he died he was still applying it, in a treatise on the services of the lowly earthworm.

Scientifically, it is a short step from homely and charming ecological tales to the universal "struggle for existence." Psychologically, that short step is hard to take because it seems superficially to have bone-chilling ethical implications.

But "nature," however it works, is not more competent to tell human beings how to behave than the Ten Commandments are to decipher the links between cats and flowers, or salmon and redwood trees.

The ethical and social "implications" often glibly drawn from Darwin's work are, for the most part, mutually contradictory nonsense. As Jonathan Howard says, "If socialism, laissez-faire capitalism, wishy-washy humanism and sociobiological fundamentalism can all find support in Darwin's work, then we must believe either that Darwin was absurdly unclear and inconsistent in his arguments, which he certainly was not, or that the theory of evolution has little if anything to do with ethical prescriptions."

If there was ethical challenge to mankind in Darwin's genius, it was a challenge on the grand scale: the deep conviction that what seems mysterious in the working of nature can be explained if the unifying mechanism can be grasped.

Even if, like the wife of the Bishop of Worcester, you are disconcerted by that possibility and wish it could be hushed up, there is much in Darwin's life and work to be simply enjoyed. Everyone presumably approves of clover, cats and bumblebees, if not pigeons.

—*November 27, 1982*

Other Side of the Sex Barrier

"I was three or perhaps four years old when I realized that I had been born into the wrong body, and should really be a girl."

That is the startling opener of Jan (formerly James) Morris' account of her longing, from earliest childhood, for sexual transformation. Most us, strangers to that obsession, find it a weird

31

and uncomfortable subject. And not only such deep disorders of sexual identity as afflicted the eminent British journalist, but the question of sexual roles and identities generally.

I have encountered people who are resolutely avoiding Dustin Hoffman's hilarious new movie, "Tootsie," which treats the subject satirically. It may be good, they say, but the subject is vaguely ominous.

In fact, the mild role-reversals in "Tootsie" have little or nothing to do with obsessions to cross the Adam-Eve barrier permanently. It is the urge to survive chronic unemployment, not transsexual longing, that leads the unemployed actor Michael Dorsey (played by Hoffman) to create "Dorothy Michael," who then becomes a hot soap-opera star.

Since it deals playfully with a powerful social taboo, this movie could have slipped into the usual coy farce or slapstick. Yet it is completely controlled and disciplined—a thoroughgoing dramatic success.

"Tootsie" is, in fact, a Chinese box tour de force: Hoffman is an actor playing an actor impersonating an actress playing a soap-opera role. It is a risky role, but Hoffman performs it brilliantly. Moreover, once Hoffman's hero puts himself, rather shakily, into corset and high heels, there is a sort of Pygmalion Effect. It is this that makes the film, if you will pardon the heavy-handedness, interesting.

Hoffman's Michael Dorsey doesn't exactly fall in love with his female double: his creation Dorothy is no Galatea. But he gets to like his creation well enough to be stung when people make slighting remarks about her looks or personality, calling her plump or a "wimp." When he has finally bailed out—the pretense has become unmanageable—he says: "I was a better man as a woman." Hoffman has been saying much the same in recent interviews.

Whatever preachy point about feminine assertiveness Hollywood thinks it has worked into the story, the real point seems to me less hackneyed. The good news about "Tootsie" is that it takes on the uncomfortable tyranny of rigid man-woman roles, and actually leaves you with a pleasant and paradoxical point about them.

Stereotyped sexual roles are perhaps less rigidly insisted upon in American society than they were 25 or 30 years ago, but they still exercise a tyranny, even when satirized. (One thinks of the dress-up revues that are said to afford after-hours levity at all-male enclaves.)

Without plunging into the murky depths of psychotherapy, one way of putting it is to say that Hoffman's actor, playing "Dorothy Michael," has given a workout to his "anima." That's Jung's metaphor for the bottled-up female spirit that lurks in every male, no one being absolutely one or the other. It is also the idealized woman inside every man.

Most of us, fortunately, are completely at home with our sexual identities. Oh, we might enjoy some mild flouting of male-female stereoptyes—ironing or vacuuming, let's say—but are faintly embarrassed if our friends catch us at it. Most men have difficulty discovering their Dorothy sides, hence never discover the interesting paradox that they're better men for doing so, which is the old point that "Tootsie" makes in a fresh way.

"Tootsie," in short, isn't so much about sexual confusion as it is about sexual clarification, the kind of clarification that comes from imaginative role reversal. This was once, presumably, a commonplace of the stage: in Shakespeare's time and later, men often played women's roles.

"Tootsie," perishable as it no doubt is, uses that old comic convention to make a thoughtful point about the benefits of imagining yourself on the other side of a barrier.

Adam, may I present Eve?

—January 4, 1983

Tremulex Ossa

Lines composed after falling asleep over a medical advice column:

Sir: The condition you describe, though sometimes confused with a common tennis elbow, is a gradual atrophy of the dorsal medusa, with complex inflammation of the joints. It is often found in sedentary men over the age of 35, and severe attacks often occur during the 7 p.m. network news programs. Your symptoms are not unusual—a tic of the lower left eyelid and a tendency to make involuntary buzzing noises with the tongue. Owing, perhaps, to the relative harmlessness of this disorder (Kaltenborn's syndrome) medical science has not yet developed a cure. But Dr. Fritz Milton of the Utah Medical Center has found the condition to be associated with vitamin G deficiency. I often offer my private patients the famous advice of Dr. Satchell Paige: "If your dorsal medusa disputes you, lie down and pacify it with cool thoughts."

Madam: It is obvious from your letter that you suffer from Infanticomitatus, which the old herb doctor knew as premature paralysis of the will. The standard specific in homeopathy was gooseberry juice. The epidemiology is not well understood, although the fact that you live in Hamtramck and have 10 children corroborates a recent study in the Nebraska Journal of Medicine. I once treated a woman, a native Australian, for Infanticomitatus and found that it responded to a mixture of aspirin and quinine water. Acute cases have been cured by radical tonsilectomy.

Sir: Your condition is shivered timbers. I suspect that X-rays would reveal a slight ripping of the tripex major, aggravated by your program of jogging and yoga. Shivered timbers (tremulex ossa) has only recently appeared in this country, and some physicians believe it to be correlated with the importation of foreign compact cars. I would advise you to stop jogging and begin a moderate program of specific exercise for the affected limb. Try rotating the left foot counter-clockwise (or the right foot clockwise) when you awaken in the mornings, taking care not to spindle the knee. While relatively new to this country, shivered timbers was well known to physicians in the ancient world, at least before the decline of the chariot. The familiar Biblical treatment (Exodus 1:3) is: "If thy left leg offend thee, cut it off and cast it from thee." This unnecessarily radical treatment is still common in the Soviet Union.

Madam: Modern medicine was moving toward the conquest of Ribaristic follica, commonly known as runaway hairline, until a rash of frivolous malpractice suits in California halted research. This condition is associated with prolonged matutinal slumber and often strikes without warning. Your symptoms are fairly common. You say that you first noticed a tormenting auricular itch at the bridge table but were embarrassed to excuse yourself while a bid of six no-trump was being played. One of my own patients has found it convenient to carry a feather-duster in her purse for temporary relief during sudden attacks.

Sir: Verdant moriartis is the technical term you are looking for. Green stains begin to appear on the fingers and toes, usually after the vernal equinox, and take on a deeper color as the grass-cutting season progresses. You needn't be alarmed—many of my own patients have found that normal color returned to the extremities after a few weeks' abstention from gardening. Hot baths with lemon juice are sometimes helpful. If you need further help, send 25 cents for my booklet, "Coping With Garden-Variety Verdant Moriartis."

Madam: Since you are of Irish descent, I am not surprised that you suffer occasionally from Rotunda megalotopica, which was first diagnosed near Dublin during the Troubles, and is often known as "O'Reilly's Complaint." Sufferers from this fairly harmless condition experience severe distention of the metatarsal sacs and uncontrolled risibility. The late Dr. Henrich Thorple, working with white rats at the Thorple Clinic, left few questions unanswered about the etiology of O'Reilly's Complaint. Thorple's rats, after ingesting small quantities of heavily buttered Irish potatoes, began to breathe heavily. Dr. Thorple, in his celebrated paper, "The asthmatic rats," suggests that potatoes activate enzyme reactions in the lower extremities. If, after switching to another starchy food, you continue to burst into howls of sudden laughter you might try facial submersion into lukewarm salt water, which tends to inhibit the symptom. Chronic rotunda should be observed and treated by your doctor.

—May 13, 1976

Typewriters and Other Deadly Weapons

While I had always been aware of certain tensions between Washington and New York, it was not until I came to work in this city some four years ago that I began to grasp the sharp differences in their habits of mind.

At a New York dinner party honoring a Washington journalist friend, where the company ran to writers and editors from both cities, I was astonished to hear Norman Podhoretz, editor of *Commentary,* declare that even his closest friendships are sometimes jeopardized by serious disagreements. Such is the intensity of doctrine along the Hudson.

35

If Washington felt this way, blood would run in the streets, and government grind to a standstill. New York, I found myself thinking, retained an almost medieval sense of the reality of abstractions, though most of them were secular rather than religious. The intellectual dividing line was not between one opinion and another—either of which might be wrong, both of which might be half right and conditioned by quirks of temperament. No, it was truth against heresy. New Yorkers might no longer drag the losers of debates to the stake. But measures short of burning seemed to be approved.

In Washington, people were necessarily more "politique" about ideas, especially political ones; at ease with the inevitable variousness of opinion. In Washington it would take more than a disagreement to rupture a friendship.

Having now read Mr. Podhoretz's fascinating political memoir of the '60s, *Breaking Ranks,* I understand more about the New York view of ideas. *Breaking Ranks* is an extended epistle from Mr. Podhoretz to his college-age son, who had asked if his father had really believed "all that stuff," the creed of 1960s political radicalism. Mr. Podhoretz *had* believed it, in fact. He candidly describes his own pilgrimage into, and out of, radicalism. It is a fascinating appraisal of the fluctuating ideological fashions of the '60s. And for a student of the New York style, it is a revealing glimpse of the intensity, usually unleavened by irony, with which New York intellectuals quarrel over ideas.

Of course, as the editor of a journal of opinion (in my view the best of its kind) Mr. Podhoretz is a specialist in the trade, a broker of ideas, an assayer of their reputability and value. When he took over *Commentary* in 1960, he set out to promote a new "radicalism" that would offer fresh perspectives while avoiding the Stalinist illusions of leftwing politics in the '30s. He gave a forum to the primitive communitarianism of Paul Goodman, the neo-Freudianism of Norman O. Brown and to other avant garde notions. Yet it wasn't long before the radicalism in social thought he had promoted went sour for him, especially when seized upon in a simplistic form by youthful university-wreckers who thought the Vietnam war not a blunder but a crime. He repented at leisure, then switched *Commentary* onto a course that was about 125 degrees in the other direction.

All this ideological to-ing and fro-ing is of great interest, especially as Mr. Podhoretz describes his personal enmities and grudges in confessional detail. Yet he seems remarkably unaware of the striking oddity of the story. How is it that mere ideas are taken so seriously if intellectual fashions change so swiftly?

36

As he presents it, the New York commerce in ideas sometimes seems almost as erratic (in a refined way, to be sure) as the movement of the hemlines and lapels in *Women's Wear Daily*.

Mr. Podhoretz can, with a straight face, describe intellectuals as "specialists in ideological conflict" and assign them a "traditional role as *fanatical* devotees of the dream of a good society." This view of the intellectual life will seem a bit militarized to most readers, I suspect. It did to me. Besides, the fleeting alignments over which friendships and crockery are shattered nightly in Manhattan seem to depend less on "ideas" than on attitudes—attitudes, moreover, that are governed less by reflection than by mood, temperament and events, and distinguished above all by their mutability.

No wonder that New York and Washington are often at odds over their mindsets. Washington, Mr. Podhoretz parenthetically suggests, is characterized by a "philistine attitude toward ideas." But what strikes New Yorkers as philistinism is often, I suspect, a difference of requirement. In Washington an idea must come within some nodding range of policy; and that is too seldom true of New York intellectual fashions, which so far as I can see rarely sit still long enough for close inspection.

These New York-Washington differences do not, I believe, establish the superiority of either place. They do explain the persistent rivalries between the political capital and the cultural capital. I propose an exchange of ambassadors. I further propose the appointment of the stimulating Mr. Podhoretz to the New York City embassy, somewhere on Massachusetts Avenue. But to get along in the capital, he will have to check his typewriter and other deadly weapons at the door. —*November 1, 1979*

Skills Are Not Enough

Are you more bewildered than enlightened by the great debate over American education—including the recent and unwelcome news that teacher pay has actually fallen, in real terms, over the past decade?

Welcome to the club.

I became a charter member of debaters' anonymous some years ago when the educational faddists abruptly turned against

37

the "open classrooms" and giant consolidated schools they had so recently and enthusiastically touted.

Now the issue is whether merit pay would be a cure-all (Secretary of Education Bell) or a catastrophe (National Education Association). Bell surely holds the higher ground. But even if merit pay overcomes NEA obstruction, it cannot itself solve the underlying problems which have little to do with money.

Americans are very serious about training. It is a national faith. At all levels we maintain a staggering array of schools teaching skills and methodologies: law schools, journalism schools, cosmetology schools, barber schools, business schools, "vocational" schools galore.

Training may be valuable, but it is too easily confused with education.

You can sharpen the distinction by asking yourself what, in your own schooling, would be of value if you found yourself in the Robinson Crusoe dilemma—cast up alone on a gadgetless island, with months or years of self-diversion to face.

Boy Scout survival skills would be handy, but once you built your lean-to and your fire and found food, what then? What stock of the world's rich lore could you recreate from memory, for entertainment or solace? It would vary, no doubt, but not long ago I ran across this bleak exclamation by Alfred Kazin, a distinguished teacher and writer:

"Donne? Dante? Don't make this professor laugh. I encounter graduate students who don't know the date of the Russian Revolution, who have never heard that 'the unexamined life is not worth living,' (and don't know who said it), who ask...what 'a Garibaldi' is, and read Yeats without knowing what happened at Easter 1916. No one who does not teach in America has an idea of the depth and complacency of our ignorance." But, you say, Kazin is speaking of advanced students, presumably dedicated to the life of the mind. What is substandard for them isn't substandard for everyone. Quite right. But this failure of general education is epidemic, at all levels.

The noble experiment in mass education got off the track when its theorists imagined that training (the necessary inculcation of useful skills) could be substituted for education (preserving and passing along a tradition of "the best that has been thought and said").

Ironically, the divorce between training and education is nowhere more deeply rooted than in the so-called schools of education. Not even law schools or business schools are as dedi-

38

cated to the single-minded marketing of methods, skills, "learning tools," at the expense of substance.

Yet the schools of education, linked in most states to the central teacher-certifying authority (usually dominated by their graduates), dictate conditions of certification and employment.

Those certification requirements are usually heavy on training (often of the most mind-numbing sort) and very light on education. You can know all there is to know about Yeats and Socrates, but if you haven't taken dozens of hours of method and theory you will be ineligible to teach elementary grammar.

It might recharge my own interest in the great educational debate if we began with all the unaddressed questions about what we really want from the schools. Skills, of course. But what else? It would be even more encouraging if we could take bulldozers to most of the schools of education, then disperse their charges to departments where they might learn a fact or two to teach.

But having watched so many great debates over the schools come and go during the past quarter century, I expect this one too to fade without a trace. As usual, the educationists will hunker down and wait it out.

—*September 5, 1983*

"Baptist Rhetoric" and Secular Tremors

In 1960, when the religion of a presidential candidate last grew controversial, Protestants of the Southern Bible Belt thought long and hard about John F. Kennedy's Roman Catholicism, but ultimately voted for him. The ancient cry of "rum and romanism," so damaging to Al Smith 32 years earlier, vanished and has not been raised since. Between them, President Kennedy and Pope John XXIII buried the Southern Catholic phobia for good.

Now that fortune smiles on Gov. Jimmy Carter of Georgia, who embodies the very marrow of Southern Protestantism, one hears it asked whether "America is ready for a Christian President from the South." That's how Joseph Kraft put it the other day.

39

The short answer is that the country was ready for one in 1912—that arch-Calvinist from the valley of Virginia, Woodrow Wilson, who was nurtured in a Georgia manse. The long answer awaits the ballots of July and November, but its factors are complex. Governor Carter must yet be tested in Northern urban states where, as Mr. Kraft observes, "Baptist rhetoric runs way behind bread and ideology."

That is an accurate, if condescending, way of saying that Governor Carter's religion disconcerts the secular impresarios who like to set the nation's political tone.

It was acceptable, this "Baptist rhetoric," on the tongue of a prophet; Martin Luther King Jr. rang the mystic chords of brotherhood and faith as none since Lincoln. But how is a virtuous pagan to react when it appears as transparently earnest, in the speeches of a white peanut farmer from Plains, Ga.—a place so far removed in distance and spirit from Georgetown as to occupy another planet? What are we to make of this talk of serious counseling in the piney woods with a sister who is a faith healer, this talk of second birth, secret missionary journeys, brotherly love, and even prayer in the anterooms of the governor's office in Atlanta? Such intensity is not in the best of taste.

There is a ghost to be laid, now as in 1960. Before Senator Kennedy laid the first, ranting parsons had stuffed the Southern Protestant imagination with dread: The election of a Catholic President would surely bring a reversion to medieval superstition, followed by the governance of papal legates.

John Kennedy successfully dispelled these lingering fears in his answers to the Houston ministers. If the Carter thing goes far enough, perhaps the governor should submit to a similar inquisition by Northern priests and rabbis, and a representative or two of the Ethical Culture Society.

The apprehension underlying Mr. Kraft's question, after all, can only be that Mr. Carter's evangelical religion would interfere undesirably with his political conduct. Unlikely. Governor Carter, less intensely private than Mr. Kennedy, has the same well-compartmentalized mind. His public statements hint at no danger that "Baptist fundamentalism" would blight his keen analytical abilities, which as Mr. Kraft himself certifies "follow with a sure grasp the component parts...of complicated arguments."

As a practicing Baptist, moreover, Jimmy Carter is presumably commited to a quite private view of religion. Baptists all but invented religious pluralism. That notable Southern Baptist, the late Hugo Black, constantly invoked, in decision and dissent alike, Jefferson's "eternal wall of separation between church and state." His views on the meaning of the First Amendment establishment clause were notoriously restrictive.

Yet to say all this obviously does not close the subject. Something peculiarly Southern, something exotically regional, lingers. W. J. Cash, who left few corners of the Southern mind unexplored, thought there *was* a difference; he considered that a certain "Celtic" religiosity was imperishably native to the Southerner, reinforced by both temperament and geography:

"Even when he was a sort of native pagan, knowing little of the Bible and hooting contemptuously at parsons, he was nevertheless at bottom religious. Ancestral phobias grappled him toward the old center, and immemorial awes, drawn in with his mother's milk, whispered imperative warning in his ears." And the climate! "There are days when the booming of the wind in the pines is like the audible rushing of time—when the sad knowledge of the grave stirs in the subconscious and bends the spirit to melancholy; days when the questions that have no answers must insinuate themselves into the minds of the least analytical of men."

And, we might add, the *most* analytical of men as well. This regional propensity is not to be minimized; it is probably basic to an understanding of this Georgian who would be President. The old-time religion is central to the way people approach life, answer "the questions that have no answers," down in Plains, Ga. Say what one will of the Plains metaphysic, it is a far cry from the dried-out secularism of our time.

—March 25, 1976

The "Engineering" of English

A disconcertingly close reader of a recent editorial "Presidents and words" complains that the piece was strewn with teasing asides about the craft of writing that beg defense and elaboration.

She particularly mentions the cryptic observation that "language, too, has its engineering" and the claim that it was by "trickery" that Abraham Lincoln "tuned his language to high effect at Gettysburg."

41

"Engineering"—I now quote her directly—"is a crude analogy, since engineering involves scientific and mechanical principles and writing is basically an art. And Lincoln knew so much good prose and poetry by heart that his writing must have been an exercise of the ear, not a bag of tricks."

Both points are well taken. Engineering *is* a crude analogy; and writing, for a master like Lincoln, cannot have much resembled the building of bridges. But with that partial concession, let us explore the issue further.

In the term "engineering," we had in mind not the elements of grammar and syntax, with which any sound rhetorical constuction starts, but the classical rhetorical patterns which critics like Gilbert Highet (whose essays on the Gettysburg Address we quoted) have discovered in good prose.

Mr. Highet, for instance, finds two in Lincoln's famous speech—*antithesis* and the *tricolon*. Notice, he says, the antithesis in this well-remembered passage: "The world will little note nor long remember what we say here; but it cannever forget what they did here." Indeed, to dwell on the obvious, President Kennedy had antithesis in his ear, if not consciously on his mind, when he said: "Ask not what your country can do for you, but what you can do for your country.' Same thing, with the following difference: In Ted Sorensen, Mr. Kennedy had a speechwriter of excellent style with a fondness for antithesis, so that it became a sort of rhetorical tic. Like all the rhetorical devices that we inherit from Latin by way of the 18th Century, antithesis needs a strict sense of occasion. It can be absurdly trivialized: "Always close the door before you leave, but never leave after you have opened the window."

As for the tricolon—"the division of an idea into three harmonious parts, usually of increasing power," as Mr. Highet defines—consider: "government of the people, by the people, and for the people" or "we cannot dedicate, we cannot hallow, we cannot consecrate this ground."

Discussing the prose music of the *Book of Common Prayer*, Prof. C. S. Lewis mentions a couple of other classical devices of prose engineering—the *cursus* and the *idem in alio*.

The first consists of "certain regular distributions of accent at the end of a sentence or clause," as in *"help* and *defend* us," *"written* for our *learning," "them* that be *penitent,"* and *"glorious* resur*rection."* Each subtle variation of meter has a name, but all exhibit the *cursus*.

My own favorite example of the *idem in alio*—literally, "the same in another form"—is Shakespearean. Lady Macbeth, in one great soliloquy, speaks of a hand made indelibly bloody by murder. Not even oceans can cleanse it. "It would the multitudinous seas incarnadine, making the green one red," she says. A Latinate, polysyllabic statement of the idea is followed by four hammer-stroke English monosyllables.

You can argue forever about why these patterns, well executed, dress up a passage of formal prose. The argument would plunge us far into the mysteries of aesthetics, or the deeps of the mind *(idem in alio!)*. Why is a Roman arch beautiful as well as useful? Why does the division of an idea, a musical bar, a theological doctrine into three harmonious parts please the senses as well as bind the memory? Why three, and not two or four?

You can also argue, long and hard, about the degree of self-consciousness that expert writers bring to their work—or more often, perhaps, their revisions. Professor Lewis, after counting the frequency of *cursus* in the prayer book, was persuaded that learned critics probably find more instances than the translators consciously intended. Self-consciousness certainly varies from writer to writer and from age to age. The Augustans of the 18th Century were more deliberate writers than their Victorian grandchildren, obviously.

Finally, there is the eternal question about conception and execution. Muddy thought gorgeously expressed is as dispiriting to read as keen thought clumsily expressed. I believe—and to this extent agree with the critic of our editorial—that pleasing prose is the mirror of clear thought (and emotion), and that artful expression springs from deep, if well-tutored, instinct which is usually the product of hours and hours of attentive reading and writing.

Yet good prose has its engineering and trickery. The fact is as inescapable as the legendary eyes of Texas.

—February 2, 1978

Spiro's Chocolate Dictionary

Spiro T. Agnew's technicolor comet first ascended in national politics when he ran for governor of Maryland—a heroic figure, according to admirers in what he now calls "the national

43

impact media," saving decency from the menace of the early prophet of ethnic purity, George P. Mahoney.

Next we saw him during the urban riots of the Sixties, wigging the Baltimore black leaders for their lack of spunk.

Then, suddenly elevated to the vice presidency, we had Agnew the scold of the elitist press and the "nattering nabobs of negativism"—the Agnew who deplored the Kent State shootings as the expectable result of dissent's excesses.

Today, after another dizzy reversal of fortune—and a long silence—Proteus strikes again. We have before us yet another Mr. Agnew, with yet another provocative line—that the major U.S. news organs are disproportionately controlled and managed by Jews.

One of the characters in Mr. Agnew's novel *The Canfield Decision,* a Persian writer, states the thesis more boldly than Mr. Agnew himself stated it in a recent Q&A with The Star's Bill Delaney: "American Jews exert an influence on American opinion that is far heavier than their numbers would indicate. They are the strongest single influence in the big media—the media with worldwide impact. They control much of the financial community. Therefore, they heavily affect, through propaganda, the majority of Congress." The voice is fictional, but the view is clearly Agnew's.

It would be a mistake, just as this fictional Agnew surrogate declares, to scream "anti-Semitism" at the latest Agnew theory. Not only is there, as in all his previous theories, a curious deficiency of the malice that one associates with outright bigotry; it is also a simple fact, as he says, that "brightness" and "inventiveness" (and in certain instances rarely mentioned by Mr. Agnew, the laws of inheritance) have given American Jews a large hand in the press.

What is missing in this new Agnew line, as in so many of his prior fancies, is a nice sense of the impact of language—not only of how things may be said but of how they may not be said. In short, a failure of taste.

Mr. Agnew is obviously a man fascinated—not to say intoxicated—by words and the theories one may spin from them, as some are fascinated by Morris designs, others by the parts of motor cars, and still others by flora or lepidoptera. When he indulges this fascination he is nearly always off-key by a half to a quarter tone (at least)—like a monotone with a passion for singing Bach arias whose technical mastery outstrips his native instrument.

One is reminded of W. J. Cash's observation of the culture affected by the new-rich planters of the Old South—that "it was not an emanation from within, but a fine garment put on from the outside." In Mr. Agnew, there is the constant sense of a man living beyond the means of his intellect, art and taste—aspiring to ease in a domain not quite within his natural range. If I am not mistaken it was just this shared unease that underlay the affinity Richard Nixon felt for him: the fraternity of thwarted aspiration.

I do not believe that Mr. Agnew is a malicious man—that he means to wound or defame American Jews any more than he meant to wound or defame the reporters and commentators upon whom he poured the popgun fire of his earlier rhetoric against the elitist press.

What seems to be lacking—what could be more dangerous than he imagines—is an ear for the overtones of words and phrases. Perhaps there is a functional anti-Semitism, as in Mr. Agnew's scourging of the press there was a certain functional demagoguery.

The disconcerting thing about Mr. Agnew—the functional mischief—is not so much what he says or how he says it, but that this shallow and tawdry stuff seems to command an instant and enthusiastic audience. It is as if, in his offkey way, he sounded a chord of submerged obsession in the American people.

For there is an audience for Agnewism, past and present—as there was an audience for McCarthyism, whose manifestations could be considerably uglier than their instigator. Sen. Joe McCarthy, as Richard Rovere portrays him in that astute biography of a few years ago, was altogether a rather amiable and blundering man, poking about in notions beyond his ken, but lacking the malice attributed to him by his more hysterical critics. There was nothing amiable or blundering in the passions his demagoguery released.

We must therefore hope that as he goes from talk show to talk show, from interview to interview, with his line about Jews in the "high impact media," Spiro Agnew will eventually stop to ponder not only what he says but what he is heard to say—and heard to mean. But that may be asking too much of a man whose dictionary is his whiskey and chocolate.

—May 27, 1976

Salute to an Unquiet Olympus

Few but college newspaper editors enjoy godliness in their time. One who has since resumed ordinary clay may perhaps be pardoned a salute to his former Mt. Olympus. I am thinking, of course, of the Daily Tar Heel, student newspaper at the University of North Carolina, which last week celebrated its 70th birthday.

Its editors, remarks the incumbent, "often assume the role of campus god—for lack of any other vaguely responsible element to fill the vacuum." That is essentially true. But the grinding task of issuing a four-page daily with one foot in the classroom permits little basking in this godliness. Indeed, it was only when stripped of his thunderbolts and released onto the tennis courts late in 1956 that this god learned from a charming co-ed: "I always wanted to stop you as you dashed about the campus—but you seemed so remote, so busy, so important, that I was afraid to try."

What power! What infallibility! I should have suspected it in time, recalling how one walked trembling into the Tar Heel's dilapidated sanctum in the student union as a freshman. The mirth of the gods, which Homer called inextinguishable, seemed so then. The editor was Barry Farber, a gangling wrestler who spoke, they said, six languages and wrote his editorials with a number of gorgeous Scandinavian girls hovering at his elbow—and wrote well, too. Another immortal was Chuck Hauser, now an editor of The Charlotte Observer, who seemed the most professional journalist imaginable. Every day he dissected the front page with a big red crayon-pencil, and hung it up to bleed on the bulletin board. And there was Rolfe Neill, the blunt-spoken, who in the McCarthy period reduced a hard-faced FBI man to tears for snooping on college students. This consortium of reigning immortals lacked no sense of the paper's majesty—or its infallibility.

How was one to become a part of it? My first attempt at Tar Heel punditry—a column about dogs in the Albert Payson Terhune vein—fell flat. Neill rejected it: "I don't like it," he said, "it's no damned good." (Profanity was de rigueur.) One accepted the rejection as a sort of journalistic purple heart, considering its source, and lived to write an equally intolerable inquiring reporter column called "pulling the grass roots," and also bad pieces on Thomas Wolfe, who as an earlier Tar Heel editor seemed an appropriate subject, if an unfortunately prose-style model.

Anyway, the point is right: Daily Tar Heel editors were gods. And even if now the illusion of editorial omniscience has passed I am glad the Daily Tar Heel feels chipper on its birthday. It must. It has always specialized in blatant deeds and sayings. One day in my time it loftily observed that the university at Chapel Hill had sunk to the level of "a teapot in an academic tempest." "It is as though," this immortal broadside continued, "our tubes had been tied off...We sit here, the calm eye of an academic storm raging elsewhere." An April Fool's Day edition of the same era revealed that Sen. Joe McCarthy (our standard bete noire) would convoke an investigation of big-time college athletics. A photo of the senator, peering with a magnifying glass at the nether end of a horse, adorned the exposé.

Plainly, the Daily Tar Heel specializes in effrontery. "No one is safe from its barbs," boasts the current editor, "from chancellors to student legislators, from coaches to magazine editors." True; and salutary, I believe. But the mystery is why Chapel Hill, unlike the more timid universities that muzzle their embarrassing student press, benevolently tolerates its cheek.

I thought I had an insight when Chancellor Robert House (emeritus, as he now is) confronted me in the lobby of the Carolina Inn, just before my year on Olympus was to end. He noted my impending graduation. "Well, Yoder," he asked, "do you think the unversity can survive without you?" Here, the good old man had probed to the deepest, the unthinkable truth. The Tar Heel in its most frenzied tantrums could do no permanent damage. The editorial heavens could shake and thunder, but the campus endured forever.

Most college administrators do not comprehend that amusing truth, and would have avenged their injuries by requiring a pound or so of student flesh. That has never happened to the Tar Heel. Phillips Russell, who edited the paper in 1903 or thereabouts, tells how he was one day summoned to the office of President Venable, who expressed a desire to read Russell's editorials before they saw print. Mr. Russell assented. But he told the president that he must come to the Daily Tar Heel office to do so. Dr. Venable never did.

So the Daily Tar Heel continues to thrive on a diet of benevolent administrative tolerance and the special illusion of its youthful editors that all questions are answerable, exclusively, from their angle. That is what the incumbent means by "the role of campus god." All things considered, there have been less constructive deities.

—*March 5, 1963*

Memoirs of Sergeant-Startling

Before me as I write is a newspaper photograph of a pleasant-looking young man, David Miller of Syracuse, N. Y. Miller, who is burning his draft card with great concentration, is a hero of the anti-war movement. A more militant member of this new legion is one Pieter Romayn Clark. On the day of his Army induction, Clark signed up 21 recruits for an antiwar petition and—what is even more startling—"shouted down a startled sergeant." He was sent home; the sergeant's reaction was not reported.

I suppose that fiercer patriots than I will take care of the denunciation of Miller and Clark, but to a sometime sergeant-startler Clark's unadmirable but gamey venture brings back memories.

I was of a generation too young to have had a good war and too old to qualify for matrimonial exemption, and in the days of which I write draft-card burning would have been thought irregular, to say the least.

So, with draft cards intact, we all arrived one freezing February night at a noted basic training camp, well out on the plains. It was there that I saw my first sergeant. He mustered us against a convenient airport wall and then said, menacingly: "I suppose you know you are all in for the hitch." He seemed to mean 20 years, which was not our understanding, but as he darted his firece little eyes from face to face no one ventured to say him nay. Fortunately, he turned out to be only an airport greeter; we never saw him again.

The real sergeant, it developed, was a roughhewn Arkansan with slitty eyes who immediately laid down extensive regulations governing the consumption of what he called "sody pop" and prefaced every directive with "take and...," as in: "If your belt is too long, take and cut it off." At first gruff, the Sergeant emerged as an admirable and skilled professional, dedicated in his humorless way to carving disciplined troops from this horde of uppity civilians. But he was a tormented man. As the weeks passed, I came to despise his tormentors.

Chief among them was a faceless higher echelon known simply, as in some Kafka tale, as "Group." On a base where rank was scarce and a master sergeant floated about like a deity, we never saw Group. We only knew that Group would someday sweep down unheralded on our firetrap of a barracks (it was estimated that it would burn completely in 12½ minutes), to mete out swift

48

justice for dirty shoes, ill-tied laundry bags, bunks that wouldn't bounce a coin, wooly-woolies and countless other violations of military polish. Many a day, the Sergeant, cast down over the condition of E Barracks, would put his face in his hands and plead with us to consider what Group would think.

It was inevitable that Group would evolve from a nameless terror into a joke. It became the pleasure of some popinjay in the rear ranks to shrill, in a falsetto voice, "Group is coming!" as the Sergeant shuddered. It is perhaps of only antiquarian interest that Group did, in fact, come one day as we were cracking 10,000 eggs on KP in a distant mess hall. Old newsreels of Marshal Hindenburg and various obergrupenfuhrers in full Wagnerian kit, spiked helmets and all, convey just the vision that Group suggested to the mind's eye. Actually, it was a bored major and two lieutenants. Several beds in the upper bay refused to bounce the major's quarter. At least 5 pairs of shoes were out of alignment, and several lint-balls could be seen skittering about the linoleum floor in the midday breeze. Group had come at 10:45 and by 11 a.m. one of the lieutenants had savagely unrolled all of Airman Basic Orin McNabb's underwear; and all that was wrong in E Barracks was that no strawberries had been declared missing, as in *The Caine Mutiny*. "Who?" the major shouted dramatically, "Who lives here? What animals?" The barracks sentry, who reported all of this later, understood the question as rhetorical and did not respond. When the major and his aides left, they had awarded 184 demerits, an all-time record, it was said. It was a historic disaster, but, strangely, the Sergeant did not scold. He put his head in his hands for a very long time, as we stood at strict attention on the troop walk, wondering what was to come. At length, he raised a suffering face and announced sternly: "By God, there'll be no goin' to the sody-pop machines today." We took our medicine without protest.

There were other torments for the Sergeant, for instance, names he could not pronounce. There was also a silly, grinning Tennessee boy who, with his law degree fresh on his sleeve, patronized the Sergeant. He got away with it because one day, at mail call, a letter came for him with a congressional frank on it. The contents were not disclosed; it became his license for what bordered on insubordination.

Another, lesser sergeant, let's call him Trent, occasionally filled in. He was as lax and cynical as the Sergeant was intense. I will never forget how he loooked when I galloped into his office early one morning on the shoe alignment stick.

49

It must be explained to those who have had no military experience that shining shoes is as important, as meticulous a craft in basic training as carving prayers on pinheads. It followed that aligning the shoes properly, once polished, was an exacting art whose completion before the 7 a.m. whistle could induce almost manic exhilaration.

It was in such a mood, not of buffoonery or fatigue, that I rode the shoe-aligning stick into Trent's little office, not knowing that he lurked there, and hardly knowing what to say when suddenly I confronted him. We stared at one another in mutual disbelief. Something in his pinched face signaled me to dismount and withdraw, and I did.

I could continue—about the confiscation of the Bible that one recruit had brought in a paperback edition, and which the Sergeant mistook for pornography; about other episodes. But enough. Whatever one may think of the Millers and Clarks of our day, they really should not assume prefabricated attitudes towards sergeants. Many come to jeer and stay to admire, as I did. Had Clark, in those days, undertaken to "shout down" the Sergeant, he would have been told to "take and" do something unpleasant, and I suspect that he would have done it—double quick.

—October 20, 1965

Einstein and "Common Sense"

Albert Einstein, born a century ago yesterday, once accepted this thumbnail summary of his noted theory of relativity: *There is no hitching post in the universe.*

The inspired metaphor was not his. It was coined by one of the many popularizers who struggled to make Dr. Einstein's physics accessible to the unmathematical. Certainly Einstein's universe illustrates the rule that "common sense" can be a treacherous guide to actuality, physical or otherwise.

Copernicus dealt the medieval outlook a hammer blow when he "stopped" the sun and set the earth revolving around it. It has been no less jarring to us to learn from Dr. Einstein, in utter contradiction of the senses, that fixed "space" and "time" are illusory, and that "energy" and "matter" are fungible.

50

In fact, the 20th Century revolution in physics has been even less accessible to common sense than usual. If it wrecked the commonsense world ("Heaven knows," exclaimed Alfred North Whitehead in 1925, "what seeming nonsense may not tomorrow be demonstrated truth"), it depended on drastic refinements of scientific instrumentation. For ordinary purposes, Newton's old laws of mechanics still hold; it is only at unimaginable velocities at or near the speed of light that Einstein's theories matter. And they are demonstrable only in the esoteric world of "subtle and ingenious experiments," recorded by subtle and ingenious instruments like Michelson's interferometer.

But arcane as it is in scientific terms, the idea of relativity—the absence of "hitching posts in the universe"—deeply affects our general outlook. When material absolutes crumbled in the laboratory, comparable absolutes in art, music, morals, theology and social theory could not be far behind.

Or could they?

William Stockton tells us that "in 1920, the most dedicated relativity opponents held a large, public, antirelativity meeting at Berlin Philharmonic Hall," a meeting which a laughing Einstein himself attended. It was a fatuous meeting, there being no known instances in which the findings of experimental science—or their supposed social effects—were nullified by rallies, marches, speeches or manifestos. But rarely for want of effort. The antirelativity rally in Berlin was of a piece with the inquisitions of Copernicus' time, the anti-evolution rallies of the Victorian years, and the anti-Mendelian genetics later officially promoted by Stalinist Russia.

It is perhaps the most interesting puzzle in the history of ideas in this century whether, or to what extent, Dr. Einstein's theory of relativity influenced the collapse of other absolutes. A cause-and-effect connection between science and culture is often postulated in the history of ideas—is, in fact, a textbook cliche. Thus the Renaisssance (man as the measure of things) is linked to the Copernican heliocentric universe as, in a later age, baroque art and music are seen as connected with Newton's orderly "clockwork" universe. The connection is certain; its exact nature, however, is not. Is it cause or coincidence?

We can see an abundance of interesting parallels between physics and other arts and sciences in our time. Did Dr. Einstein abolish absolute notions of time and space? So, in fact, did Freud in psychology, Proust in fiction, Picasso in art, Stravinsky and others in music.

In Freudian psychology, childhood traumas influence the adult; the lapse of years between the childhood scar and eccentric ("neurotic") adult behavior, while chronologically long, is psychically short. Proust, musing on time and change, shows that sensual memories do not fade with years. A long-ago visual impression of Venice, the taste of a certain teacake and the childhood scenes associated with it, can be more vivid when evoked than the trivial impressions of the day before yesterday.

Here, too, are forms of "relativity," that baffle our usual linear sense of fixed space and ever-flowing time—as, in a sense, do abstract painting and atonal music, both defiant of "common sense."

Was Dr. Einstein the architect of all this? Or did he express in science what minds and sensibilities of comparable power were expressing in other disciplines? It may be an unanswerable question, since it is beyond the ingenuity of intellectual historians to trace such connections precisely. Yet the query is not trivial. If we imagine the physicist as but one of many pioneers, along with the artist, the psychologist, the novelist, the composer—all responding to the same spirit—we must then imagine a world even stranger than the one Dr. Einstein pictured for us.

The thought is, at any rate, mind-boggling. And when the mind boggles, it is time to stop.

—*March 15, 1979*

Wouldn't You Rather Have a (1927) Buick?

My mechanically-minded 14-year old son is scandalized that I continue after many months to drive a car with a broken heater fan. He reminded me of that during a recent discussion of our mutual foibles.

In fact, he doesn't know the half of my tolerance of the personalities of automobiles, since he does not know the story of the John Foster Dulles. I shall tell him the story someday; he is not yet mellow enough to appreciate it.

The John Foster Dulles of which I write was not the secretary of state of that name but a car named for him—a 1927

52

Buick touring car bought in London, in the spring of 1957, with the aim of driving from Oxford to Rome by way of Paris.

To appreciate the story you must accept a fundamental difference among people. Some of us, though living in truce with complex modern societies, take a fatalistic view of the whims of motor cars. Vulgarly speaking, it is the view that certain cars are lemons; metaphysically speaking, it is a kind of animism, reminiscent of the belief of certain remote New Guinea savages that an abandoned American bomber was a god. In this view, a car has a spirit quite beyond the wit of mechanics to alter. If a car *wants* to have a broken heater fan it will have one. If you fix it, an obscure gismo under the hood will blow just to show it's not submitting.

There are, needless to say, those who regard all this as nonsense.

The John Foster Dulles episode began with a casual remark. The way to take a spring vacation in style, said an English friend, was to buy an old London taxicab—the old square boxlike kind—which could be had for about 50 quid. You could drive it around the world and then get what you paid for it.

Thus originated a consortium of five, of which Van Ooms and I were designated purchasing agents. Ooms and I spent an early March Saturday prowling the back lots of Bayswater for this bargain. No one had heard of a used taxi for sale. What was to be found—it would be tedious to say how—was a 1927 Buick tour car, slate blue with buff fenders, belonging to a Captain Buckley-Johnson. The captain would sell it for 55 pounds. He seemed almost eager to do so. He would even undertake certain repairs; we could send for it in a couple of days. Done, we said.

It was on the shakedown cruise that the car first disclosed a temper. Willie Morris and Dick Baker were ferrying the car from London to Oxford. Puffing up the Chiltern Hills, the Dulles's radiator boiled over with a great effusion of steam and noise. Morris, at the wheel, took his usual comic view of the radiator. Baker, who took the rational view of cars, was angry. This for 11 pounds? He announced his withdrawal from the consortium and fastened himself in his rooms at Christ Church.

On the day of departure, Baker now appeased and the radiator mended, ceremoniously christened with a Coca-Cola, the John Foster Dulles stood poised at the ancient gates of New College. At mid-afternoon, five merry tourists chugged southwest into the green English countryside. Not far into Berkshire, suddenly, with a loud blast, a rear tire expired. Only cows looked on. But as if miraculously, a little man from the Royal Automobile Club roared up by motorcycle, dismounted, saluted, and bent himself to patch the tire. He asked no questions; he demanded no fee. Was there no limit to civility?

We rumbled on, darkness falling over the countryside but our spirits rising. Rome, now, or bust! It happened as we were passing through a small village of Surrey, looking for a pub. A certain sinister scraping sound was to be heard as the Dulles negotiated a sharp corner, then a horrid bumping sensation.

"Now look what's happened," exploded Baker in a tone of bleak accusation, regretting that he had not defected after all. *"The wheel's come off!"*

The wheel had not, in fact, come off. But no matter, another ancient tire was in shreds. A garage man announced that tires for *that* sort of Yankee car—he eyed us as he might have eyed five men astride a harnessed mastodon—had not been sold in Southern England since before the War, if ever.

We spent the night—it was April, and warmer than we had a right to expect—perched at a strange angle in the leather seats of Captain Buckley-Johnson's machine. We were perched at an angle because the car was hoisted at the rear of a towing truck. In the dim light all one could see on either hand were derelict cars.

The intractability of a car that could be bought for 55 pounds suggested itself as the subject of a dialogue between the amused and the unamused. It was that discussion that revealed to me, for the first, a truth about human attitudes.

To some of us, it was obvious that not all the mechanics or Royal Automobile Club dispatchers in the Kingdom could have doctored this car as far as Rome, or even Dover. Like an old dog that knows his master's boundaries, the Dulles had adapted to a territory. The boundaries could not be breached, and there was an end of it.

This was not the view of Baker. In his view, we had bought a wreck. The wreck had performed just as a wreck might be expected to perform, and that was that. No nonsense about the souls of automobiles.

I was not there when Captain Buckley-Johnson learned, late the next day, that he still owned a 1927 Buick touring car, slate blue with buff fenders, but an insufficiency of tires. They say he reacted as an officer and a gentleman.

—January 12, 1978

54

Christmas:
The Stumbling Block

Christmas is above all a season of poetry and story, and no poet has caught its divine paradoxes more agreeably than John Betjeman:

"And is it true,
This most tremendous tale of all,
A Baby in an ox's stall?
...That God was man in Palestine
And lives today in Bread and Wine.

Is it true? That must obviously be a matter of personal belief. But we know that the human thirst for divine visitation is abiding—the eternal search for some sign that the primal powers of the universe are benevolently interested in this troubled and mutable world, interested enough to take human form and intervene in it.

Science, for all its power to explain, cannot satisfy it, having centuries ago differentiated itself from "final causes" and ultimate truth. So the craving can be satisfied only by storytelling.

All stories are not fiction, and some are of ultimate importance. The novelist, Reynolds Price, has put it this way: "We crave nothing less than perfect story...We are satisfied only by the one short tale we feel to be true: *History is the will of a just god who knows us.*"

The original Christmas tale is just such a story. Its peculiar twist was that it was the tale of a divine visitation to a world dominated by the Greek intellect, a world that had already mastered the categories of understanding familiar to us—poetic, mythic, scientific, epic.

The Greeks, of course, told themselves the divine tale in a very different way. The divinities of their ancient Olympus were at once cozier and more remote, more human-like yet psychologically distant, not only powerful and provident but playful, capricious and meddlesome.

The idea of godly attention embraced in the Christmas story came to them as a shock, for it was very different. It was in a way grander than theirs, but in the first instance homelier.

There was in it what Christians theologians call "the scandal of particularity," a startling assertion that the divine could

55

assume fully human form, with all its frailties and vulnerabilities. It was the story of a child born in circumstances of shocking ordinariness, a message of hope mixed with a most ungodly vulnerability to suffering, humiliation and even a criminal's death. It was a "stumbling bock," even as St. Paul said, a radical revision of the Greek and Hebraic conception of the remoteness and invincibility of gods and even heroes.

It is small wonder that so strange a tale remained suspect. For Christmas is indeed the newest of the main Christian festivals. It was hardly observed at all before 200 A.D.; it was sanctioned by only two of the four gospels (Luke and Matthew), unmentioned in the most telling, human and authentic (Mark) or in the most exalted and mysterious (John).

So the wariness that has been felt about Christmas was there from the start. And perhaps advisedly, for there is about Christmas an overlay of fancy and sentimentality that is alien to the deeper fabric of Christian belief. It was a pretty tale—shepherds in the fields, singing in the skies, an infant on a bed of straw—whose ingredients and colors are to a degree evasive and mythological.

Still, there is a quality about the Christmas story that appeals to the deepest quarters of the heart: the proclamation of a divine gift to humankind exemplifying generosity, good will, kindliness, the hope for universal reconciliation and peace. And all these are at all times scarce in a naughty world.

Today the story remains a scandal—a stumbling block— and it is easy to understand why. In our time, the power of story to explain ultimate things is greatly diminished by the habit of scientific thought. Our typical form of knowing is the form that traces all mysteries to "natural" causes, from the known limits of starry space to the microscopic world of biochemistry.

At Christmastime, thus handicapped, we are sharply reminded of the need to rediscover the powerful uses of story and myth, and above all the perfect story that "history is the will of a just god who knows us." It is both incredible and indispensable, not the least of the great paradoxes of faith.

"And is it true…this most tremendous tale of all?" It will be truer, certainly, if we admit that life is more than the sum of its natural elements; if we allow the possibility that the universe is pervaded by a purposefulness that science discarded as irrelevant to its uses centuries ago; if we acknowledge the truth of a stubborn and persistent intrusion of divine love into mundane affairs of which not even the wonders of Greek intellect can ever give a full account.   —December 24, 1982

The Tranquil Way We Were

In the eyes of others older or younger, whose composure has been rattled by wars or political passions, the class of 1956 (too young for Korea, too old for Vietnam) must seem fortunate. Or unfortunate, if you think us stuffy and unscarred, as some do.

Even at a 25th class reunion, our generation's theme remains elusive. We were never a "silent" generation, as charged. Having learned to talk before "you know" stopped all conversational gaps, we were actually rather articulate, and had the habit of speaking our minds. We also knew how to enjoy ourselves; and Chapel Hill was a place, the Fifties the time, to do so. You could also work a bit under excellent tuition if you wished to do that. And a surprising number of us did.

According to the reunion class survey, a majority of us now call ourselves "conservative." With an average family income of almost $70,000 and a taste for Masterpiece Theater that is not surprising. We have, we are told, 2.6 children on average and want them to excel academically—preferring a filial Phi Beta Kappa key to a varsity letter.

Most of us would send sons or daughters to this enduringly lovely and beguiling place. Indeed, many of us already do. But that is not surprising either, since many of us were sons and daughters—even grandsons and granddaughters—of alumni. The teachers we remember best were all in the old humanistic studies: an archeologist whose overflowing Egyptology lectures were good for the grade average; three historians; a professor of Bible studies; three of English.

The town has a timelessness about it. McCorkle Place, with its overarching oaks and 18th Century buildings, is among the lovely academic sites in the country. But all is not changeless. On Franklin Street, the Goody Shop is no more. Gone are the front-window tables where rowdier classmates could be seen at almost any hour with ranks and files of beer bottles at their elbows. Hogan's Lake, not a proper lake but a muddy cowpasture pond where combos blared on matchless spring afternoons, has been filled in, they say, its pleasures unknown to latter-day students. A condominium is rumored to be there now.

At a 25th reunion, the shock is the state of long unseen faces. It is not just that they are older, and some also wiser, though they are. It is also that they seem at first glimpse blurred, like an undried instant snapshot: familiar but undefined. Bev Webb, the class president, put it wittily, as usual: "You want to ask, who *were* you?" But even as you stare, the faces begin to focus out of the blur of graying hair and wrinkles. And the longer you stare the younger they look—the portrait of Dorian Gray in reverse.

We were never a pious lot, however conventional we were (and are) in other ways. The class has its clergymen but none was at hand when, after refreshment of Virginia Gentleman and other elixirs, the cry went up for an invocation before dinner. We are, after all, Southern and church-bred. But it also seemed in character that the grace came to be pronounced by the only known pornographic novelist of our class, a Yadkinville boy with a nasal drawl who has always conversed easily with the Almighty.

As he thanked the Lord for sending us to Chapel Hill, I remembered the day long ago when he stood at a microphone hawking tickets to an outdoor dance. It would be on the tennis courts, he was saying, when a voice said, "unless it rains." "By God, it had better *not* rain," he brayed, craning his long, doleful face skyward. His invocation, in the same amiably irreverent vein, was applauded. Still, this class has undoubtedly produced more sinners than saints or zealots. And if anyone claims to have been born again, the experience is not remarked in the class profile.

When I think back on our time here, I think of a line from a Robert Graves essay we all read in our Brooks and Warren *Modern Rhetoric* books, in freshman English: "It was a stable world." This old town, which the local newspaper and radio stations still call a village, *was* a village then, the university providing its only business. Save for Mr. Morehead's planetarium, the "new" buildings were of the Twenties and Thirties, were few, and discreetly hid themselves among the trees.

There were about 5,200 of us, including the graduate and professional schools, and you knew everyone but the recluses. Ike was in the White House. Our only flirtation with activism was a "Joe Must Go" rally, supporting Sen. Sam Ervin's decision to vote to censure the Wisconsin senator. And it was punctuated by wayward beer stops.

The campus traditions, some very old, were readily observed. Professors left the room during quizzes and exams, and knocked before re-entering. There must have been some cheating, but I never saw any. There were "characters" around town like James Street, the writer, and Mary Gilson, the retired sociologist, who conducted a merry but unending quarrel over the merits of the sexes. That was of its time, too. Equality of the

58

sexes was at a barely experimental stage, 25 years ago. There were seven men for every "coed," as we still brazenly called them.

Now one of those coeds and I have a daughter here, as do others among our intermarrying classmates. What she finds here is very different, if also well loved, and she takes a more guarded view of the human prospect than I recall taking at her age. But who can blame her? It is a stable world no longer.

—May 21, 1981

A New Look at an Old Town

The town where I grew up is, and was, very much like the town where you grew up—a bit older perhaps. In colonial days thrifty Scots-Irish settlers at Haw's Old Fields, who on Sundays worshipped John Knox's stern God in a church built 230 years ago and still in use, traded there with the lingering Indians. Along a neighboring road, a few years later, Cornwallis' Redcoats marched to their fateful rendezvous at Yorktown. Colonel M, the local grandee, gave his name to the town, which bears it still.

When I was growing up there, the founding family—a branch of it anyway—survived in reduced estate living in a ramshackle house with slave quarters still standing behind it. One cold November night, in a year impossible to specify now, the lone male scion had too much to drink (as, by rumor, he often had) and fell in the way of a delivery truck. The line came abruptly to an end.

The town was, as they say in the South, sot in its ways. The furniture factory whistle, summoning its craftsmen to "The South's Oldest Makers of Fine Furniture," punctuated the day, at seven, noon and five—except for a two-week July holiday, when its silence became penetrating.

There were four distinct classes of people in my town, if you counted the farm folk who lived at country places called Hebron and Woodlawn and the millworkers of "Mexico" whose cottages perched in rows near the abandoned clay mine. All the town's known Republicans were tagged, like exotic migratory birds, and it was unkindly whispered that they all descended from carpetbaggers. On a fine Sunday morning you could set your watch, the furniture factory whistle being silent, by the ferocious roar

59

of Miss Emma H's old auto, as with elaborate stuttering and popping she readied her noon departure from the First Presbyterian Church. Traffic parted to make way, like the Red Sea before the Children of Israel.

It was small enough, my town, to blend gradually into the surrounding country, where fields of grass and briar—good quail and rabbit country—parted woods of loblolly pine, hickory and beech, poplar and oak. On certain autumn days in the woods the rattle of hickory nuts on dry fallen oak leaves and the fussy bickering of squirrels were positively symphonic. In May, in town, the dogwoods lining the main residential street blossomed in clouds of white; and in the fall, following the rhythms of the year, companion maples flamed in incandescent hues of red, yellow and orange.

The town where I grew up has changed now—as, no doubt, has the town where you grew up. We walked around it recently, on a quiet and misty Christmas day, taking the old road through the woods that once led to the baseball park. The park is now startlingly overgrown with pine. We passed the field, just under the power lines, where rough tackle football was played, its scale now dwarfed to belie memory. The trail has surrendered to wild shrubs and generations of leaves, and is littered now with the rubbish of the instant food age: throw-away bottles and beer cans, frozen food cartons. The road at the end, unpaved when I was a boy there, dusty in summer and muddy in winter as only red clay can be, is smoothly blacktopped.

What we mostly noticed, as we walked, was how the new houses, all brick suburban look-alikes, are untidily jammed into the open spaces. On the main street, the prosperous old houses, still lined with maple and dogwood, look a bit forlorn. One doesn't know, as one certainly knew 30 years ago, who lives in them, or how they spend their time, or what their family secrets are. Some houses are elaborately remodeled, honest Victorian slicked over into imitation Williamsburg, with a weathervaned cupola on the garage.

Here, looking worn and down at the joints, is Miss Ella B's big house, once a kindergarten where naughty boys were sent to stand, humiliated, behind the upright piano. Miss B must be dead now. She seemed to be living on borrowed time 30 years ago, when behind her frail but straight back her charges mimmicked her strange flapping footsteps. And here, a block or so beyond, stands the pleasing old bell tower of the church, showing its age, the window-casings blistered and yellowed. Beside it the new church, more conventional and less pleasing in de-

60

sign, observes the execution of time's sentence on the mother church.

These towns endure, even with new faces and houses and habits. Perhaps it is fancy to believe they were more interesting then, in their cloistered and time-set ways—more interesting than, to tell the truth, they seemed at the time. Were they more interesting when familiar people sat on the front porches on hot summer evenings, counting the fireflies and listening to the crickets, than now when unfamiliar people sit unseen in back rooms watching fantasies on their television screens? *O lost, and by the wind grieved, ghost, come back again!* cried Thomas Wolfe.

But these musings do not last long on a Christmas day walk. The air chills, the light fades, the eggnog waits amid the littered wrappings at home, and there are long distances to go tomorrow.

—January 1, 1976

II. American Portraits

W. J. Cash after a Quarter Century

IN FEBRUARY 1941 Wilbur J. Cash, an erratic North Carolina journalist who wrote editorials for the Charlotte *News*, published *The Mind of the South*, a volume instantly recognized by students of regional analysis as a classic.* Subsequent works on the same subject have almost been footnotes.

Until Cash really showed how crucial the historical dimension is to an understanding of the South, its eccentricities were inflated by admirers, scoffed at by reformers. Profiles of the region ran to one of two unhelpful extremes. One saw either a bizarre wonderland full of hotheaded "Southrons," or a sterile waste from which social scientists had removed the people, whose vagaries were simply matters of poverty, pellagra, and poll taxes. In the first, the past was distorted out of all recognition; in the second, it was ignored. *The Mind of the South* recalls Carl Becker's observation about Jefferson: he felt with his mind as some think with their hearts. Cash was not the first to explore the Southern mind—"a fairly definite mental pattern, associated with a fairly definite social pattern," as he defined it. But his map remains the most plausible we have.

To understand *The Mind of the South*, its muffled bitterness, its permanent value and fascination, one must understand Cash's mind—and its obsession with cotton. He was born and spent his boyhood in a cotton mill town, Gaffney, South Carolina, where his father operated a company store. When he later composed a rather self-consciously romantic autobiography for H. L. Mencken's *American Mercury*, where his early essays appeared, Cash recalled that "the keening of the five o'clock whistles...drilled me in sorrow."

---

*But the author did not stay around to collect laurels. Taking a Guggenheim grant, Cash, then forty-one, went to Mexico City. There, a few weeks later, his nerves apparently shot, he hanged himself in a hotel.

Those whistles, beckoning the millworkers—the "lint-heads"—to the spindles were the characteristic sound of Cash's South. When he thought of cotton, it was not of wide fields but of an altogether different and drearier picture: "company houses," clouds of lint, and lung diseases. Cash saw a Hardyesque pathos in his early life. He was a sensitive boy, nearsighted from secret reading, restless, as he wrote Mencken, at "the Baptist preacher's too graphic account of the Second Coming"; he expected an apocalypse every sunset. He was out of sympathy with the brutalities of his childhood setting and with the economic nexus that brought them about. When he saw a rich cotton-mill manager passing down the street, he felt that some ingredient in the traditional myth of a sympathetic and gracious South was being betrayed. Hadn't the "Confederate captains," as the old gentry are called in his book, built the cotton mills for humanitarian reasons, to salvage the sinking tenant farmer from economic ruin? And what was one to think of the hopeless mental primitiveness of a culture, all too typically represented by the fulminations of the parson—a civilization which had not even begun to come to terms with Darwin and Freud?

From this difficulty at reconciling myth and fact there sprung, initially, a lively if unoriginal iconoclasm. Like all enterprising young journalists of his day, Cash wrote in the manner of Mencken. It was in fairly good imitation Mencken that he fired his initial salvos in the pages of the *Mercury* at his childhood villains. But as Cash matured, so did his tactics. Reading back now over the bombastic essays he published in the *Mercury* in the late 1920s, one might suppose that in time he grew tired of firing point-blank and began to contemplate a more subtle strategy for solving the regional anomalies. He stopped writing for Mencken and began to look deep into the political, psychological, and social evolution that had set the South apart. This scrutiny, lasting twelve years, was to culminate in *The Mind of the South*.

That mind, Cash came to believe, is primarily a frontier mind, bearing the marks of a rough and ready beginning. It is, he writes, "a tree with many age rings...but with its taproot in the Old South." The period of its formation was 1830-1860, the setting the South beyond the coastal settlements in the back country, "the man at the center" the upland cotton planter. In a dense but powerful style, Cash imagines how this prototype of the Southerner scrambled precariously to imitate the coastal Old Regime whose more genteel ways he both hated and envied. The upland Southerner's struggle to assimilate the way of life of the tidewater "Virginians" covered little more than a generation before the Civil War. This process was never concluded, and it is not surprising that Cash could write of the manner of this kind of Southerner: "It was ultimately not an emanation from the proper substance of the men who wore it, but only a fine garment put on from the outside."

Furthermore, Cash concluded, the characteristic sectionalism of that frontier mind was a defense—a reaction. Before the war, the Abolitionist assailed the immorality of slavery. After the war, the Carpetbagger and Radical so plundered the South, always with high moralizing, that the Southerner was driven to assume that he *was* "different," if only in self-defense.

The ruin of the economic system was so complete that the frontier was reopened. Poverty and social ferment—"the frontier the Yankee made," Cash calls it—returned. So this new man who in antebellum days had never fully defined himself was once again cut adrift in a world that rewarded his cunning and calculation—and sometimes violence—at the same time that he espoused a romantic view of the past. The Southerner imagined, in a setting dulled by ruin, a never-never land in which his unrealized aspirations to ease, grandeur, and graciousness had once been realized after all. That this myth was false was beside the point; it became a vital factor in his mentality. Cash thought he had found the key to an enigmatic culture that pretended to mellowness, but could be crass; that pretended to chivalry, but could be savage; whose legendary hospitality consorted with political demagogy, violence, anti-intellectualism, and a fundamentalism on basic principles which found an occasional outlet in what Cash calls "the savage ideal"—the ideal of total conformity.

At several points the historian must, after twenty-five years, quarrel with Cash. Revisionist historians of the Reconstruction period—among whom a Southerner, Francis Butler Simkins, is notable—now tell us there was more to that period than Yankee piracy and the brutal economic imperialism of Cash's "tariff gang." Other critics have found Cash's treatment of Southern religion superficial—"the trivial booing...we heard so much in the 1920s" says Donald Davidson.

These reinterpretations aside, has the essential behavior of the South as Cash described it changed radically in the last quarter-century? On the whole the answer seems to me No—notwithstanding obvious economic and social modifications that are often heralded today, as in the 1890s, as constituting a "New" South. In truth "the mind of the South" seems today to defy the impersonal forces. When you put aside the spread of television sets, the advent of jet air travel, the larger cash incomes (all consistent with national developments), you are left with a mental pattern familiar to Cash: the race picture, though increasingly subject to federal legal pressure, is mostly as Cash saw it—status politics still intact. The South is still given, more than any single identifiable region, to unholy repressions of wrong thinking. Its economy, though diversified, though emancipated from the cotton mills on which Cash obsessively spent almost a third of his book, has yet to transform the South into a truly industrial or urban society. Its habits are still tied to the land.

But let me specify.

No sane person denies today, North and South, the existence of a second American revolution in race relations. But it is easy amidst the one way flow of legal and legislative mandates from Washington to lose sight of those durable Southern habits which, being more subtle than most critics suppose, defy political command. Race preoccupies the South today as much as (if not more than) when Cash wrote in 1941. In flippant moments, Southern newspaper editors still call it "Topic A," a label rarely applied without a weary sigh that such a preoccupation should stand, virtually immovable, between the South and its dream of modernity.

Cash's analysis of the "proto-Dorian convention" still applies:

> If the plantation had introduced distinctions of wealth and rank among the men of the old backcountry, and, in doing so, had perhaps offended against the ego of the common white, it had also...introduced that other vastly ego-warming and ego-expanding distinction between the white man and the black. Robbing him and degrading him in so many ways, it yet, by a singular irony, had simultaneously elevated this common white to a position comparable to that of, say, the Doric knight of ancient Sparta. Not only was he not exploited directly, he was himself made by extension a member of the dominant class—was lodged solidly on a tremendous superiority, which...he could never publicly lose. Come what might, he would always be a white man. And before that vast and capacious distinction, all others were foreshortened, dwarfed, and all but obliterated.
>
> The grand outcome was the almost complete disappearance of economic and social focus on the part of the masses...

Even today, the enduring presence of Negroes in large numbers forbids, except in the most tranquil moments or truce between Washington and Birmingham or Jackson or Albany, Georgia, the practice of genuine interest politics. For whatever the South has chosen to accept in the way of racial practices, it has not yet accepted in any state that entire division of political opinion along lines of natural economic interest that could make Negro votes decisive and thus raise what Francis Butler Simkins calls "the bête noire of Southern politics—the election of Negroes in considerable numbers."

Governor Wallace, for instance, understands the Cash analysis. Though by the Bilbo-Vardaman standard the Governor of Alabama is an elegant refinement, his political appeal rests on a canny insight into the "proto-Dorian" standing of the Southern poor white—the fixture that he must never be threatened with submergence below the mass of Negroes in the social and political heap. Naturally, the new Southern demagogue has updated his vocabulary. He is much given to denunciation of foreign devils. He rarely uses the word "nigger" in public. But when he attacks parts of the federal Civil Rights Bill for threatening hiring and firing rights of the longshoremen's local in Mobile, his listeners recognize, however cleverly sugared for distant consumption, the cry of status politics.

To say that Cash's anaylsis of race politics is still pertinent is not to say, of course, that it will always remain so. The present stage may be transitional. Certainly Southern politics of even the most diehard kind must come to terms with Negro voters newly enfranchised by the registration sanctions of the civil-rights laws. And their votes will carry more weight if the Supreme Court persists in its current attack on malapportionment. Only another spell of fatigue such as overcame the national political consensus by 1877 can postpone this showdown; and Senator Goldwater's failure to find and exploit the rumored "white backlash" in the 1964 election makes such a prospect dim. Still, it is well to remember that the Goldwater-Wallace axis did exist, however weakly, and that it formed a precedent of sorts in American politics.

If an absence of radical change in race relations is discernible, the same is true of what Cash called "the savage ideal"—"that ideal whereunder dissent and variety are completely suppressed and men become, for all their attitudes, professions, and actions, virtual replicas of one another." The South's ideals of tolerance are today hardly those of John Stuart Mill, or even Thomas Jefferson. Doctrinal diversity, questions about the basic assumptions of the social and economic system, are largely confined to the intelligentsia. Cash was guilty of a great exaggeration, of course, when he likened the savage ideal of his day to the mad authoritarianism then in vogue among European dictators. After all, the key word is *ideal*. When repression-minded Southern legislators curtail freedoms of speech, organization, teaching, or movement, it is usually, so they say in all good faith, for the sake of a higher good. The Southern vigilante strikes out at threatening scientific or social ideas with a Rotarian highmindedness and sobriety that has little in common with Hitlerian nihilism. When fundamentalist parsons throng (they recently did) to meetings of the Texas State Textbook Committee, hoping to put Darwin in his place; or when North Carolina legislators shut state college campuses to pleaders of the Fifth Amendment, as they did in June 1963; when a professor is given walking papers in the Deep South; when these things occur they are usually said to protect school children against dangerous thoughts. Even today the apologists for a closed society in parts of the South fall back on a premise—sometimes unspoken—that the Southerner cannot analyze an idea. And it is ironic evidence of the continued pertinence of Cash that in making this observation himself, he even borrowed on that arch-scold of the South, Henry Adams.

In the Southern economy, change is most obvious to the casual eye and durability is difficult to spot. Here I think Cash himself was partially deceived. If *The Mind of the South* has a major flaw, it is a naïve faith in the power of specific changes in the Southern economy to revolutionize social, political, and mental patterns. To say this is not to scoff condescendingly; John Kenneth Galbraith was hardly the first to tell us that Productivity is, for Americans, a sovereign index to society. What is strange is that Cash, having for some two hundred pages sought to show the basic indestructibilty of the Southern mind under a barrage of economic changes, should then profess to believe that the mere unionization of cotton millworkers would herald a new day. Of course we have heard of the "New South" for generations; and for every generation, the meaning of the vision differs slightly, though it usually has much to do with industrialization or industrial sophistication. It is typical that in Robert Lerché's *The Uncertain South*, a recent study of Southern voting patterns in the House, the author ends an exhausting exercise in statistical gymnastics with the old conclusion that industrialism and urbanism will end the "uncertainty."

Were it that simple, the South would long since, I think, have put up or shut up. The trouble with the industrial panacea is that it rests on too simple assumptions about what makes society run. It is as tired as the anecdote Henry Grady used to tell about the Georgia funeral for which that underindustrialized state supplied only the corpse and the hole in the ground.

Were Cash writing today, what might startle him is that the wholesale unionization he saw in prospect never came. It was beaten by right-to-work laws, by a plentitude of "Anglo-Saxon labor" out of the hills, and by high-priced legal talent. But an even more important deterrent was that fierce individualism, that aversion to regimentation, that could be noted— as Cash recorded—in the behavior of the Boys in Gray, who elected their officers and took unkindly to sharp command. Why Cash, having sketched "one of the world's most remarkable individualists" in the person of the Southern cracker, nonetheless believed that he could become a dutiful and disciplined modern labor unionist I cannot say. But he did so believe.

Even more to the point are the observations of Professor William H. Nicholls of Vanderbilt, recently president of the Southern Economic Association. Nicholls speaks not only as a devotee of industrial progress but as one whose firsthand inspection of the effect (or non-effect) of foreign aid has given him insights into the riddle of the Southern economy. The more he has seen of the infusion of capital into economically "backward" lands, he says, the more he has been convinced that profound economic change does *not* produce social change—but rather vice versa. Regional "progress" will not come about so long as the South remains bound by "agrarian values, the rigidity…of the social structure, the weakness of social responsibility, and the conformity of thought and behavior"—just the catalogue of qualities which advocates of the various "New Souths" have usually sought to relieve by industrialization.

The picture I draw, then, assessing Cash's book twenty-five years after, is one in which stability outweighs change. Oddly, this state of affairs seems to me reinforced, and in a way made respectable, by a succession of writers and professors who with genuine critical detachment tell Southerners—and outsiders— that it is not so bad to be different. Reviewing Cash's book for *The Nation* in 1941, James Orrick noted: "What makes the mind of the South different is that it thinks it is." And while C. Vann Woodward's conception of the difference in his superb book, *The Burden of Southern History*, departs drastically from that of neo-Ku Kluxers, everyone joins in the refrain of "Viva la différence."

The Southerner's attachment to this "difference" in the Southern mind has two sides—one defensible in down-to-earth terms, the other admittedly difficult to reduce to sociological paraphrase.

In 1941, Cash could conclude by saying of the region:"Proud, brave, honorable by its lights, courteous, personally generous, loyal, swift to act, often too swift, but signally effective, sometimes terrible, in its action—such was the South at its best. And such at its best it remains today, despite the great falling away in some of its virtues."

On the practical side, by way of apology for the Southern mind, it is hard to better Vann Woodward's formulation: that in a nation conditioned by a happy history to victory, plenty, and a consequent optimism about the susceptibility of human affairs to beneficial innovation, the South has been a tempering force. Knowing defeat, scarcity, and failure to root out an intractable social evil the South has a sense of common destiny with the larger world (which has shared defeat, poverty, and tragedy). This departure from the unmarred triumph of the national experience has surely helped the South supply more than its quota of creative statesmen on the world scene, from Wilson and Hull to Johnson and Rusk and Fulbright. And it is the sense of abiding tragedy that has enriched Southern fiction and made it pre-eminent.

The mystical side is best approached through Southern literature, where one encounters directly the fetishes of family, physical place, and tradition that are so important, or were, in the Southern mind. The curious difficulty of communication here is beautifully illustrated in Faulkner's great novel, *Absalom, Absalom!*, when Quentin Compson pauses from his obsessive narrative of the rise and fall of the Sutpen dynasty, and is blandly interrupted by Shreve, his Canadian roommate at Harvard:

"So he just wanted a grandson," Shreve said. "That was all he was after. Jesus, the South is fine, isn't it. It's better than the theatre, isn't it. It's better than Ben Hur, isn't it. No wonder you have to come away now and then..."

In a highly commercialized and mobile society that has replaced ties of blood and household with abstractions of a fairly impersonal sort, one is apt to confront these bloody and tortured

Southern iliads just as Shreve does. They will seem out of date to some, melodramatic and perverse to many, and so, I suppose, they will remain.

Perhaps, then, Cash defined the "difference" beyond improvement—and hence gave us the key to his own continued pertinence—when he chose his title. Being Southern *is* a state of mind—a condition of chronic introspection reaching its highest imaginative pitch, perhaps, in Faulkner's reflective heroes like the Reverend Gail Hightower and Isaac McCaslin.

Cash himself is a case of this. He did much by writing his book to enhance regional self-consciousness as an ideal per se—and so reinforced the tacit alliance that reaches down from the rarefied meditations of professors, authors, and journalists to the inchoate consciousness of the leather-jacketed hot-rodder who sports a Confederate battle flag on the rear bumper. These improbable allies differ in almost everything except the proposition that the South is and should remain "a nation within a nation" and so much the better so.

Naturally, I am not suggesting a continuity of motives or objectives here, let alone a dark conspiracy. It is a fair guess that the fine points of the Southern mystique are of more interest to Cash's successors than to the "hell of a fellow" (to borrow a good Cashian phrase) who puts the Stars and Bars in the same decorative class with foxtails, Spanish moss, jeweled mudguards, and twin exhaust pipes. And it is an open question how much the meditations of the regional intellectuals and creative writers sustain this unholy alliance.

There is, however, little doubt that if the South lacked working mythologists to go on holding up a mirror to "the mind of the South" this mind would vanish as a distinctive study in self-consciousness. But I confess my own relief that Cash's successors remain at work. It is not only that human variety is instructive, if not always pleasing to the moral sense. Self-knowledge remains, one assumes, the virtue it was for the ancients—not only for the South itself but for a nation which too often supposes in pride and vanity that it will eventually remake mankind in its own definitive image.

From Harper's
September, 1965

Louisiana's Kingfish

"Oh, hell" growled Huey P. Long one day from a hotel bed as newspaper reporters, gathered as if in court around him, mused about his political style. "Just say I'm *sui generis* and let it go at that." More than three decades after his assassination Long's self-characterization still stands up. His uniqueness is the theme and gist of this long, masterly work* by an American historian who is also, by adoption, a fellow Louisianian. I know of no better American political biography.

For his astounding detail Harry Williams has relied, apart from the usual sources, upon the oral history techniques developed at Columbia University, interviewing hundreds of surviving associates and allies, foes and detractors, relatives and sidekicks of the Kingfish. To those who know something of the mechanics of state politics in the South, the book has the ring of authenticity both in its analysis of motive and its assessment of outcome. Sustaining suspense and interest throughout, Professor William's portrait of the principal player in this astonishing drama is admiring, sometimes laudatory, and wherever possible exculpatory—though only rarely to the point of special pleading. Williams has assumed the role of counsel for the historic defense; and I believe he sustains his thesis that the man who dragged Louisiana kicking and screaming into the twentieth century is both misunderstood and underrated.

The main cause of Huey P. Long's somewhat tarnished reputation is perhaps the tendency to dump all dissident Southern politicians into a bag neatly marked "Southern demagogues" and thus to obscure their merits and telescope their vices. Of political vices (and personal ones) Huey Long had his share. Reformer and autocrat, dictator and democrat—a strange blend of Roman emperor and benevolent *caudillo*—he knew the way to the ordinary man's heart, and he knew that that way is often paved with ribaldry and excess. Yet it is not true of Southern demagogues, as Governor Reagan is reported to have said of redwood trees, that once you've seen one you've seen them all. Long, for one, defies all the clichés one might contrive. He differed from others of the genus as Louisiana differs from other Southern states; and it took an *echt*-Yankee like the late A. J. Liebling to perceive that Louisiana is in fact "the Westernmost of the Arab states," Mediterranean in its relaxed political ethos.

Huey Long, by T. Harry Williams (Knopf, 1969)

Huey Long's immunity to the usual pratfalls of Southern demagoguery lay, that is, not only in the singularity of his character and background but in the uniqueness of Louisiana politics.

More than most angry men who rise on the periodic tides of "cracker" discontent, Huey Long was literate, although his was the literacy of the self-taught. Without benefit of formal schooling in economics, he anticipated the anti-Depression techniques later expounded by Keynes, and he could handle a bank crisis with skill at least equal to that of his contemporary, Franklin D. Roosevelt. (Once, desperately searching for an excuse to proclaim a bank holiday, he found it in the little-noted fact that Woodrow Wilson had on that date severed diplomatic relations with Germany; with a pinch of Long boldness it served to save the banks.) As a boy he developed an intimate acquaintance with that staple of Southern provincial eloquence the Bible, where, in the laws of the Old Testament, he claimed to have discovered the basis for his "share the wealth" nostrum. He read Ridpath's history of the world and almost yearly perused *The Count of Monte Cristo*, once explaining: "The man in that book knew how to hate and until you learn how to hate you'll never get anywhere in this world."

Yet, curiously, Long was not a hater. Unlike so many of the emissaries of Southern rustic rancor, the Longs of Winn Parish, Louisiana, were not sprung from grinding poverty. They came of a substantial small-farmer stock; and historically their parish straddled the great gulf, economic and doctrinal, between the hill country and the delta. If Huey Long was, as Professor Williams notes, one of the few Southern politicians of his time who "did not oratorically employ or exploit the Confederate tradition," perhaps it was because the Winn Parish dissidence from Confederate orthodoxy dated to Civil War days. It had been cool to secession. Later, it would emerge as a stronghold of Populist sentiment when that meant resisting the do-nothing Bourbons.

Equally decisive, in the singular mix that was Longism, was the nature of Louisiana politics itself, mercurial and entirely restrained in its reaction to corruption. "Louisiana politicians," writes Professor Williams, who has watched them closely for years, "were and are much like feudal barons. They operate as rulers of geographical principalities or personal followings, independently, calculatingly, and sometimes irresponsibly or petulantly...Leaders break, ally, rebreak, in an endless chain of combinations."

To understand the thrust of the Long movement, which began with his election, at age twenty-five, to the Louisiana Rail-

74

road Commission (utility regulation), one need only note the incredible recalcitrance of those who had ruled the state without challenge for decades. Before Long demolished it, Louisiana suffered from what Harry Williams calls "government by goatee"—which, even by Southern standards, was a political fossil. As late as 1928, when Long was elected to the governorship, the doctrine that government should or could be more than a caretaker of established interests or a source of jobs for decrepit patricians was untested, if not unknown. Not, in fact, since the young carpetbag Governor Henry Clay Warmoth had a politician managed to tweak the goatees.

Occasional ripples were stirred by Governors with mild, Milquetoast programs of reform, acting from well within the goatee ethos. One such notable, still represented as the best of the breed, was Governor John M. Parker, who was mildly infected with Progressivism. He agreed in principle with Huey Long, then a railroad commissioner, that the oil companies and lumber barons were not bearing a tax load equal to their spoils. But Parker sought to tame the oil companies by bargaining on their public spirit, even when a dollar was at stake. When they balked at his severance tax proposal, he summoned their lawyers and begged them, as gentlemen, to agree on their own tax law. At this point, Huey Long thought gentlemanliness was being carried too far and accused the Governor of being a tool of Standard Oil. He had to pay a token libel judgment for the remark, but his moral victory was much noticed and enjoyed among the bayous.

The fatuity of "government by goatee" found no more typical ornament, perhaps, than U.S. Senator Joseph Ransdell. Having once helped salvage Ransdell from defeat, Huey Long in 1931 challenged him for his seat. Opening his campaign against the Kingfish at Lake Providence, the Senator received from a delegation of housewives a symbolic feather duster, clearly meant to suggest contrast with the disreputable vigor of Long's governorship. "I feel deeply honored," the Senator responded, "that the women should turn over to me this almost sacred emblem of cleanliness in the home. The feather duster has been used by wives, mothers and grandmothers for centuries past to clean the sanctuaries of their homes." Apparently the ceremony (and the Senator's response) were without irony.

Fatuous as these gentlemen of the goatee set were, they could be venomous when aroused. Once they realized that Long was not to be bought off, cast out by impeachment, or swept away by a feather duster, the opposition became fierce. There were mutterings quite anticipatory of the mid-1930s' opposition, on the national scene, to FDR.

Were the indignation and alarm justified? Perhaps, if politics were a matter of manners. But at the highest estimate Louisiana before Long had just over 300 miles of paved roads and few if any state-maintained bridges. Its adult illiteracy rate was as high as any in the nation.

At the cost of some personal meddling, Long left behind Louisiana State University. State spending rose almost 200 per cent during the Long régime, most of it supported by the now reputable form of bond issues. By any measure of activist government the Long record seems rather tame; it was flamboyant only because his operations left a good deal to be desired in the manners department. The Kingfish and his administration were in fact the antithesis of "government by goatee." His predecessors were polite and responsible and did nothing; he was rude and at times irresponsible, but he built bridges, paved roads, secured free textbooks for school children, vastly increased the budget for education, and provided considerable entertainment the while.

Gradual in form, Huey Long's political changes were revolutionary in implication, for he not only shattered patrician control but tamed the entrenched New Orleans political machine. Traditionally, New Orleans was the key to Louisiana elections. Statewide offices could not be won against its determined opposition. Unlike so many Southern insurgents, Long systematically broke down one political machine and built another. Funded by levies on the salaries of state employees, the Long "machine" at its peak strength controlled the governorship, the two Senate seats, and, by 1935, at Huey's death, an estimated 25,000 jobs. Long and his candidates could muster a vote of about 125,000 in a poll that usually totaled 300,000.

Yet it would be false to suppose that the Long machine, the instrument as well as the by-product of his program, rested wholly on spoilsmanship. He was the most charismatic of figures, loved for his impudence, his color, his boldness in the face of any adversary, however daunting. From Standard Oil to railroads, majority leaders to Presidents, no foe was too big. What scandalized the drawing rooms—the Governor strutting in front of a college band, or sitting on the bench with "his" LSU football team, or shouting directions like a coxswain to "his" legislature, or involved in a nightclub brawl—merely entertained the less exacting.

Somewhere in that special Valhalla reserved for lovable ro-

76

gues Huey is no doubt shaking his head just now at the recently publicized exploits of his son and heir, Senator Russell Long. A zealous Associated Press reporter has found that the Senator in recent years realized several hundred thousand tax-free dollars from his Louisiana oil leases—tax free by virtue of the 27½-percent depletion allowance which he does not blush to defend, as chairman of the Senate Finance Committee, as essential to the republic's survival.

"I don't regard it as a conflict of interests," said Long *fils*. "If you have financial interests completely parallel to your state then you have no problem...[and] if I didn't represent the oil and gas industry I wouldn't represent the state of Louisiana."

One thing Professor Williams makes clear is that the Kingfish marched to power over the protest of the oil interests. His son may confuse the interests of Louisiana with oil and gas, but Huey never made that error. When Russell Long sets himself up as the U.S. Senator for oil and gas, old Long buffs will agree that the family's magnificent effrontery has bred true; but somewhere a gene has slipped. Russell has gone over to an old foe— this, one supposes, being one of the ghastly perils of the generation gap.

The uniqueness of Long *père,* of which one sees a mild, hereditary glimmer in his son, was impatience with niggling distinctions between *pro bono publico* and *pro bono Longo.* Yet Huey could practice corruption without being tainted by it. At the height of his power, which he reached after his election to the Senate in 1932, he all but owned the Louisiana legislature and ran an engine of unparalleled state patronage. Operating through his creatures (who included the Governor) he could enact any fancy into law. In his personal keep was a cash box fattened by contributions from state employees and well-heeled admirers and the cream off state highway contracts. As his power grew so did his taste for fancy suits, silk shirts and ties. Yet it is striking how much of his idealism survived, unsoured, the temptations that undo lesser tribunes of the people.

Moreover—and here the departure from the pattern is total—the Kingfish's grip on the sympathies of ordinary Louisianians depended not at all on race-baiting. He left undisturbed the Jim Crow laws that Louisiana shared with the South, he was not above a racial jest, yet he refused to exploit the easiest of paths to Southern political power. Like few insurgent Southern politicians, he understood that the race issue is largely a dodge, evil in itself and evil in the real issues it obscures. His inclusion of Negroes among those to whom were due the benefits of his "Share Our Wealth" movement (which was never as radical as it sounds) had, for its time, revolutionary implications.

At the time of his assassination in the capitol at Baton Rouge in September 1935, Huey Long had become an influential figure in America. In Washington he treated President Roosevelt, a sometime ally, with his customary irreverence. (A White House aide was indignant when he saw the Kingfish talking to the President with his hat on, removing it only to slap FDR's knee for emphasis.) In the Senate he ignored or disdained fellow Southerners unless they were mavericks like himself, and found his niche among Midwestern and Western Progressives like Borah and Wheeler. For a Democratic administration, in truth, Long posed a problem more political than ideological. When Roosevelt described Huey as "the second most dangerous man in the country," he had in mind the voter appeal that helped re-elect Mrs. Hattie Caraway to the Senate in a whirlwind Arkansas campaign, the spreading appeal of the Share Our Wealth clubs (more than 27,000 of them by 1935 with an estimated 4.6 million members), the coziness with Father Coughlin and other prophets of the radical right, not to mention the fact that Long had clearly tamed and overridden the opposition in Louisiana. FDR the politician had to respect Long; as President he deplored him.

FDR's wariness was well grounded. For, in accordance with his lifelong ambition, Long meant eventually to grasp at the Presidency. He would, he had told intimates, put together a radical coalition, sapping Roosevelt's strength on the Left and throwing the election in 1936 to the Republicans. The economic condition of the country would worsen and the nation would be ripe for Huey by 1940. "It was a bold plan and also a coldly calculated one," writes Professor Williams. "He was willing to let the country suffer for four years so that he could then save it." But on a September night in 1935, just over a year before the election, Dr. Carl Weiss's bullet made the Long problem forever academic.

"It was a bold plan and also a coldly calculated one" is a good epitaph for the Kingfish. Immune to ordinary personal corruption, Long suffered from an appetite for power that knew no limits. Ultimately, fulfilling Lord Acton's dictum, he was pressing the Louisiana legislature for a law that would have placed the state militia under the Governor's (for which read his own) personal control, without so much as a judicial check. Would he have used such power in the time-honored Louisiana way—to meddle with ballot boxes and registration lists—or for more sinister ends?

All we may conclude, with Professor Williams, is that Long was, as he said, *sui generis*—part upstart rural *führer* but mostly ingenious American politician. Concede as one will the beneficence of his program, concede too the orneriness of his opposition, his style was at the last impermissible in a land of limits and laws. His grip on Louisiana, seized legitimately, was illegitimately maintained, for he erased every countervailing force save the assassin.

This is not to exonerate the dreary "government by goatee" he overthrew nor to scoff at the idealism that remained very real in him. Huey and his foes, in keeping with the Newtonian laws of politics, were well met. Professor Williams persuades me, however, that, in more ways than it has ever liked to admit, Louisiana was lucky to get the Kingfish.

—November 1, 1969

The Faces of Robert E. Lee

The face of Robert E. Lee—in the national imagination and in what used to be called down South the cult of the Lost Cause—is as rigidly set in alabaster as the face of his lifelong model, George Washington. It was the historian Charles A. Beard, who should have known better, who told us with stunning irrelevance that Lee's lips "were never profaned by an oath, whiskey or tobacco"—thus erecting for the contemplation of a whole generation of neo-Confederate ladies a saintly piety and Prohibition.

But one has only to visit the still-undisturbed little office at the Washington and Lee library to see the conventional image belied. Photographs taken of the general after the war show us another Lee. It is a face in ruins, furrowed and darkened by immeasurable remorse. It almost seems to freeze on paper the terrible portrait in Dr. Freeman's biography—Lee wandering the stricken sward at Gettysburg after Pickett's charge, murmuring "Oh, too bad, Oh, too bad."

If, as we may suppose with Beard, General Lee's lips were not "profaned" by strong words or drink, his face reflects the

79

worst of human torments: The torment of divided loyalty and bitter regret. They were common emotions of that time and episode. Whole families were riven by them. "Three brothers of Mrs. Lincoln died for the South," write the historians Morison and Commager, "whilst near kinsmen of Mrs. Davis were in the Union army. In a house on West 20th Street in New York, a little boy named Theodore Roosevelt prayed for the Union armies at the knee of his Georgia mother, whose brothers were in the Confederate navy. At the same moment, in the Presbyterian parsonage of Augusta, Ga., another little boy named Thomas Woodrow Wilson knelt in the family circle while his Ohio-born father invoked the God of Battles for the Southern cause."

Robert E. Lee, the most brilliant military figure of his generation, knew and felt this anguish. A brave and effective soldier in the Mexican campaigns, later superintendent of the U.S. Military Academy where he had stood second in his class, he was a figure ensnared by the quarrels of stronger, more elemental wills. His was the fate that befalls temperate men when, as Yeats put it, "the best lack all conviction, while the worst are filled with passionate intensity." Yeats' lines might stand, in fact, as epigraph to the Lee story, as to the Lincoln story, as indeed to the whole story of the Irrepressible Conflict. Not that he lacked conviction. His convictions were not convenient and did not lend themselves to easy choice. One of them was that the new President, Abraham Lincoln, was dead right about the great issue of spring, 1861.

"In your hands, and not in mine," Lincoln had told the secessionist hotheads in his First Inaugural, "is the momentous issue of the civil war. The government will not assail you. But I hold that, in contemplation of the universal law and the Constitution, the union of these states is perpetual. No state, upon its own mere action, can lawfully get out of the union." Many (including at one time the arch-abolitionist Horace Greely) disagreed. Lee agreed. Secession, he declared, "is nothing but revolution." But another, stronger conviction eclipsed his agreement with the President about the illegality of secession. He thought it would be monstrous "to raise my hand against my native state, my relatives, my children and my home." When the Virginia convention, following others, voted to secede, Lee sadly rejected field command of the Union armies. In mid-April, 1861, he crossed the Potomac to what simpler, hard-bitten men would call treason: A harsh term for a profound preference.

Our age, which finds supreme importance in political abstractions, which often betrays personal loyalties in their name, would not find Lee a congenial figure. And it was all the more baffling that after making his choice and seeing it through to Appomattox, he walked away from this war he had not wanted, for a cause he had regarded as illegal, whose ruin and fratricide tore at his spirit, with not so much as a word of explanation or apology.

Perhaps it was that infuriating self-containment, that patrician neglect of the memoirist's convenient hindsight, that helps account for what one must view as a national indecency—that Robert E. Lee remains, after a century, a man without a country. Congress, one reads, is at least moving in its leisurely way to rectify this disgrace. But the long neglect is a comment on the poverty of our sense of history. Lee's anguish, no less than Lincoln's, summed up the divisions of an era—divisions too deep for casual judgment, and certainly too sad for revenge.

—June 26, 1975

The Cosmic Fatalism of Mr. Justice Holmes

Like most amateur students of the Constitution, I learned early on to venerate Justice Oliver Wendell Holmes Jr., the father of the modern American doctrine of free speech.

Holmes not only thought inventively, he wrote with unforgettable pithiness; and that tends to ingratiate him with any ink-stained wretch who draws his pay for writing opinions. We owe to his pen phrases like "clear and present danger," "freedom for the thought we loathe"; and it was he who memorably denied that free speech included the right to shout "fire!" falsely in a crowded theater and cause a panic.

Lately, however, two influences prompt me to wonder if the Holmesian view of free speech, for all its grandeur, is destined to survive. One is the controversy over the Nazi demonstration in Skokie, Ill.; the other is Prof. Walter Berns' fascinating analysis of "the strange case of Oliver Wendell Holmes" in *The First Amendment and The Future of American Democracy*.

The argument over the Nazi right to exercise "freedom for

the thought we loathe" in Skokie exposes the shallowness of the conventional Holmesian free speech view. How, for instance, does one answer Professor Berns' argument that, taking Holmes at his word, "the only meaning of free speech turns out to be that it is worse to suppress the advocacy of Stalinism or Hitlerism than to be ruled by Stalin or Hitler"?

By protesting, perhaps, that this was not what Holmes said? But what else can he have meant in his famous dissent in the Abrams case? "...When men realize that time has upset many fighting faiths, they may come to believe *even more than they believe the very foundations of their own conduct* that the ultimate good desired is better reached by free trade in ideas,—that *the test of truth is the power of the thought to get itself accepted in the competition of the market;* and that truth is the only ground upon which their wishes safely can be carried out. That, at any rate, is the theory of our Constitution." (Emphases mine).

Professor Berns, having studied the history of the First Amendment, insists that this is *not* "the theory of our Constitution." The U.S. Constitution attaches fundamental value to "a republican form of government," explicitly guaranteeing it to all the states and by implication valuing it over dictatorship. That is the constitutional bedrock, not a cosmic political relativism. Holmes, then, was wrong to say in his *Gitlow* dissent: "If, in the long run, the beliefs expressed in proletarian dictatorship are destined to be accepted by the dominant forces of the community the only meaning of free speech is that they should be given their chance and have their way."

In Mr. Berns' view—which I find persuasive—this is not "the only meaning of free speech." Justice Holmes insinuated into our constitutional doctrine the heresy of "unlimited pluralism" in the guise of free speech theory.

The really interesting question is not whether Holmes was right in what he said about the First Amendment—that is most debatable—but why Holmes held that view. What personal experience and belief underlay it?

Justice Felix Frankfurter, a disciple and admirer who wrote an admirable sketch of Holmes for the Dictionary of American Biography, believed that "the Civil War (in which Holmes fought and was thrice dangerously wounded) cut more deeply than any other influence in his life. If it did not generate it certainly fixed his conception of man's destiny."

And what was that conception? It seems a kind of Darwinian fatalism: the view, not unfamiliar in his time, that life was essentially a lottery in which puny mortals are "humble instru-

82

ment(s) of the universal power." Justice Holmes was, moreover, a kind of battle snob, the survivor of a "good war" who never forgot the arbitrariness of human fortune. Since "time has upset many fighting faiths" there are limits to the zeal of sensible and urbane men for such faiths, however fundamental they are.

Is it fanciful to see a connection between this credo and his almost cavalier vision of a republican system that must, at least theoretically, envision its own eventual self-destruction? I think not. Even Justice Frankfurter concedes that "by conventional standards...his opinions not infrequently appeared to dispose rather cavalierly of controversies that were complicated in their facts and far-reaching in their immediate consequences." That is certainly true of the famous dissents in free speech cases. They *are* cavalier; they breathe a soldier's cosmic fatalism.

Of course, the Holmesian vision of free speech had great dignity, force and eloquence if not logical coherence. There is, however, something flippant about it—as if to say that it is beyond our power to resist whatever ultimate political fortune destiny has in store for us—even if "the thought we loathe" emerges triumphant and puts an end to the system by which it has triumphed.

—May 25, 1978

Jonathan Daniels Remembered

If North Carolina produces a distinctive journalism—or journalists, which comes to the same thing—Jonathan Daniels, editor of the *Raleigh News and Observer,* who died last November, was an important part of the explanation.

He and I belonged to different generations, but started with a common bond. In 1954 I was a sophomore at Chapel Hill, writing editorials for the student paper he had once edited—"in an early and golden age," as I had put it with youthful exuberance in a tribute to another of our number. A few days later there was a note from him in the mail. His era, he said, "did not seem so golden then, and I wish it did not seem so early now." He added that I must drop by to see him in Raleigh where he edited the family newspaper.

Please understand that for a young, wide-eyed student jour-

83

nalist this was a summons to a sort of summit. Jonathan Daniels was by then a totemic figure in the state: the friend and companion of Thomas Wolfe, a White House press aide for FDR and Harry Truman, one of the original writers for Henry Luce's *Fortune*, the author of good and influential books like *A Southerner Discovers the South*. Above all, his editorial voice forced itself, by bravado and wit, upon the notice of everyone who took an interest in North Carolina politics. "The Nuisance and Disturber," as its subscribers always called it, was mandatory reading even among its enemies, from the standard rape-trial story below the front-page fold to Jonathan's pistol-whipping editorials. The voice had an unmistakable resonance.

The figure I saw for the first time that autumn afternoon in the early 1950's, in his office overlooking one of Raleigh's city parks, fit the advance billing. As we talked newspapers, an artist in one corner dabbed away at a portrait of Daniels. From an adjoining room that looked a bit like a broom closet his trusty editorial deputy "Fleet" Williams (who was said to write "more like Jonathan than Jonathan himself") darted in and out with copy and galley proofs. At one point the phone rang. It was Kerr Scott, the former governor of North Carolina, then a U.S. senator, stung by a *News and Observer* editorial suggesting that he was getting too cozy with the big-oil lobby. "I see your point, Kerr," I heard Daniels say, speaking of a controversial natural-gas bill, "but it's a dangerous vote." I was impressed. To an 18-year-old it seemed an enviable situation: to be painted for the ages while admonishing a senator by phone upon some distant but presumably important issue in Washington.

I must not leave the impression that Jonathan Daniels was pompous or self-important. It was true that he affected a homburg hat (at least until Dwight D. Eisenhower adopted the homburg as the official headgear at his inauguration in 1953). But he liked puncturing pomposity, especially when it emerged, as so often it did, from his favorite editorial target, the North Carolina General Assembly. In one unforgettably vituperative valedictory he had observed that a certain legislature had wasted scores of days at the taxpayers' expense while passing only one bill of value: a fireworks ban, including cap pistols. "The Cap Pistol Legislature," he called it, quoting Cromwell's famous dismissal of the Long Parliament: "In God's name go! You have been sitting here too long for aught you have been doing."

That the North Carolina legislature was a favorite Daniels target was natural. In those days before reapportionment it was solidly dominated by rural grandees from the very conservative, sometimes frivolous, fun-loving eastern part of the state. This was *News and Observer* country, but by circulation rather than by political inclination or social outlook. (Kerr Scott himself had once explained the failure of eastern North Carolina to develop a dairy industry by observing: "No one has yet invented a cow that doesn't have to be milked on weekends.") The General Assembly was, then, a redoubt of traditionalism, and Jonathan Daniels was no traditionalist. His *News and Observer* preached "national" Democratic doctrine to a region whose outlook mingled sentimental affection for the house of the fathers with a distinct unenthusiasm for many of its national causes.

Daniels's standard counsel to aspiring journalists, offered at our first meeting and often thereafter, was that a newspaperman should work for himself at least part of the time. He himself did so. Even while editing the paper and writing editorials for it daily he found time to produce a stream of books.

Whatever the form, Jonathan Daniels was always readable, whether he was excoriating corrupt legislators for drinking the trucking lobby's booze or seeking, as he supposed, to rescue some long-dead scoundrel from the toils of false legend. There was a sturdy, sensitive eloquence in Daniels's prose. In"Poet of the Boom," a fine reminiscence of his friend Thomas Wolfe, he recalls helping carry the novelist's coffin up an Asheville hillside to his final resting place: "I remember while we moved toward the long hole in the yellow clay that O. Henry was buried somewhere in the same cemetery and that he had looked at the mountains around us without getting an idea into his head. But Tom had been a mountain man who could see city streets as well...at home in both."

I was not there when Daniels himself was buried, but in his way he left a legacy as important as Wolfe's. He was a craftsman who found an interesting balance between the life of the lively amateur historian and the life of affairs. He spoke articulately and fearlessly for progressive causes. And, as my own youthful experience shows, he took a keen interest in the next generation. He knew that a tradition survives only if the elders keep their eyes open for new recruits, however raw and green.

From Washington Journalism Review
January/February, 1982

"The Jefferson Scandals":
A Historian's Assessment

That Thomas Jefferson, sage of Monticello and third president, had a secret love affair with the slave girl Sally Hemings, siring five children, is (to paraphrase Gibbon) deemed by a few historians equally certain, by a novelist or two equally useful, and by most Jeffersonian scholars equally improbable. Who is right?

Negatives can't be proved. But in his new book *The Jefferson Scandals,* Virginius Dabney files a powerful brief on the negative side. A distinguished editor and a historian of Mr. Jefferson's university, Mr. Dabney may be regarded by some as an interested witness. And so, in a sense, he is.

But interested in what way? The late Fawn Brodie, whose "intimate history" of Thomas Jefferson (1974) revived the Sally Hemings legend for a credulous mass audience, insisted that she was only rounding out our picture of Mr. Jefferson, adding a human wart or two. Others like to expose the "hypocrisy" of one who wrote that "the amalgamation of whites and blacks produces a degradation to which no lover of his country, no lover of excellence in the human character, can innocently consent." Still others, as Mr. Dabney notes, relish any tale that debunks the great.

But this presupposes that the issue is the character and reputation of Thomas Jefferson. Actually, the issue is the responsible use of historical evidence—a topic less exciting to most of us than the private sex lives of famous people, though not without a special fascination. But this is Mr. Dabney's interest.

The legend of the Jefferson-Hemings affair rests on one contemporary source: the writing in the Federalist Richmond *Recorder* of one James Callendar, a character assassin once as violent in the Jeffersonian cause as he was, by 1802, for Jefferson's foes. Mr. Jefferson had refused to appoint him Richmond's postmaster; and it was thereafter that Callendar began to report with embellishments the Monticello gossip that Mr. Jefferson had a slave mistress and a brood of mulatto children.

As Mr. Dabney shows, the tale drew some credibility from the story, also spread by Callendar, that as a young man Jefferson had, as he later put it, "offered love" to the wife of a friend,

86

a Mrs. Betsey Walker, in his absence. Jefferson admitted it; but to friends he flatly denied the stories about his alleged liaison with Sally Hemings.

Decades later, in 1873, the editor of a Pike County, Ohio, newspaper coaxed from Madison Hemings, Sally's son, the story that his mother had become Mr. Jefferson's mistress when she accompanied his daughter Polly to Paris, and had there become *enceinte,* as he quaintly put it. (Madison Hemings, barely literate, knew no French. He also claimed to recall events before his birth, or in the first year or two of his life.)

The evidence on the negative side is also sketchy, as evidence on such matters usually is. But most Jefferson scholars believe that Mr. Jefferson's nephew, Peter Carr, was the father of Sally Hemings's children. So said Thomas J. Randolph, Jefferson's grandson. "Colonel Randolph," wrote one 19th Century Jefferson biographer to another, "informed me that Sally Hemings was the mistress of Peter (Carr) and her sister Betsey the mistress of Samuel (Carr)—and from these connections sprang the progeny that resembled Mr. Jefferson...The Colonel said the connection with the Carrs was perfectly notorious at Monticello and scarcely disguised by the latter—never disavowed by them."

In any forum of historical plausibility the testimony of Randolph, who grew up at Monticello and knew its lore well, would weigh more heavily than hearsay of a Federalist pamphleteer or the ghost-written reminiscenes of an ex-slave too young to remember the events—who might well have been told by his mother that he was Jefferson's son.

The late Julian Boyd, editor of the Jefferson Papers, summed it up: "In confronting partial or contradictory evidence, the historian may and indeed must employ inference, conjecture and hypothesis...legitimate tools of his craft. But the one thing he cannot do is regard his own inferences and conjectures as proven facts...The real danger is that the methods of historical investigation (Mrs. Brodie) has employed may, if allowed to go unchallenged, begin to pass as intellectual coin of the realm."

This tarnished coinage is the real issue—not the character of Mr. Jefferson, and not the silly belief that Jeffersonian scholars observe some code of discretion requiring them to shroud the "intimate" Jefferson from our blushing age.

But in biography there is no arbiter. We can choose to believe scholars who have long studied Jefferson's character and who have no good reason to suppress "discreditable" stories about him. (Quite the contrary, the discovery of conclusive evidence of a hidden love affair, whatever the sort or condition of the mistress, would be a great find for any biographer.) Or we can believe the spinners of fanciful yarns from selective and manipulative use of the evidence. Mr. Dabney believes the scholars. So do I.

—June 11, 1981

Justice Douglas: Emancipation from History

Justice William O. Douglas was, of all recent Supreme Court personalities, the cynosure of judicial liberalism—the underdog's advocate, the libertarian, the foe of what our grandfathers called "the interests." There was generosity of spirit in these views; and yet he could be a prickly, unceremonious man, and beastly to his law clerks. Or so one is led to believe.

A keen student of politics to whom I mentioned this Janus-like reputation said: "Easy—liberals are almost never as nice as conservatives." Conservatives, his theory went, usually oppose what is conceived to be political benevolence and, feeling guilty about it, go out of their way to show that they aren't ogres. Liberals, on the other hand, assume they are on God's side on every issue and hence feel free to be ornery in private life.

I distrust facile theories of behavior, even when they're as entertaining as that one. But whatever else explains Justice Douglas' contradictory reputation, he was certainly free of the conservative's exacting sense of accountability to the past.

The justice's utter emancipation from mere history probably accounts in part for the years of friction on the Court between him and Justice Frankfurter. Both were "Roosevelt justices"; but while Frankfurter lived *in* history, Douglas lived beyond it. The first was endlessly preoccupied with the knotty texture of precedent, historical and judicial; the second, with his darting mind, usually cut swiftly through complications that troubled others.

88

Not that one approach is "right" and the other "wrong." A close attention to history is seemly in a judge, but invention has its claims. I would guess only that a justice who undertakes to root his work in the past and its complexities has a better chance of seeing his doctrines survive him.

When one thinks of Justice Douglas' freedom from the anchor of history, a host of instances spring to mind.

In 1963, the Supreme Court finally mustered the votes to overturn what had long been one of his *betes noires*—Georgia's county-unit system of electing governors. There was a reasonable case against it. But Justice Douglas, typically, did not stop with that case. He came up with an oracular formula calculated to sweep aside all objection: "The conception of political equality," he wrote, "from the Declaration of Independence to Lincoln's Gettysburg Address, to the 15th, 17th and 19th Amendments, can mean only one thing: one person, one vote."

It sounded wonderful, but this resounding formula read into American political history a "conception of political equality" at war with many institutions and assumptions that predated the Gettysburg Address and the Civil War amendments—the U.S. Senate and the electoral college just to begin with. Again, the contrast with Justice Frankfurter was instructive. In the legislative reapportionment cases that had preceded the Georgia ruling, Justice Frankfurther, the dissenter, searched Anglo-American history to buttress his view that "one person, one vote" is too simple a doctrine to contain freedom's essence. And he was right.

Another of Justice Douglas' celebrated dicta, in a freedom of religion case of the 1940s, was that "we are a religious people whose institutions presuppose the existence of a Supreme Being." It was, for some, an agreeable theory. But what were the historical antecedents? It appeared to be conjured out of thin air. And indeed, as a constitutional notion, it had no future. It would not control even the justice's own future votes in Establishment Clause cases.

In the spring of 1970, Justice Douglas put his jaunty historical style on public display in a little book very much attuned to the rebellious spirit of the day, *Points of Rebellion*. He praised the French revolutionaries of 1789 who, as he charmingly put it, "shook up the Establishment of that age." Elsewhere in its pages, he seemed to equate U.S. antiwar protesters with the "loyal opposition" in England, not pausing to consider that England's loyal opposition is not exactly a revolutionary bureau but a device for institutionalizing dissidence within the fold of constitutionality, even for paying it a salary. Nor that its strictures on the exercise of power are tempered by the certainty that if it topples a goverment it must take office.

I join the homage being paid this week to the justice, who served the nation long and faithfully. Still, I can't help wondering whether the curiously ahistorical judicial style to which his impatient brilliance led him will remain a lasting force in the law, or whether it will be buried with its formidable architect.

—January 24, 1980

C. B. Deane and the Next Generation

When former Rep. C. B. Deane died last week, those who remembered Tar Heel politics in the mid-1950s recalled his refusal to sign the so-called "Southern Manifesto" of March, 1956—an act of conscience that cost him his seat in Congress.

"He was a man," said his daughter, "more interested in the next generation than in the next election."

It is an interesting distinction at this time, when most politicians strike the young as dedicated to political survival at all costs. They have become, in fact, remarkably cynical. There is in that "next generation" a certain cool heartlessness about acts of conscience once meaningful that remain so no longer. Certainly the controversy over the Southern Manifesto, with the dust of 14 years upon it, signifies little. Many of that "next generation" would say, presumably, that the architects of the Manifesto were so dead wrong, and the few dissenters so dead right, that refusing to sign it was the least a moral man could do. And so what—so what in A.D. 1969?

Perhaps they are right. Nothing is deader than a controversy that time has resolved. But if the Southern Manifesto fight is ancient history, it is instructive all the same.

It was hatched, this dignified document against the U.S. Supreme Court, in the spring of 1956 by some 20 Southern senators who believed then that if the South presented a solid front against the Court its decrees ending racial segregation in the

90

schools might be stayed. The air was thick with bogus constitutional theory out of the 1830s, 40s and 50s.

According to one historian of the episode, the late Sen. Harry Flood Byrd, a leading draftsman of the manifesto, believed that solid resistance, were it lawful, would save segregated schools. He also felt Virginia should lead the way, for "if Virginia surrenders the rest of the South will go down."

In the background were other, less quixotic thoughts. More than one of the 20 senators knew that school segregation involved issues of justice that lofty rhetoric about "constitutional principles" could not hide. They condemned the Supreme Court decrees as "a clear abuse of judicial power...encroaching upon the reserved rights of the states and the people"; but in the back of their minds they suspected—a fear that was political, but not dishonorably so—that the figures loosed in the South might dislodge the best of their number.

It might, for instance, dislodge senators like the late Walter George of Georgia, who had come to the Senate with Klan backing in 1922 but had lived down that taint in the nation's service. Senator George was up for re-election; Herman Talmadge (the unreconstructed "Humman" of that day) waited in the wings.

So the Manifesto was, in the main, another of those endless acts of Southern realpolitik instigated by moderates who convinced themselves that they must periodically toss a few scraps to the yahoos, lest the yahoos overturn them.

When the Manifesto came to the House, 24 southerners refused to sign. Three North Carolinians—Deane himself, Thurmond Chatham and Harold D. Cooley—stood among them. Deane and Chatham fell in the 1956 election, Deane almost certainly because he had not supported the Manifesto, Chatham perhaps for other reasons. (His challenger, Ralph Scott of Danbury, did not use the Manifesto issue.) Cooley survived, to be conquered finally by Jim Gardner 10 years later.

Never, so far as I know, did Mr. Deane ever think of himself as a hero. His austere code of personal conduct—he was for years a Baptist lay-leader and was also deeply caught up in the worldwide Moral Rearmament movement—did not permit such posturings.

But the poignant tribute of his daughter suggests that his act was not without significance to him. Perhaps he believed, a bit crazily perhaps, that one generation is generally an improvement on the last, and that the "next generation" cannot

91

thrive on admonition alone but needs examples of behavior that cost something to the giver.

The question is whether the best of that next generation, in their capacity for moral certainty and their abrupt judgment of a past they often do not trouble themselves to understand, will make a small effort to understand a man like C. B. Deane. It seems a modest favor, since he evidently had them much in mind at a crucial point in his life.

—November 29, 1969

Last Bard of the Melting Pot

In late 1958, when I took up newspapering in Charlotte, all the shoptalk was of two colleagues, one a ghost and the other an antic presence.

The ghost was Wilbur J. Cash, the editorialist who had published "The Mind of the South" in 1941 and then hanged himself the same year in Mexico City. The antic presence, very much alive, was Harry Golden, the editor, publisher and only contributor of the Carolina Israelite, a tabloid that issued on an erratic schedule from Golden's house on Elizabeth Avenue.

Harry claimed, and for all I know it was true, that the Israelite's unscheduled appearances signaled the overflow of the old cracker barrel into which he tossed pieces as he wrote them. But these were merely the mechanics; the interest lay in the substance.

Harry Golden's personal journalism had long since won a discriminating local clientele. It had been the recent publication of a collection of Israelite classics (e.g., the short Pascalian essay on the infinite distances of galactic space entitled "Why I Never Bawl Out Waitresses") that made him a national celebrity and a figure on the television interview shows. The book was called "Only in America," and was selling faster than his publishers could print it. That was not surprising to those who had been Israelite fans for years. "Only in America" might have put Harry on the national map. He had been on the North Carolina map—a fact of importance to him as I shall suggest—for more than a decade.

Just how he had gotten there—just how this roly-poly son

92

of Galician immigrants from the New York sidewalks, of all people, had chosen, of all places, a starchy southern town like Charlotte as his perch—I do not know to this day. Perhaps no one does. Not even his closest friends knew in 1958 what was soon to be disclosed by an unfriendly leak to a New York drama critic: that he had once served a prison term for stock fraud. Perhaps he had come south seeking the anonymity it might offer to a stranger with a past.

His obituaries (he died last week at 79) really give no inkling of the complexity of the niche he found for himself in a somewhat insular state where, nonetheless, some eccentricity of character was tolerated, and, by its better spirits, even treasured. And where a witty pen would find an audience.

It is certainly a mistake to portray Harry as a crusader. His influence leavened the racial climate, but he did not approach the evils of Jim Crow as a long-faced moralist. He flanked them as an ironist, making even the segregationists (at least, those who had a sense of humor) smile in rueful recognition at the absurdities of the race barrier. His "white baby plan" (which recognized that a black servant shepherding a white child was welcome anywhere) and his "vertical integration plan" (it was when sitting, not standing, that whites seemed to object to black propinquity) were ingenious formulations of home truths.

My own personal exposures to Harry Golden were mostly at the soirees given occasionally for him in those days by his friends, the David Wallaces. There, perched like a Buddha with a fat cigar and a circle of eager listeners munching lox and bagels and sipping bourbon, Harry would hold forth on art, song, politics, history and poetry. Simmons Fentress, then a Charlotte Observer editorial writer, played the straight man: "Harry, tell us about the time when..."

These scenes were repeated in after-hours seminars that often followed Chapel Hill meetings of the state press association, with dozens of people squeezed into one of those small sweat box suites at the old Carolina Inn. There Harry would vie with Jonathan Daniels, William Polk, Phillips Russell and others at the art of storytelling. In these rivals, all natives, Harry found kindred spirits, who knew something of the world and shared an appreciation of classical literature, the magic of politics and the color of provincial tradition.

But Charlotte? Charlotte was at this time one of those booming towns of the "New South" where the Chamber of Commerce was more important than it should have been, and the city had not yet shaken free of the chrysalis of textile manufacturing and Presbyterianism. But as I think about it now, it must have been the Calvinist climate that was in some mysterious way congenial.

Southern Presbyterians, who abounded in Charlotte, might be strait-laced. But they took the Old Testament seriously and knew a lot about it. In one of his best Carolina Israelite pieces, Harry had mused on the possibility that in view of their intense absorption in the lore of the Pentateuch, southern Presbyterians might be one of the lost tribes of Israel.

Having established himself in this rather improbable setting—a child of New York in the southern provinces—it amused Harry to inquire from time to time on what terms one might finally come to be regarded as an authentic North Carolinian. Am I a Tar Heel? he once asked, in an Israelite editorial. In those days such a question did not go unanswererd. From Raleigh, Greensboro, Smithfield and elsewhere, the answer was a resounding affirmative. Yes, Harry, you are a Tar Heel. Being so is a state of spirit, not origin.

I am glad the answer was affirmative. For it was true. Harry Golden gave us in those days a taste of distinguished personal journalism whose decrease, with the disappearance of journals like I. F. Stone's Weekly and in 1968 the Israelite itself, has removed something savory and expressive from the profession.

Not only that, Harry Golden was, I suppose, one of the last bards of the Melting Pot. His successful entry into the Waspish preserve of Tar Heel journalism, was one of the last and best examples of its solvent power. Say what one will of the "new ethnicity," the older enthnicity assumed improbable brotherhoods under the skin and unities in colorful multiplicities; and in that it was appealing. Yes, Harry Golden was a Tar Heel; one of the best.

—October 9, 1981

The Lesser Caldwell

After a recent evening's struggle with my young son over American history (history, I fear, was the loser—what's the Missouri Compromise to a 13-year-old?) I got to thinking about how we learn history when and if we learn it. And that made me think of J. R. Caldwell, Jr.

I first saw him in a Chapel Hill classroom in the autumn of 1952, where 20 edgy freshmen prepared to study under him the course known, I believe, as "Contemporary Civilization in the West," one of those two-semester tours of the past from Charlemagne to Churchill.

He was, he announced, "the lesser of the two Caldwells." The greater, by this reckoning, was a colorful professor of classical history full of eccentric boasts. One was his boast that he graded quizzes by tosssing them up (or was it down?) his staircase, the heavier ones getting A's and those of fluttery and insubstantial weight failing.

In his deliberate and methodical way, J. R. Caldwell brought the past to life; at the least he made sense of it. As the last echo of the bell died, he would stub out his pre-class Raleigh 903 cigarette, prop a foot upon the handiest desk, and begin: "When the bell sounded, gentlemen, we were examining into..." *Examining into!* That was the trademark phrase of his teaching; it seemed novel and attractive to those of us for whom, at this stage, history remained an unmemorable muddle of dates, names, personages, treaties and other matter vaguely known and certainly of no practical consequence. History something to be "examined into"—not a static or fixed pattern, not a lie agreed upon, but something for scrutiny? Here was something new.

I shall not urge the claim, here, that J. R. Caldwell was the most spectacular lecturer of his time; he was merely the most effective. If the subject was Napoleon—"a man on horseback," as he invariably called him—J.R. Caldwell gave you five reasons why Napoleon came to power; and when the proper time came, he gave you five reasons (all equally plausible) why he fell.

E. B. White recalls that his favorite English teacher, William Strunk, spoke in triplets, repeating his grammatical admonitions three times. J. R. Caldwell, lecturing without a glance at the notes before him from a memory of startling retentiveness and accuracy, said all the important things twice. It was enough. His notes parsed; they were beautifully studiable; they were, more than that, interesting.

Like all historical accounts, J. R. Caldwell's account of modern history was of course an artifice, as a good parquet floor is an artifice. You knew that the design was imposed by human craft upon an odd assortment of rough-hewn lumber. But there was no looseness about it, no ill-fitting joints. It would bear weight.

95

He graded tests with precision and care, rewarding almost any visible effort with a little personal note. "An excellent product" was his highest praise; if less than that, it might be a "good product" or a merely "satisfactory product," but it was always a product.

I would, in due course, encounter other and different kinds of history teaching, but none had the memorable force of J. R. Caldwell's "Contemporary Civilization." What he did, as I look back on it, was to move his students from the naive view that history was "facts" to the more intriguing view that it was at least a process in which believable people had been involved, whose motives were sometimes mysterious but in their humanness worth examining.

It was a stroke of luck to be one of Caldwell's "boys," for even then the dreadful publish-or-perish pressures (from which he kept a healthy distance) were building up and beginning to sap the foundations of undergraduate instruction. Besides, one might in other hands encounter the hazards of callow freshman teaching—shallow iconoclasm, superficial cleverness, obnoxious displays of pedantry, unrefined cynicism, sarcasm. Of these familiar academic vices he was altogether free.

Many Americans, I find, never encountered their J. R. Caldwells at the right age or time. They were less lucky than we. Or else they collided at an impressionable age with one of those dreadful "textbooks" that wring all credible passion and drama from the past. Or they succumb to the typical American view that history is at best a bore, at worst a positively dangerous branch of knowledge. Think of poor Miniver Cheevy, who grew lean with yearning for the romantic past!

Henry James, the novelist, believed that something in the American air was inimical to the sense of the past. Indeed, many of our ancestors, when they came here, were in flight from history and sought a new slate to write on. The past for them was complicated, oppressive, chastening; the future could be simple, liberating, emancipating. *History is bunk,* said Henry Ford; Americans cheered. The cheering hasn't stopped.

We need more history teachers of the Caldwell stripe, but we aren't likely to get them. I learned with regret the other day that he is retiring this year in Chapel Hill. I doubt that there are many of his like—who, like Chaucer's scholar "gladly teach"—waiting in the wings.

—May 19, 1977

Was Richard Russell Miscast?

Among connoisseurs of the governmental skills, Richard B. Russell, "Democrat, of Winder, Ga." (as his laconic entry in the Congressional Directory described him) was perhaps the most widely admired legislator of his era. A senator's senator, he was the man who ran the club that ran the Senate.

As the nation viewed it, he was also a southerner's southerner—in an increasingly antiquated sense. Our last glimpse of Russell at work is a sad one: the old gentleman, wracked by emphysema, pounding his desk and crying, "Order! We must have order!" as the Senate galleries crowed over the rejection of Judge Carswell.

James Reston, groping for a gracious summation of Russell's career, sees in it the tragedy of the Old South, overtaken by history. And so it was in part, but only in part.

Richard Russell was not really of the Old South, never wholly comfortable in its mystiques and rituals. In his early Senate career as a staunch New Dealer (and he remained a Democratic loyalist long after most of the Southern Bourbons had jumped ship) he thought of himself as a liberal and a progressive. Journalists as informed as Rowland Evans and Robert Novak suggest that Russell "was almost surely suspicious of Lyndon Johnson's New Deal background," as the two collaborated in the early 1960s. But Russell had the same background, the same basic convictions about American politics.

Georgia remembers Russell as its best modern governor—his efficient administration paralleling that of O. Max Gardner in North Carolina. In 1936, running for his first full term in the Senate, he raised a decent standard against racist, ribald Eugene Talmadge, who with the backing of the Georgia Power Company shrieked that the New Deal crowd was "a combination of wet nursin', frenzied finance, downright communism and plain dam-foolishness."

In later years, ironically, Russell's junior Senate colleague will be Ol' Gene's son Herman, an adjustable man more easily bent by the winds of change.

Whatever else it may be, Russell's is not a career out of the Old South, but out of the New South as progressive and liberal-minded southerners conceived it before the world war and the civil rights movement swept away the old terms of reference.

97

Would a man of Russell's caliber, one asks oneself, have stuck in this crumbling mold except for what happened to him between 1948 and 1952? Both were pivotal years for the Democratic Party and the South—the Dixiecrat movement (which Russell shunned; he supported Truman); the rise of Mayor Hubert Humphrey of Minneapolis, shedding "the bright sunlight of human rights" on the Democrats; the drafting of his kinsman Adlai Stevenson for a spot that Russell himself very badly wanted—the Democratic presidential nomination.

For Russell, those years brought gloom and disappointment: the realization that a southerner of superb abilities was forever barred from the presidency for no better reason (or so it seemed to him) than that he was Southern. Those who knew Russell best said that 1952 was the watershed for him.

None but racial, perhaps, is crueller than sectional bigotry; and beating his head against it seems to have had permanent effects on Richard Russell. On one side it brought out his generosity and highmindedness: Convinced that he could never lead the Democrats, or even all the Senate Democrats, he searched for an alternative and his eyes fell on the brash but gifted new senator from Texas, Lyndon Johnson, who as a border state man carried no sectionalist burdens. Russell's patronage and influence projected LBJ; the latter's talents did the rest.

On the other side, however, the bitter disappointment of 1952 pushed Russell into habits of thought and reaction best described by the writer who called the Senate "the South's undying revenge on the North for the Civil War."

A man of greater resiliency and less pride might have made adjustments. Many do. As Paris was worth a mass to a Protestant French prince, many a governmental perquisite has been worth a perfunctory nod in the direction of civil rights by southerners—so much so of late that as Robert Campbell recently put it, "It's getting hard to tell the players even if you've got a program."

Seeing sectionalism as a handicap, Russell might have fought it; or, as many of the better Southern senators do, he might have neutralized it by developing an expertise not burdened or embarrassed by the racial obsession—as Fulbright did in foreign affairs, Lister Hill in social legislation, Sam Ervin in constitutional rights. Or he might have observed philosophically how a mere accident of constituency may emancipate a southerner, as the Supreme Court emancipated Hugo Black, or the executive branch Lyndon Johnson—making his peace with a quirk of government.

But Russell didn't. When there was a sectional fight to be fought, he led it. When there was a "Southern" posture to be struck, he struck it, albeit honorably and decorously, often at the cost of seeming more Bourbon than he was.

Some may find weakness or cynicism in this. But it seems to be a perfectly plausible, if regrettable, reaction for a strong, proud man who knows that the world has failed to identify his character and talents accurately. He would not, therefore, rage against the iron dictates of circumstance, he would embrace them as if they had been justly ordained. He would affirm a sectionalism all the more uncompromising for its having been thrust upon him.

"Since you insist upon viewing me as a stereotype," he seemed to say, "and since you insist on limiting my role accordingly, very well, I will play the role to the hilt." And so he did—a fine player miscast; a man of national abilities wasted in lesser roles about which he must, at times, have had his doubts.

—January 27, 1971

Ralph McGill and the Future

Reading of Ralph McGill's sudden death in Atlanta, I recalled with greater appreciation two recent columns, typical of his best, that had lodged in the mind.

One began by noting the death of an old Georgia woman, nearly 100, whose family had committed her as a girl to the state asylum for women at Milledgeville—committed her, then promptly (and guiltily, McGill thought) abandoned her. For 50 years no loved one or friend had visited. Locked in friendless isolations she had long since lapsed into hopeless schizophrenia. Reflecting on the case, Ralph McGill visited his divine indignation on the obscure relatives of this obscure woman, ending with a tart "good riddance" to the good old days when a mental illness was a hush-hush matter to be dealt with furtively and in shame.

In the other piece, McGill broke a firm resolve to keep his silence about the Kennedy-Onassis marriage, provoked to marvelous sarcasm by the letters of snide women whose empty lives

99

(or so he imagined) drove them to the envy of a beautiful woman.

Ralph McGill's front-page columns in the Atlanta Constitution for decades explored, often with a drop or two of acid, such by-ways of the news. Like all who write against a daily deadline he wrote his share of humdrum pieces. But when aroused, as often he was, by misery or meanness, loneliness or injustice, his pieces flamed to life on the page, the imprecations of an Isaiah. The live coal was on his tongue.

Though identified with streamlined Atlanta, Ralph McGill sprang from among the substantial and individualist farmers of the Tennessee Valley—a peaceful, almost alpine bend in the river named Soddy-Daisy. A big, rumpled man, his coat pockets bulging with notes and clippings, he somehow resembled a country preacher and loved the evangelical tone. But few masters of the pulpit had his gift of language, or his command of human psychology.

For the most part, the preoccupation of the South in our time, the race problem, was his also. He explored this regional vexation fearlessly, without grandstanding or compromise. Not many years after the Supreme Court decision of 1954, sentiment spread through Georgia that the schools would be better shut than integrated. Georgia avoided that self-spiting act; and many Georgians credited that fact to a wise, courtly and conservative old gentleman, John Hart Sibley, who moved through the state holding public hearings and putting the choice directly to the people.

Mr. Sibley and other impeccable figures of the Georgia establishment played a large role, unquestionably. But behind their success lay a spirit of accommodation to change almost single-handedly implanted over the years by Ralph McGill. The same might be said of Atlanta, the boom-town "too busy to hate." McGill was in but not wholly of the tradition of Sidney Lanier and Henry Grady, who deplored Georgia's backwardness but could swallow Jim Crow and low wages to cure it.

Like many other interesting commentators, Ralph McGill was very judgmental. It usually struck him that there was a right side and a wrong side to most public questions. He was often righteous but never self-righteous. Calvinistic in tone as they were, his views were not always to be swallowed smoothly—nor meant to be. His appreciation of the famous Agrarians who had gone to school with him at Vanderbilt was, for instance, slight—he thought of them as apologists for racism. His relentless criticism of the foes of desegregation rested on the view that to talk of resistance was to court hoodlumism and violence. When a snarling mob of white mothers pelted or spat on a Negro child seeking entry to a school in New Orleans, and the moreso when worse horrors occurred, he would train his fire on apostles of genteel resistance. It was they, he claimed, who made mobs respectable. His text was: Sow the wind and reap the whirlwind.

It was a troublesome theory of the potential dangers of free speech, even for those who agreed with Mr. McGill that laws must be obeyed.

In the ultimate balance of his career, it was of minor consequence—one of the quirks that makes a great man interesting. Ralph McGill exemplified courage and conviction for a whole generation of southerners who wanted their region to throw off the crippling obsessions with race. At his death the harvest in Georgia and elsewhere was mixed. Georgia had voted in November for George Wallace, in so many ways his antithesis; and the Governor's chair was occupied by Lester Maddox, the obstreperous little restaurateur. Had Ralph McGill been given to bitterness or irony, there was food for both. He was not. He persisted in what he believed to be right and trusted the future to vindicate him. I believe that it will.

—*February 5, 1969*

Francis Warrington Dawson Revisited

Francis Warrington Dawson, who edited the *Charleston News and Courier* from its founding in 1873 until his violent death in 1889, has been called by one successor "the one who introduced modern journalism into South Carolina." No journalistic tradition, if so, could have a more arresting Father Abraham. At a casual glance, Dawson seems an inviting subject for one of those odious psychobiographies now so fashionable. I suppose that anyone with a beginner's knowledge of 19th Century South Carolina journalism would know the rudiments of the story: How a penniless London lad of 20, filled with romantic sympathy for the Confederate cause, begged his way aboard the

101

Confederate cruiser Nashville at Southampton in 1861 and thus began a voyage that would in time make him a power of Southern journalism and politics.

But beyond a certain point, fact shades into speculation and speculation into the uncertain hues of apocrypha. The Dawson entry in the *Dictionary of American Biography,* so far as I can judge, contains at least two serious errors in as many columns of type—typical in this of the obscurity and myth that wrap Dawson's origins. Why, for instance, did he change his name from the prosaic Austin John Reeks (as he was christened at birth) to the more sonorous Francis Warrington Dawson? According to one story, the new name was his spontaneous invention when his father begged him not to embark on his quixotic knight-errand for the South and said he would be ashamed to have a son hanged as a spy. His more reliable chronicler, S. Frank Logan, to whose unpublished Master's thesis I am indebted, says rather that Reeks became Dawson in homage to a wealthy maternal aunt, childless widow of a Captain Dawson of the British Army, who financed his meager formal education at a minor Roman Catholic preparatory school. (In this period, Oxford and Cambridge were still exclusively for Anglicans; otherwise the young Reeks might well have qualified.)

Not only the change of name but the decision to uproot himself presents that theme so tempting to the speculative biographer: the change of identity. One may also wonder why an apparently promising career as a London playwright should have been so casually abandoned. Herbert R. Sass, in his informal history of the *News and Courier,* writes that Dawson "wrote four or five plays which were produced in London"—a precocious beginning not lightly to be cast aside in a fit of youthful romance for the lesser arts of war, politics and journalism. But again, Logan has searched the manuscript books among the Dawson papers and found there only one play, a two-act comedy revealingly entitled, "Never Judge By Appearances," dated June, 1859. Logan puts the number of plays actually produced in London at two; but he does not indicate the source of his information.

There are other mysteries about the young crusader. Logan tells us that Reeks' father, once a man of wealth, had lost a fortune trying to corner the English wheat market. To one who knows something of the economic history of the period, that seems unlikely. In the year of Reeks' birth, in one of the great political upheavals of the Victorian age, Sir Robert Peel engineered the repeal of agricultural protection, ushering in an age of free trade in foodgrains. This at least complicated the hazards of speculation. I am led to believe, or at least to guess, that the tale of his father's ruin in wheat speculation was a product of Dawson's ample fancy; perhaps he had written a youthful theater piece on the subject.

In any event, we know that the young Reeks, now Dawson, was a young man uprooted and in search of a new identity and role. He found both in the war-torn Confederacy, where he served honorably and adventurously in both army and navy. He was an ordnance officer under Longstreet, he suffered wounds, he was captured and was briefly a prisoner of war.

In the autumn of 1865 he took his first newspaper job on the old *Richmond Examiner,* a paper whose predecessor of the same name had been Thomas Jefferson's paper. There in Richmond he struck up a friendship with his future partner, Bartholomew Riordan, and in time followed Riordan back to Charleston and a job on the *Mercury.* With the other Charleston papers, Riordan found the *Mercury* "very slow and old-fashioned" and it was not long before the two men had acquired the *News.*

The regional and even national reputation that Dawson was to make on the *News* (which became the *News and Courier* in 1873) has, I judge, suffered historical distortions that ought to be dispelled. His two decades of editorial leadership were, of course, crucial for South Carolina, the South and the nation: still very hotly contested ground among historians. Prof. C. Vann Woodward, in a classic book on the disputed election and compromise of 1876-77, has characterized the era as one of "reunion and reaction"; and in *The Origins of the New South* he lists Dawson—Captain Dawson as he now was—among the reactionaries. At least, in Woodward's portrait, he becomes a commonplace booster:

> In Dawson's metropolitan and unprejudiced eyes there was nothing in old Charleston that could not be improved with an eye to Pittsburgh...He preferred "a cross between the Bostonian and the Chicagoan." Although Dawson and his compatriot Godkin, who preceded him to the New World by five years, chose opposing sides in the civil war of their adopted land, they saw eye to eye on the deeper consequences of that unpleasantness...Dawson and Godkin spoke with the voice of Manchester to the New South.

This predominantly economic interpretation of Dawson's outlook and significance is echoed elsewhere. "No journalist after 1880," writes Paul Buck in *The Road to Reunion,* noting Dawson's belief in the community of intersectional interest and how it tempered his politics, "no journalist...added an idea or word to the preachments of F. W. Dawson on the gospel of labor, the need of manufactures, and the desirability of agricultural diversification." Woodward, again, calls him a "forceful propagandist" for cotton mills. This is a true but partial characterization. Dawson did take a healthy interest in the economic recovery of his state and region. But to paint him as a grim Manchesterian, a sort of journalistic Gradgrind panting for dark satanic mills, is seriously to distort the significance of his career. One who reads, even selectively, through the editorial crusades of the postwar years, in all their variety, gains a wholly different impression. He knew well the grim limits of industrialism, and he did not hesitate to write about them in the *News and Courier*. At times he sounds very current in his observations. In June, 1880, while serving as a Democratic convention delegate in Cincinnati, and being fed by the hosts there on such delicacies as crab salad and fricasseed frog, he was overwhelmed by environmental nuisances. Cincinnati, he reported in a long piece of front-page editorial correspondence, was "an exceedingly unpleasant place":

> ...The coal used in Cincinnati makes more smoke than any other coal that I have ever met with, and as the city itself is in a basin surrounded by high hills, the smoke beats down upon the city, obscuring the sky, covering everybody and everything with soot, and making breathing more difficult and unprofitable. The water, of which there is a copious supply, is as rich in its color as the smoke. It can best be compared to thin chocolate. Columbia water in its worst form is as clear as crystal in comparison.

It was not the observation of an uncritical admirer of industrial cities.

If by modern journalism his admirer William Watts Ball meant journalism of variety and independence, and even a certain elegance, Dawson provided it. One can, of course, find Dawson editorials on economic subjects, some quite knowledgeable in contemporary economic theory. He did not neglect the subject. He also kept a standing editorial caption, "Bring the mills to the cotton," and under that heading he plausibly argued from time to time that it would be to the advantage of New England textile firms to build new plants in the South. He took an interest in Charleston's continuing development as a port city, es-

104

pecially as a funnel through which, unvexed by tariffs, "the wares of Europe" would flow to "the mighty cities of the West." The thought of it could stir him to rhapsody: "Along a mighty line, traversing empire states, are hosts of eager men who shall sigh for the day when the wares of Europe shall come to them from a South Atlantic port."

However heartfelt—and there is a certain perfunctoriness about the writing—these editorial causes were fitful by comparison with Dawson's commitment to the overthrow of dishonest government, the reduction of casual violence, and the welfare of the Democratic Party. He was a deeply political man. With most white southerners of his adopted caste and time, Dawson regarded Republican (or as he invariably called it "Radical") Reconstruction with disgust. Up to the advent of the Chamberlain administration in the mid-1870's the editorial columns of the *News and Courier* are replete with denunciation of printing scandals, the waste of public money and various swindles. As much as Dawson craved the restoration of the old regime in South Carolina, however, he is not to be called a Bourbon who ignored or forgot the lessons of the Civil War. He took what was, for his time and place, a detached and independent view of the race question, not condoning the violence and chicanery by which some of his fellow Democrats wanted to regain power. He agreed with James S. Pike's description of South Carolina as "a prostrate state," and promoted it in his pages. But when Senator Charles Sumner introduced his famous civil rights bill of January, 1874, Dawson noted without complaint that South Carolina already had a state act assuring the same rights, although he did complain that when a Negro plaintiff sued under the act the burden of proof would be on the accused. Otherwise, the Sumner bill did not disturb the *News and Courier*. South Carolina, Dawson observed, "cannot be expected to fall into paroxysms of grief because Massachusetts, for instance...may be at last herself to taste its flavor." Dawson's own long-range strategy for the restoration of Democratic—that is, white—dominance was in part the encouragement of wholesale German immigration to the state. He returned to the theme frequently, not indicating the underlying purpose.

Nowhere is his relative independence of mind on the civil rights question more clearly or admirably illustrated than in the *News and Courier's* response to the so-called "Hamburg Massacre" of July 4, 1876. This gory incident, whose origins were disputed, came just as the Democratic Party's bid to recapture control of South Carolina from the "Radicals" reached a crucial stage. According to reports reaching Charleston and printed in the news columns of the *News and Courier,* a rowdy mob of white vigilantes had tried to disarm a black militia drilling on the main street of Hamburg; later, seven of the disarmed Negroes had been shot down in cold blood. Although it could not have been a popular position, Dawson's editorials caustically assailed white lawlessness. To be sure, the paternalistic and patronizing racial attitudes underlying these editorials qualify their excellence in our ears; but it does not mar their eloquence, force and character. In "The Bloody Work at Hamburg," Dawson warned that the Edgefield vigilantes were sowing the wind and would reap the whirlwind. He declared, in an argument calculated to penetrate the dullest white skull, that "the higher intelligence and culture of the white imposes on them the duty of self-reverence and self-control." On the 11th of July, already taxed with protest from readers, Dawson refused to yield ground. There could be, he wrote, no double standard of justice:

> ...There is only one right and one wrong for those who look to superior intelligence and virtue rather than to rifle and saber, as the means of restoring to the whites the control of the state. We shall, come what may, give our cardinal judgment upon every public act, whether it is done by Democrats or Republicans...Indeed, we could not condemn the passionate Negro who...applies the torch to a dwelling-house or barn if we did not condemn the conduct of white men in killing defenseless Negroes.

Sensitive as we may be today to the limits, as well as the correctness of Dawson's argument—which was quite bluntly pitched, it would seem, to the overriding expedient of restoring white political mastery—Dawson's denunciation of the "bloody work" at Hamburg commands admiration. He consistently advocated the rule of law, as we shall see in the case of his stand on duelling, but with the single distressing exception that the *News and Courier* condoned lynching for certain offenses. Thus a headline for July 28, less than a month after the Hamburg fray and Dawson's eloquent editorials, screams:

A BLACK BRUTE LYNCHED

The subhead echoes: "Swift and Deserved Penalty For A Terrible Crime." With this single most regrettable exception, Dawson and the *News and Courier* held up to their influential audience the ideal, and the practical advantages, of equality before the law.

The editorial flavor of Francis Dawson at his best may, I think, be found in his celebrated campaign against duelling, for which Pope Leo XIII, in November, 1883, made him a Knight of the Order of St. Gregory the Great. The campaign is interesting on several accounts. Not only did the editor of the *News and Courier* rise to an impassioned eloquence, arraying all the techniques of moral suasion, sarcasm, ridicule and logic in his arsenal; also, the former penniless immigrant who had once had nothing to his name but a postage stamp and a gray uniform asserted a strong independence of the values of his adopted class. In doing so, indeed, he exposed himself to scurrilous charges of cowardice. But in the end he drew along with him the whole of the South Carolina press and most of its political leadership.

The event that crystallized Dawson's passion was the duel at DuBois's Bridge in Darlington County, July 5, 1880, in which Colonel Boggan Cash shot and killed Colonel William M. Shannon. The origins of this affair, as of many duels, were obscure. The challenge stemmed ultimately from an imagined offense to Colonel Cash's wife in some long-forgotten financial matter. "Remember," whispered Colonel Cash's son to his father as the duelling pistols were handed out, "how poor mother was treated."

Duelling, which had been outlawed in South Carolina for almost 70 years, was a sport of the gentry. As one might recall from the famous caning of Senator Sumner by Preston Brooks after Sumner's "Bleeding Kansas" speech, the code duello prohibited challenges to social inferiors. Nor was satisfaction to be gained by returning an insult for an insult. Its class character was one of the things that bothered Dawson most. The dimensions of this gentleman's vice, formal and informal, have been entertainingly suggested by Francis Butler Simkins:

> South Carolina, with less than one fourth as many people as New England, had three times the number of homicides...The newspapers before and after 1900 were crowded with accounts of homicidal frays among lawyers, planters, doctors, even preachers, and particularly editors. (He cites the violent deaths of both Dawson and N. G. Gonzales.) Homicide was an important means of preserving the Southern code of decorum and puritanical chivalry. Sometimes lives were exacted for offenses as trivial as an argument over a dog.

Just when Dawson himself became an impassioned foe of duelling cannot be fixed exactly; indeed the question presents another of those biographical mysteries I spoke of earlier. In his *Reminiscences,* Dawson recalled that as a young blade just out of the army in Richmond, he challenged a Mr. George after an imagined discourtesy to his lady companion at a ball. The young lady was so impressed—perhaps that is the point, after all—that she accepted his suit for marriage; but the engagement hardly survived the challenge, which was patched up. She married another.

Perhaps it was his marriage, after the death of his first wife, to the lively Sarah Morgan of Louisiana that shaped his view finally. Sarah Morgan Dawson, as a young girl, had lost a brother in what Edmund Wilson correctly calls a "puerile" duel in New Orleans, a duel sparked by, of all things, a rendition of the song "Annie Laurie" in the Morgans' parlor. As Wilson tells the story, paraphrasing Sarah Morgan's diary, "an old gentleman got up to leave, and this old gentleman's son, an obnoxious outsider to the Morgans' world, who may or may not have been under the influence of opium, imagined that the son had offended his father. Harry Morgan denied this, and the outsider called him a liar. '…Quick as a thought Harry sprang to his feet and struck him across the face with the walking stick he held…' A duel followed and Harry was killed." After such an incident, Sarah Morgan, whom Dawson greatly loved, could not have taken a kindly view of the code duello.

Dawson's crusade against duelling in South Carolina, following the Cash-Shannon affair, resulted almost immediately in a tightening of the laws. It may indeed account for the demise of duelling after that encounter. Dawson hinged his argument on two major themes. He did not—it is an interesting study in editorial strategy—assail duelling directly on moral grounds, although he had at least once declined a challenge as a Roman Catholic. Instead, calling the duel "ceremonious manslaughter," he bore down upon its decadence: its decline from an institution that might once, he conceded, have had some practical use, to an elaborate and stylized ritual of which, "as the niceties and elegancies…have been perfected the mortality has diminished." There was, he wrote, now heaping ridicule on the custom, "much correspondence and little bloodshed" in this "foolish…illegal practice." A more serious argument was the risk of gross injustice: the risk that a man who had wronged another might escape condign punishment while the aggrieved party lost his life. This, he said, had happened in the Cash-Shannon duel.

108

"There is about as much sense," he wrote, "in allowing a common murderer to engage in a single-rope combat with the hangman as in inviting the scoundrel who has perpetrated a mortal wrong to try his hand at murdering the one who has been injured."

Perhaps the most telling argument, as he put the case to *News and Courier* readers, was the familiar plea for a uniform application of the laws to all. Duelling had been outlawed since 1812, but the duelling classes enjoyed a certain immunity. There could be, he insisted, no true civility, no rule of law, if in its application distinctions of class and caste were made. "For the people of the state," he said, "the single question is, shall the law be enforced against common offenders and be of no effect when they who commit the crime are persons of position, influence and means?" He asked that question after the coroner of Kershaw County issued a warrant for Colonel Cash's arrest; he challenged authorities either to enforce the anti-duelling statutes or strike them from the books as a mockery. "Colonel Cash and his son," he wrote, "put themselves above the law. They assert the right to maim or kill, if they can, anyone who in their judgment does them an injury...a mischievous and barbarous doctrine."

I dwell on this, among all the Dawson causes that might be discussed at length, because it shows the power and inventiveness, and true practicality, of his fine editorial mind. The crusade was singularly effective: It was not long before the legislature significantly strengthened the laws and duelling came to an end. One may speculate, as always, whether the result was Dawson's doing or whether he merely voiced an idea whose time had come. But he certainly focused the thoughtful minds of South Carolina upon a custom of great hypocrisy, injustice and cruelty.

When his eventual successor William Watts Ball called Dawson the founder of modern South Carolina journalism he may have had in mind just that conception of civility that the *News and Courier* urged during the Hamburg outrage and the Cash-Shannon duel. But journalism is technique as well as cause. Let us turn, then, to questions of style, craft and editorial management.

In Dawson's editorial writing, one can see editorial journalism emerging, however imperfectly, from the old habits of vitriolic sectionalism, personal virulence and vendetta that had characterized so much 19th Century newspapering. Indeed, the old journalism, the journalism represented by Dawson's Charleston predecessors, was with difficulty to be distinguished from mere pamphleteering. It is precisely Dawson's era in

109

Charleston that Frank Luther Mott chose to describe, in his classic history of American journalism, as that of the rise of independent newspapers. Mott mentions a number of factors. The Civil War had made heroes of some correspondents, and the growing thirst for information was diminishing the importance of editorializing and, correspondingly, the chain of party ties. A college education was no longer a rarity in the nation's newsrooms, and in 1869 General Robert E. Lee, as president of Washington College, had established the first known program for journalistic education. Six scholars were to be admitted "to work out their tuitions at the printing trade while taking the classical course at the college." It was an age of great editors.

To a retrospective eye, the imperfections of this emerging independence, in a paper like the *News and Courier* of the 1870's and 1880's, are sometimes as striking as the emergence itself. When Dawson is aroused, sometimes with cause, he still turns to the old language of personal abuse. General Sherman, who is never mentioned without loathing, is "Sherman the Malignant." Many others appear as rascals, scoundrels, poltroons, swindlers, etc. The followers of Pitchfork Ben Tillman, the Edgefield farmer to whose agrarian views Dawson extended urbane hospitality, become "people who carry pistols in their hip pockets, who expectorate on the floors, who have no tooth brushes and comb their hair with their fingers." I merely note, without judging, this relatively harmless vestige of personal journalism.

Another limitation on the "modernity" of the *News and Courier* for about half its period under Dawson's editorship—that is, until January, 1882—is that the editor's chair and the bookkeeper's bench are one and the same. This mingling of vital roles did not, I believe, much impair the independence nor cramp the style of the paper. The accusation leveled by political enemies of the paper that Francis Dawson and his partner, Riordan, had intrigued corruptly for state printing contracts was not sustained by an extensive legislative inquiry. But Logan turns up one unacknowledged case in which the interconnection of purse and pen may have been at work. It appears from the McGrath family papers that Dawson was not unwilling to take a fairly glowing editorial view of a business—the South Carolina Railroad—whose president was his creditor to the tune of $3,000 or more. In March, 1873, knowing that Dawson and his associate needed funds for their purchase of the *Courier,* President W. J. McGrath pressed an unsecured loan on Dawson. (Dawson insisted on putting up a life insurance policy as collateral.) Later, without disclosing this interest to his readers, Dawson would hail the yearly financial report of McGrath's railroad with assurances that its management during the business panic of 1873 had been "irreproachable." Indeed, he wrote, "no corporation in America has been handled with more sagacity." This handsome tribute was the only editorial of the day, except for a brief welcome to the South Carolina medical association, then meeting in Charleston. Two days later, the editorialist returned to the excellence of Mr. McGrath as a railroad president, extolling his "rare capacity, earnestness and culture." Again, there was no disclosure that the editor of the *News and Courier* had good personal reason to value Mr. McGrath's "sagacity." Again, I note this minor departure from strict independence, not in judging so much as observing that it was one hazard of a link between business and editorial judgment.

A more serious, at times a more compromising, limitation on Dawson's independence of judgment was his intense activity as a Democratic Party official and insider. Passionate party connection was, of course, an affliction of some of the best editors of Dawson's era, though it was declining. One thinks of Marse Henry Watterson of Louisville, and later of Josephus Daniels of Raleigh. Few carried it to such lengths. Dawson not only served as a county Democratic executive committeeman, as a national committeeman and national convention delegate; he turned his pen frequently to the writing of party broadsides and platforms. Of course, it was all quite understandable. One gets the feeling from Dawson's editorials that until South Carolina's "deliverance" from Radical rule Dawson had not been a slavish party man. His famous fight against the so-called "straightouts" of the Democratic Party in 1876 exhibited genuine independence. But after the nomination and election of Wade Hampton, Dawson's independent line tended to be submerged. His editorials became far more partisan on political subjects; the welfare of the state and the nation were often uncritically identified with the election of Democrats. In the post-Reconstruction period, more than during Reconstruction itself, one encounters a sense that in the years of Radical rule South Carolina had been a conquered and humiliated people, its neck under the heel of aliens. Among the latter, notwithstanding his sympathy for civil rights, he included certain Negro officeholders. Perhaps the process of myth-making was already at work. In any event, like the tone of personal abuse, like the hidden connection with President McGrath of the South Carolina Railroad, Dawson's intense Democratic partisanship was a limitation on his independence.

111

Whether independence is a virtue or a peril of modernity I would hesitate to say categorically; but I tend to think, the former.

Francis Dawson made his career in Charleston on the eve of mass-circulation journalism in America. The circulation figures of the *News and Courier,* though it stood among the top two or three Southern journals, reminds us that his writing, after all, was directed to and shaped the thinking of an elite. Charleston was a city of 75,000, but the entire circulation of the *News and Courier* was but a fraction of that figure. Select as it was, his readership expected and got from Dawson editorial comment of great maturity and detail. When Dawson sought to persuade South Carolina Democrats to cast their lot with Governor Chamberlain, whom he had once opposed, he laid out his case with a leisurely amplitude that the age of television and other distractions has put well behind us: a nine-part series, entitled "The Chamberlain Record," running to thousands of words and discussing the issues in the most minute detail.

Dawson, a distinguished writer on politics and economics, had interests that went beyond politics. His readers could expect literate, sometimes sophisticated comment in literature—for instance, the publication of a new edition of Bulwer Lytton's novels, or even a new anthology of devotional verse. Polygamy and the Mormons, the death of the great naturalist Louis Agassiz, new treatises on theories of capital and labor, were likely to call for editorials. In his interesting obituary piece on Agassiz's death in 1873, for instance, Dawson touched gingerly on the vexed issue of apes and angels, of Darwin and natural selection. Incidentally, he was careful to conceal his own partisanship, if he had any, on the evolutionary doctrines that had shaken the Victorians so deeply. He merely observed that with Agassiz's death the anti-evolutionists "will lose their most able champion" whose lifelong dream had been "to gather together the fruits of his research and thought and hurl them upon the head of the hydra of Evolution..." He does not sound like a partisan of the angels to me. The notice of Agassiz was not unusual, in that Dawson evidently took a more than routine interest in Victorian science, engineering and husbandry. He wrote knowledgeably on scientific agriculture; he was quick to call to the attention of his low-country readers the theory that the tree Eucalpytus Bolus might, if transplanted, spare them the dread threat of the summertime miasma. He wrote from a vast store of knowledge about trains.

Dawson, apart from his erudition, had that quality never

out of place in an editorialist, a sense of the absurd. His mode of humor was rather forced and stilted; he was no Mark Twain or Joel Chandler Harris. But he rarely missed an opportunity to turn to the sardonic mode, especially when a Republican rascal strayed into his sights. One such target was the unfortunately named Godlove S. Orth, who had returned from a diplomatic career to accept the Republican nomination for governor of Indiana in 1876. Orth had been accused by Indiana newspapers of shady dealings in Central America. Dawson wrote:

> (Orth) was not born great...but his sponsors in baptism, when they vowed for him to renounce the world, the flesh and the devil, invested him with an appelation that gave promise of divine blessings...His name was his fortune...But alas! scandal whispers that though God loved Orth, Orth loves Mammon...In spite of his name the devil will be apt to catch him before long.

It was not Mark Twain; but it would serve. Dawson, who in youth had aspired to belles lettres, seems to have had a formal, conscious sense of style—a sense of craft that went beyond the ordinary, especially among journalists. It was evident not only in the finish and grace of some of his writing, but in his insistence that even public servants and politicians should write clearly and honestly. In commenting on the public message of his bete noire, Governor Moses, he would write that "brevity is not the soul of the wit of Governor Moses, either as writer or orator...[In his message] there is plenty of fine writing. Aristotle and Plato, and Heaven knows who else, are laid under contribution and when the supply of these is exhausted, His Excellency vibrates between hackneyed poetry and fustian prose...there is no manliness, no straightforwardness in him or his official papers."

In *Patriotic Gore,* Edmund Wilson considers the transition that American prose underwent in this postwar world, "from the complex, the flowery, the self-consciously learned, to the direct and economical." The newspaper writing of the time, he observes, "had no doubt something to do with this shift: the editors were pressing for simplicity and brevity." Dawson, I should say, was very much a man of this shift. In him the transition was not complete; but his style combined formality with vigor.

Francis Dawson, though a man and journalist of his time and place and very comfortable in both, and his work subject to the limitations of scope and imagination I have mentioned, was an estimable editorialist. His readers respected and responded to his comment; his foes, and he had many, feared his influence. He could be extraordinarily generous, considering the intense partisanship of the time, to opponents such as Ben Tillman; his faults, such as they appear, were not those of meanness nor narrowness of vision, but of a loyalty carried to a fault: sectional and party loyalty, I mean. It is sad and ironic that Dawson, who held up to his readers the ideals of civility, should have met his untimely end, at the early age of 49, by the uncivil personal violence he abhorred. Angered by police reports that a Charleston physician of dubious report, Dr. T. B. McDow, was seeing his children's French governess, a young woman brought to this country under his wife's protection, he went alone one afternoon to issue a warning. In a confrontation of which his murderer later gave a highly self-serving account—including the charge that Dawson had attacked him with his cane—he was shot dead, and McDow gruesomely sought to hide his body in a storm cellar. The ensuing trial ended in acquittal, a last mockery of Dawson's crusade against unpunished violence. McDow's acquittal, morever, was applauded by some who were Dawson's enemies, or imagined they were; but he was mourned in his city, state and region. "To his infinite and lasting honor," wrote Henry Grady, "it can be said that his leadership has never been abused, its opportunities never wasted, its powers never prostituted, its suggestions never misdirected." That is a farewell any editorialist would covet.

Eckhardt of Texas

When representative Bob Eckhardt of the eighth district of Texas entered the U.S. House of Representatives in early 1967, he encountered a lot of problems—the cards are always stacked against the new boys, especially if they are already fifty-three years old and stand little chance of achieving seniority. But the worst problem was that his natural political allies in the House could not believe Eckhardt was a liberal.

In the first place, he speaks in the soft drawl of East Texas, and even after his real political sympathies had been suspected he would still horrify a correct Yankee liberal by going over to the Senate side to testify on a bill and bandying genial colloquialisms with people like Senator Sam Ervin, Jr. of North Carolina, laughing and saying things like, "But *Senatah*, isn't that like sending the possum to chase the *dawg*?" Usually there is a gold watch chain strung across the waistcoated paunch of his three-piece suit; and above the unvarying bow tie the vaguely Claghornish hair tends to tumble down to eye level. The truth is, Bob Eckhardt *looks* like a Southern tory, and when you first meet him you expect him to think like an Allen Drury caricature of a Southern Congressman.

In the second place, Eckhardt *isn't* a liberal. He is actually an almost quaint example of the genuine federalist who flourished in the early days of the Republic but began to become extinct during the stresses of the 1830s. He really believes in the balanced system of state and federal power that Madison & Company put together, but he differs from most Southerners of that apparent persuasion in that he is usually for the underdog rather than the top-dog. In a twelve-year legislative career (which included several terms in the Texas Assembly before his election to Congress) Bob Eckhardt has worked for industrial safety legislation, civil rights, arms control, conservation, consumer protection, and other generally un-Texan causes.

Still, it was quite a while after he took his seat in Congress for metropolitan Harris County (Houston), in a seat he had in fact helped design as a member of the Texas House, before the suspicious Congressional liberals began to notice him. "The hardest group to crack," surprisingly, "was the Democratic Study Group," a loose confederation of House liberals who supply each other with study papers and voting positions in an effort to dent the well-fortified House committee establishment.

Some of this suspicion was allayed, last June, when the U.S. Supreme Court delivered its decision in *Powell v. McCormack*, with Chief Justice Warren delivering the last of his great libertarian opinions and holding that the House had illegally deprived the Harlem Congressman of his seat. In reaching that verdict, the Court quoted at length from an elegant discussion of the parliamentary issue written by Bob Eckhardt in the University of Texas law review. Typically, Eckhardt regards Powell as a rogue but believes that even a rogue has his rights under the Constitution. Powell never bothered to thank Eckhardt for his pains, but that hardly matters to Eckhardt.

His advocacy of Powell's unpopular cause is only one in a series of improbable positions in which Bob Eckhardt has found himself. When the omnibus crime-control bill came to the House floor in the summer of 1968 on a tide of "law-and-order" senti-

115

ment, he joined a small group of liberals in opposing its riot-control section, believing it to be a departure from the Bill of Rights and—as important to a real federalist—an unprecedented and uncalled-for expansion of federal criminal law.

These same considerations, basically, governed a recent decision that put him among the tories. He opposed—persistently—the Constitutional amendment, passed overwhelmingly by the House last September, providing for the direct popular election of Presidents.

"I think you're being country-slicked," he told the New Yorkers, Californians, and other urban Congressmen who voted for the amendment, noting that the five largest states, containing a third of the people, control only six committee chairmanships in Congress—15 percent. Under the electoral college, he argued, the President is a "superlegislator" whose "innovative quality" the country needs. He voted in a minority of seventy.

As his progressive colleagues in the House began to perceive that Eckhardt is a man of rare independence, they began to admit him to those almost conspiratorial little cells of the like-minded that operate beneath the huge, unwieldy surface of the House. Eckhardt is active in several informal bands, in addition to the large and rather inchoate Democratic Study Group, which he mysteriously designates as the "True Believers," the "Hard Core," and another so ultra-confidential that no stranger is admitted—the "Group."

When I visited Eckhardt in Room 1741 of the Longworth Building for a week last September, I found myself barred from any spying on the Group, which was then mapping legislative strategy on defense procurement. (At that time the procurement bill, which had been debated by the Senate for three months, seemed likely to pass the House in a few days, and it did.) I did manage to visit the Hard Core, a somewhat less serious group of House activists who gather weekly over Danish rolls and coffee to intrigue against the inertia of the committee establishment.

On that particular morning, Eckhardt had ridden his bicycle all the way from his house on N Street in Georgetown to Capitol Hill, his route taking him past the little red town house where John Kennedy once lived, by the reflecting pool and the Lincoln Memorial. During those morning bicycle rides, Eckhardt ponders the coming day on the Hill and sometimes writes verses—he is an amateur versifier and cartoonist—about House colleagues. Two years ago, pedaling the same 35-minute route, he got to thinking about Representative H. R. Gross, the Iowa

Republican watchdog whom he admires at a safe ideological distance, and wrote:

> It's good enough for Mr. Bow
> To just preserve the status quo.
> And Dr. Hall will gladly tell 'em
> His status quo is antebellum
> "What bellum, then?" cries Mr. Gross.
> "The Civil War is much too close.
> I'd fain retreat with right good speed
> To England prior to Runnymede."

"Mr. Gross," Eckhardt says, "sees the world as not having changed much from the days when it was ruled by the British Navy. Mr. Gross, you know, is the one who combs the *Congressional Record* to find out how much tax money's being spent for those limousines he sees parked below the Capitol steps."

Mr. Gross, comfortably established by virtue of the seniority system, is the kind of Congressman Eckhardt isn't—and couldn't be—both because of his orthodox power in the House and because of his outlook. But it isn't as if the House were a strange place to Eckhardt, even if its usual entrees to power are shut to him. His maternal uncle, a Republican named Harry Wurzbach, was there under Harding and Coolidge, and as a boy Eckhardt once campaigned with him. "Some fool fired a pistol at him during a speech, and another time they tried to count him out but he demanded a recount and claimed his seat after the House had already convened." Another uncle on his father's side, a Bryan Democrat, sat during the Teddy Roosevelt era. His father's cousin, a "Southern bloc conservative," was in the House in New Deal days. Eckhardt's constituency in northeast Harris County provides a further variation on the family legacy. It is a labor-minority district, which reelected Eckhardt last year with a 70 per cent majority, even though there was considerable Wallace sentiment among the oilworkers and steelworkers. His thumping majority was all the more remarkable in that Bob Eckhardt has never disguised the fact that he isn't a segregationist. (In a Houston television debate thirteen years ago, he dismissed the then-fashionable revival of "interposition" as "digging up John Wilkes Booth and trying to run him for President.")

When Bob Eckhardt pedaled his bike up Constitution Avenue on the September day we were to breakfast with his friends of the Hard Core, a more or less routine week in the House was

117

in prospect—no large dramas or dilemmas but a good window on the House as an institution at this stage in its history. Most of the week's newspaper headlines generated on Capitol Hill would, as usual, dwell on the Senate. Senator Charles Goodell would pass a milestone in his countermarch toward reelection by introducing his resolution to extricate the U.S. from Vietnam. Judge Clement Haynsworth, Jr., President Nixon's nominee for the Fortas seat on the Supreme Court, would explain his stock portfolio to the Senate Judiciary Committee.

On the House side, there would be little business on the floor worth remembering, although Bob Eckhardt would speak briefly for a bill to revive railway passenger service, recalling a trip through the Rockies in a decrepit Pullman car when he and the ancient porter sought to raise the temperature above freezing. (In some ways, the House floor is nearly as removed from a Congressman's hour-by-hour concern as the Senate, which by custom is never called anything but "the other place." Every few hours the bells would ring and the lights flash on the clock above Sam Houston's portrait behind Eckhardt's oval desk, and the Congressman would scurry over for a quorum call or a vote. To a stranger looking down from the well-invigilated galleries—you may not rest your elbows on the railings or take notes—the House chamber, in its dim reds and browns, suggests a railway depot of the last century where some berserk station master is droning about legislation rather than train schedules.)

The Longworth Building, where Eckhardt parks his bike every day for a quick elevator ride to the seventh floor, is one of three House office buildings. Its offices are arranged four-square about a courtyard planted with three forlorn rows of shrubs, and looking down from a fourth-floor window you half expect to see a queue of prisoners taking the air.

On this morning, the Hard Core were meeting in the offices of Representative Dave Obey of Wisconsin, a newcomer whose office walls are decorated with peace emblems and anti-DDT posters, and whose credentials no doubt permitted him quicker entree into the inner cells of House liberalism than Eckhardt's. In fact, Eckhardt is the only Southerner in the Hard Core. Others—Representative Ed Koch of New York, Abner Mikva of Illinois, Patsy Mink of Hawaii, Brock Adams of Washington—have some seniority behind them but not enough to be part of the committee establishment that runs the House. Gathering in Obey's office, the regulars joke about the District of Columbia crime bill, a civil libertarian's delight from the Justice Department. Koch complains that post offices in his district are dumping his news letters and asks what the others do about that problem. Patsy Mink, just back from Hawaii, takes a good bit of ribbing about her new district, now mainly agricultural. "Boy, am I going conservative," she says.

The Hard Core is representative, I gathered as I listened to the discussion, of a certain group of younger, seniority-shy members who hold senior members in some affection but believe that the committee chairmen are too powerful and too independent. This they blame largely on the "leadership," a word spoken in Eckhardt's circles with a certain bemused disdain. Speaker McCormack, the ancient presiding officer of the House who is familiar to Americans as the old gentleman with the gaping mouth who sits behind the President during joint sessions, is agreed to be wrapped up in "the goody game." He is preoccupied, they complain, with housekeeping matters like the controversial extension of the Capitol West Front, improving the food service in the various dining rooms, and placating House employees. (If Mr. McCormack is somewhat remote from the infighting on national issues, he perks up at the slightest sign of disorder or discontent in the household. When one fairly prominent Midwest Democrat joined several others in speaking about the treatment of the dining room employees, he was startled by the Speaker's response. "After the speech, he telephoned to say that he's with us and followed it up with a meeting and other phone calls. You know why? If there were an employees' demonstration, *he's* the one who'd be embarrassed.") Majority Leader Carl Albert, McCormack's deputy, is suspected of secret sympathies. But as the heir-apparent to the speakership he must play conciliator. When Bob Eckhardt took me by Mr. Albert's office, I found the Majority Leader a friendly, diminutive man with twinkling eyes and a soft voice. He bristled only when I mentioned the usual clichés about the House—for instance, that it has become a less responsive chamber than the Senate.

On the Wednesday before I met with the Hard Core in Obey's office, the insurgents had won a small victory in the caucus—a resolution "adopting" the 1968 Democratic platform as the basis for legislative initiative in the 91st Congress. "You can't understand the caucus problem," Eckhardt explained, "unless you understand that it's the only House forum where people who think as I do—the activists, the impatient younger members— have a potential majority." The powerful committee chairmen despise the caucus. "Do you know the difference between a caucus and a cactus?" one asked. "In a cactus, the pricks are all on the outside." Knowing as they do that the insurgents want to

119

use the caucus to bring pressure on them, the committee chairmen yearn for the old days when Speaker Sam Rayburn controlled it, fearing that it would develop into a scene of family quarrels among Democrats, especially over civil rights.

I learned still more about the recent history of the caucus, a few days later, when Eckhardt sent me to track down Representative Morris Udall of Arizona. To talk with Udall, who used to be a star athlete, you have to stay in motion. First he would lean against the marble pillars in the hallway outside the members' entrance to the House chamber (suggestive, in its tawdry ornateness, of a Byzantine seraglio). Then something would happen, Udall would dart into the chamber, where a debate was in progress over an amendment to the Wilderness Act, and after a bit he would return and we would move out on the porch overlooking the West Front. On the run, I discovered why Udall stood as a test candidate for the speakership in January 1969 against Speaker McCormack, a somewhat quixotic enterprise in which he had Eckhardt's support. Udall would say nothing to disparage the leadership, but he pointed out that his "Dear Democratic Colleague" letter of December 26, 1968, was a matter of record, having appeared in the *New York Times*. It was, in effect, Udall's platform, and it spoke for Eckhardt and others in declaring that the House "can and should be a source of innovative programs" and that "too often House Democrats have failed to extend to our newer and more marginal members the kinds of recognition...that would give them deserved strength in their constituencies."

Udall cupped his hands, forming a sort of canyon. "In theory," he said, "when the elections come, the House is supposed to have a heavy turnover"—he swept one hand over the other, indicating a major washout—"but it takes a real flood—a 1964—to do that, and in most years only the marginal few at the bottom of the gully, eighty or so, are exposed and washed away." It still rankles with House activists that the leadership did so little to protect the so-called "Goldwater liberals" elected in the 1964 landslide from the inevitable washing away in 1966.

In the speakership race, Udall pleaded for "constructive, rational, and responsible airing of differences in caucuses." He got a meager fifty-eight votes on the secret ballot, indicating to at least one of his staff members that "there are either a lot of secret sympathizers with the seniority system or a lot of liars." But combined with other pressures, the Udall challenge brought more alterations, one of them an upgrading of the caucus. It now meets monthly, not sporadically as under Rayburn, and it debates issues rather than merely ratifying the decrees of the elders.

The change is important to Eckhardt, for with most of the Hard Core types he believes that the Democrats' loss of the White House last year drastically changed their role. "Under Kennedy and Johnson," Eckhardt says, "the leadership was a conduit of Presidential leadership and we had a sense of motion. Nixon exerts little or no pressure, and with White House pressure off, the committee chairmen are more lackadaisical and independent."

Eckhardt was excited by what happened in the mid-September caucus, the week before I visited his office. Representative Jonathan Bingham and others, with Eckhardt playing a last-minute parliamentary role, managed to pass a resolution directing the committees to seek legislative goals in the 1968 platform. The coup displeased the elders, some of whom tried to divert the attack from the Democratic committee moguls to the White House. ("You can hear the old bulls roaring when one of us gets up in the caucus," said one of the Hard Core.)

It was the visit of Mr. Ezra Schacht of Houston one morning that introduced me to the full range of a Congressman's labors in ombudsmanship, labors Eckhardt takes very seriously. Mr. Schacht, dressed in a natty brown suit with blue pinstripes and a matching striped tie, had just delivered certain legal papers to the Supreme Court in behalf of his son, who is trying to appeal a prison sentence for antiwar activity. Danny Schacht, a young electrical engineer working at his father's plant, had acted in an antidraft skit outside the Houston draft induction center two years before. Several nights later, as Eckhardt summarized the story, FBI agents arrested Danny Schacht and charged him with violating a law prohibiting the unauthorized wearing of a military uniform. In May 1969, the sentence was upheld, even though young Schacht's lawyers argued that the antidraft theatrics were protected by the First Amendment, as well as by a law permitting an actor to portray a soldier "if the portrayal does not tend to discredit the armed forces."

This "exception to an exception," as he calls it, intrigues Eckhardt. With his aides Julius Glickman and Chris Little, both lawyers, he discusses the constitutional issue. If the Supreme Court accepts Schacht's appeal, he decides, he may submit an *amicus curiae* brief arguing that the whole proceeding was unconstitutional if the theatrical use of an Army uniform must be confined to skits reflecting credit on the armed forces.

The Schacht case is one of hundreds that come to a Congressman's attention every year, making his office a sort of ganglion where the nerve fibers of governmental relations meet. The mails every day are heavy, and have been for three years, with military problems—mainly over the draft.

I asked Eckhardt for other examples of the ombudsman's role. From the files he brought out several worn manila folders concerning George Vincin, a Houston odd-jobs man who joined the Army in 1935—thirty-five years ago—and still seeks back pay for false imprisonment. Recently, Eckhardt wrote to the Secretary of the Army what is perhaps the hundredth letter in the case, calling Vincin's "the most shocking bureaucratic abuse that has ever come to my attention." Falsely accused of sodomy while in the guardhouse at Fort Brown, Texas, in 1938, Vincin served five years at Leavenworth, even though his key accusers admitted lying. His thirty-year effort to clear his name and collect back pay is incomplete: he has a pardon signed by President Johnson who took a personal interest in the case but still lacks the back pay; and unless the Army supports private legislation Eckhardt has introduced to grant Vincin his back pay, it will probably fail. Vincin, Administrative Assistant Chris Little told me, once flew from Houston to Washington to check on his case. "When I sent him down to the Army liaison office he took one look at the uniforms and fled on the next plane."

Kristina Truitt, Eckhardt's tall caseworker, handles the ombudsmanship operation, which ranges from cases as grim as Vincin's to those as comic, and as far beyond Eckhardt's miracle-working power, as that of the mother who recently wrote to complain that the Air Force band would not accept her son as a French horn player. "I can certainly understand your keen disappointment that your son was not accepted," Eckhardt wrote in a letter of skillful Haim Ginott-like consolation. "After doing his very best to perfect his skill in the French horn, he must have been crestfallen that he was not chosen."

Some pleas for help run to the bizarre. An Army enlisted man who has been in and out of military dispensaries in the Far East wrote to ask Eckhardt's advice on a drug to restore his sexual powers to normal. As we talked about bureaucratic mix-ups one morning, a Houston lawyer telephoned to ask the Congressman's help in speeding home the body of an oil-rig operator who'd died of a heart seizure in Libya.

"His wife," Kristina Truitt explained, "asked for an autopsy, which seems to have thrown the Libyan government into an uproar. She's waived the request, but they don't embalm the dead in Libya." At the State Department, Kristina found an office wholly concerned with American deaths abroad, which for a $10 cable fee will make inquiries. (Somewhere in the labyrinths of the diplomatic establishment, we speculated, there must be a deputy assistant secretary of state for death.)

Every Congressman is to one degree or another a guardian of the Danny Schachts and the Vincins and others who run afoul of the law or bureaucracies, but I had the feeling that Eckhardt's office takes its ombudsmanship almost as seriously as the legislative process itself. From the wall near Eckhardt's desk stares down Eckhardt's formidably bearded great-great-grandfather, Robert Kleberg, who came to Texas from Germany in the 1830s, seeking he said "unbounded personal, religious, and political liberty" and expecting to find "in Texas, above all countries, the blessed land of my most fervent hopes."

After lunch that day came the lobbyists, two gentlemen who wanted to discuss Representative John Dingell's bill pending before the Interstate and Foreign Commerce Committee, of which Eckhardt is a member, to curtail FCC licensing of pay television.

As the staff removes the dishes and glasses, Eckhardt explains that on an average week like this one he may see perhaps a dozen lobbyists of some kind: representatives of railway unions who are quarreling among themselves over a bill to adjust the retirement fund; the pay-television people; the Quakers, who want to enlist Congressional help for the October 15 Anti-war Moratorium.

"When I came to Congress," he recalls, as we wait for the pay-TV people, "my first reaction was, 'There's far less lobbying here than in the Texas legislature.' But it's only subtler—less obtrusive, more professional. You have to make yourself available for it. But it wasn't that way in Austin. When the Texas House would adjourn for lunch and the big doors would swing open, dozens of lobbyists would swarm outside, waiting to snare you for lunch if you'd go. I believe a man could go to Austin and live off the land for the whole session. You had to hide from them. I remember I was eating one night with my family at a place in Austin. I asked for the check and found it'd been paid. I looked across the room and there was a prominent lobbyist, just smiling and nodding. He didn't even come to the table, 'Is he a friend of yours, Daddy?' one of my little girls asked.

"The first time I ran for the Texas legislature—it was 1940, I was just out of law school and I got what I call my mandate from the people to practice law privately—old man Edmonds Travis, a lobbyist for several Standard Oil subsidiaries, told me, 'Bob, what you do is you attack all the venal interests except

123

one, and that's where you git your money. You attacked them all.' As a rule, Capitol Hill lobbyists make themselves scarce, usually hole up at the Hotel Congressional. The key point of contact is usually between a highly specialized lobbyist and the specialized staff people of a standing committee. Intimate friendships spring up there—it's the rivet point. Friendships that outlast terms. They probably have a greater influence on legislation, especially if it's technical."

Mr. Pieter van Beek, who has come to talk with Eckhardt about pay-television, turns out to be a vice president of Zenith Radio Corporation, which makes the signal-scramblers for pay-TV. An erect, Chicago Dutchman with darting eyes, a clipped moustache, and a manner of precise speaking to go with it, he looks as if, transposed to the days of the Battle of Britain, he had just stepped from the cockpit of a Spitfire. In fact, Mr. van Beek is a bit battle-shocked from the pay-television wars, and he launches into a resigned and rather doleful history of the effort of pay-TV to gain licensing by the FCC. Anticipating the point, Eckhardt breaks in: "You really want me to do nothing—right?" Nothing, that is, about the Dingell bill. As a member of the Commerce Committee, Eckhardt knows the legislation, which the local broadcasters are pushing to forestall a potential competitor. Dingell himself, as Eckhardt explained later, wants to reserve a number of the dwindling VHF frequencies for non-commercial uses, but his aims and those of the commercial broadcasters mesh. A glance at Eckhardt's mail on the subject, which was plentiful, indicated that the broadcasters are waging a fairly strenuous campaign for the Dingell bill. "We want to put you across to your constituents," the letters say, in effect, "and please drop in for a live interview next time you are in our area, but be sure you vote right on the Dingell bill." Eckhardt concludes the interview with Mr. van Beek by saying that he is "disposed" to vote against the bill, a way Congressmen have of signifying hope without airtight commitment.

Eckhardt is a do-it-yourself man when it comes to bill drafting, which is unusual in a chamber where it is admitted that too much legislation is either written or rewritten under the influence of specialized lobbies. In recent months, the House of Representatives has suddenly developed for the first time the practice of cosponsoring legislation, too, which means that there is a constant flood of bills begging for every Congressman's signature, whether he knows what's in the bill or not.

Eckhardt has a philosophy about writing legislation. "For instance," he said, "Lyndon Johnson's Great Society legislation

124

suffered in some cases from the fact that he is what I call a legislative entrepreneur—result-oriented—not a craftsman. Too little of that legislation was governed by a firm view of what a bill is supposed to accomplish and how.

"Look, for example, at the contrast between the Economic Opportunity Act and, say, the Wagner Act, which was modeled on a functioning New York law. Congressional acts, like the common law, ought to move carefully from precedent to precedent.

"But I'm the first to admit that it isn't easy to be a good legislative craftsman—not with twenty thousand or so bills coming into the House every year. That's why the committees up here are so important. To survive them, a bill must gain the attention of a committee and surviving a committee means passing muster with men who've spent a lot of time mastering the details of taxation, say, or trade regulation, or judicial procedure."

("One thing you ought to say about the House," I was told by one of Eckhardt's colleagues as we marched through the cavernous corridor that joins the office buildings to the House chamber, "is that a man's committee work is his life here, if he's serious. The real legislative craftsmen are in this house. Time is so short that when someone is allowed to speak he usually has something to say—not like the Senate, where you might hear almost any Senator talking in a half-assed way about almost any subject. You won't often hear it over here. Too little time.")

Too little time; too many members. During a week of prowling through the U.S. House of Representatives and talking with Bob Eckhardt about his job, these are the constant refrains. Because of them, the House is a pyramid resting on its apex, where legislation is usually marked pass or fail at a narrow, closely confined level. During the week I visited in Room 1741, the Commerce Committee was meeting almost every morning to complete the drafting of a complicated piece of airport legislation, and although the sessions were closed, its final action and vote would almost certainly determine the bill's fate on the House floor. "Back in Texas," Eckhardt told me, "a committee report might be overthrown or not—nobody thought very much about it. Here, almost never." In the House conveyor belt for legislation, subcommittee chairmen defer to each other, committees to subcommittees, chairmen to subcommittee chairmen, and the House as a whole with very few exceptions to its committees. Often bills come to the floor under so-called "closed rules," with

125

amendments barred. Democratic in theory, the legislative process is elitist in practice.

Bob Eckhardt, who brought an expert knowledge of federal labor law to the House, concentrates in the field but doesn't confine himself to it. I sat in late one afternoon as he and his aides, Glickman and Little, chewed over Eckhardt's "consumer-class-action" bill, a piece of legislation reflecting his passion for the fine points of federalism, combined with his interest in consumer protection.

"Today," he told me, "it costs the average consumer of, say, a defective box of breakfast cereal so much in legal fees that it would be silly to sue the company that made it. But if a number of similarly defrauded customers could pool their resources and bring a suit under the more liberal federal class-action rules, maybe some redress would be forthcoming.

"The victimized consumer ought to be able to get to court and collect when he's victimized by fraud, but a good piece of legislation will enable him to do so as elegantly as possible—without cluttering the law. You ought to be able to do it without writing a whole new federal law of deceit." (Eckhardt's federalist fastidiousness drips from every word.)

"But isn't the problem really that the courts would construe the law too narrowly, rather than too broadly?" asks Chris Little.

"Maybe," Eckhardt concedes, "but if we define deceit too broadly the bill wouldn't pass anyway. It'd be like a Nixon program—all good intention and no action."

By 6:30 p.m. the House has usually adjourned and most of the staff have left. Eckhardt, Little, and Glickman end the day by deciding that Glickman will continue to consult with Senator Tydings' office, which is also interested in the class-action legislation for consumers, seeking to pool their efforts in a definition of fraud large enough to incorporate state laws but narrow enough to oblige Eckhardt's federalist qualms. A version of the bill was introduced in May 1969, and if Eckhardt and his cosponsors are lucky either the Commerce or the Judiciary Committee or both will arrange hearings for the bill. Only then, months after the first discussions and possibly jostled by several competing bills, would it reach the full light of legislative conflict as most Americans see it and understand it. But in the House, that would be the end, not the beginning.

—*June, 1970*

126

Allard K. Lowenstein:
A Reminiscence

Readers of this page, whether or not they knew Allard K. Lowenstein, may recall at least one unusual thing about him. He was probably the only liberal activist ever endorsed for Congress by William F. Buckley, Jr. That was two years ago, before he fell victim last week to an unhinged gunman.

The Buckley endorsement was one measure of the catholicity of Al Lowenstein's charm. It also reflected the recognition, common to all his admirers and friends, that this unembittered exponent of the politics of dissatisfaction was a wholesome force in a cynical age. And force he surely was.

I cannot claim to have known him really well, despite our common connections—few did, I suspect. He was always on the wing. To see him, you had to wait patiently, as for Godot.

Once, about 10 years ago, I tried several times to interview him for a magazine piece on the House of Representatives, where he was serving his first and only term. His office resembled a railway station in hurricane weather. Eager young retainers darted or lounged about. Al Lowenstein lay sprawled, cradling a telephone, on the leather couch where he slept, *if* he slept— organizing Biafran relief. The interview consisted of greetings and hand signals meaning wait. I couldn't. But one morning in the misty regions between midnight and dawn my phone rang. Congressman Lowenstein, the voice said, as blandly as if it were high noon, could see me now! I went back to sleep. I wish I hadn't.

I also recall an evening, about the same time, when a group of old Chapel Hill friends gathered for a visit scheduled for 8 p.m. Al came about 1 a.m., all pumped up. He had just been at Cornell, denouncing president, faculty and students for giving in to the intimidation (and bongo drums, bought with university funds) of the Black Student Movement.

For some of his older friends one story seemed to tell it all. An old friend—I think it was Eli Evans—telephoned the family restaurant in search of Al. "Oh," his mother answered, "Al's not here. He's in Spain." After a thoughtful pause she added, "You know, Al never did like Mr. Franco."

Perhaps there was a Lowenstein-led dump-Franco move-

127

ment. If so, it was probably effective in its way. His tenacity was awesome. The coiled, athletic energy, fueled on a breakfast of corn flakes and chocolate milk, never deserted him.

I was of the wrong generation to qualify as a Lowenstein disciple, and too stodgy to want to be one. But like many others, I often wondered what preserved the whirling-dervish energies from cynicism. Surely not results, which were often unsatisfying. I first met him in 1952, when he was running the national student movement for Adlai Stevenson, an effort that did not stop the Eisenhower landslide. Likewise, the crusade he organized to oust Lyndon Johnson 16 years later ran on high, uncalculating emotions and led to a most unwelcome result—the disruption of the Democratic Party and the election of Richard M. Nixon.

As an instructor at N.C. State, in 1963, Al Lowenstein organized civil rights demonstrations to beard the North Carolina legislature in its den at the Sir Walter Raleigh Hotel. The tippling legislators glared and seethed as Al Lowenstein's young hosts chanted and marched before their doorstep in the warm spring evenings. The good result was that some—a few—accommodations opened their services to blacks; the bad result was that the legislature passed a mischievous law banning "known communist" speakers (of which there were, of course, very few) from state college campuses.

The removal of this obnoxious legacy consumed the better energies of a decade. (Incidentally, the last-ditch support of this stupid act of unconstitutionality by both present U.S. senators from North Carolina didn't help). By then, when the lingering bills of activism fell due, Al had moved on to other places and causes.

A career of perpetual dissatisfaction like Al's rested, I suppose, on the honorable belief that the perceived evils of the moment aren't to be temporized with, consequences be damned. The seeds of a new and better order must be planted while the bright sun of idealism and indignation shines. The glacial pace of reform is a risky bet in a short life. So, I suppose, Al Lowenstein would have argued.

His faith in insurgent causes—always to be pursued within the rules—could be traced, I think, to the influence of an even more charismatic figure too little known outside North Carolina—Frank Porter Graham, once president of the University of North Carolina, and later a U.S. senator and a U.N. mediator.

From one perspective, Dr. Graham's life was one of unavailing struggle—as a racial liberal before his time, as a gentle man unseated from the Senate by a campaign of vile personal abuse, as a man who even tried in vain to talk the Indians and Pakistanis into agreement over Kashmir.

These disappointments left Frank Graham unembittered, hopeful, patient, stubbornly inclined to see redeeming traits of character even in his enemies when others could not. The legacy of this gentle and diminutive Carolina calvinist, a stubborn fighter for longshot causes, left its mark on Al Lowenstein. His son, named for Dr. Graham, is the living symbol of that.

The struggle for a *possible* world, however stubbornly resisted by the real one, was Al's steady business, and his dedication to it galvanized hundreds of others. No wonder, perhaps, that for so many he became a figure of political legend.

—March 18, 1980

The Importance Of
Being Earnest

As he worked on his forthcoming inaugural address in late 1976, Jimmy Carter examined all the earlier ones and fastened, typically, on Woodrow Wilson's. Perhaps, though he doesn't say so, it was significant that Wilson had also been Southern-born and a man of religious faith.*

"Like him," Carter writes, "I felt that I was taking office at a time when Americans desired a return to first principles...His call for national repentance also seemed appropriate, although I feared that a modern audience might not understand a similar call from me."

The passage is revealing. Carter sounded no call for national repentance as such on January 20, 1977. But then and thereafter, through his four years in the White House, Americans never quite escaped the suspicion that he was preaching at them—though usually, to be sure, from behind a protective

---

KEEPING FAITH: Memoirs of a President, By Jimmy Carter (Bantam, 1982).

grin. The need for sackcloth and ashes was always somewhere in the picture.

Readers of *Keeping Faith* are apt to experience the feeling again. Not that it is an obnoxiously pious or self-righteous book. But there is in it the same familiar tone of painful earnestness and moral assurance, bordering at times on the homiletic. Moreover, the austerity of Carter's precise prose leaves few channels for the richer juices of life to run. Of one thing, however, and that not insignificant in our time, we may be sure. This is Jimmy Carter's authentic voice. No ghostwriter has haunted this house.

The publication of a presidential memoir, so soon after the author's exit, is of course an American political Event, automatically. Carter's memoirs will be scrutinized more eagerly than most for clues to the lingering puzzles about him, and about his hurried appearance on the Washington stage.

He was certainly different, a card-carrying Christian and a Deep Southerner, from a family of eccentrics. But what was he like? What were his purposes? What kinds of success did he enjoy, or failures suffer, in his own eyes?

Unfortunately, the personality reflected in these pages is a bit blurred. It will disappoint those who assume that every public man floats, like an iceberg, on a hidden substructure of self-contradiction. The Jimmy Carter appearing here is the same sober, energetic, earnest Carter who stood before us for four years—friendly to a point, but with the icy eyes and the grin not quite congruent; not exactly humorless but not witty either; unschooled in and to some extent skeptical of Washington's accustomed rituals; a president who assumes, sometimes wrongly, that others take public duties as seriously as he does, and therefore act from the same disinterested and rational motives.

Sobriety and public-spiritedness are the keynotes—hard work, studious attention to detail, for instance. (Carter tells us that along with his maps and briefing books, he carried with him to Camp David for the famous meetings with Begin and Sadat "my annotated Bible which...would be needed in my discussions with Prime Minister Begin." Later, he tells us that when the cascade of White House paperwork threatened to overwhelm him he arranged to take a speed-reading course, and quadrupled his speed. No mini-memos for him!)

Carter also appears as a man to whom the revealed truths of evangelical religion are of hourly importance. He "prayed a lot"; he urged Premier Deng Xiaoping to allow freedom of worship and the distribution of Bibles in China. Learning of his wife's despondency at a hard moment in 1980 he reminded her of the New Testament verses they had read (in Spanish) the evening before: "Let not your heart be troubled..."

But in many ways, the most personally revealing aspect of *Keeping Faith* is the conventionality of its thumbnail portraits. There are neither saints nor rogues in Carter's gallery, and lots of studies in shades of gray. If he likes gossip you'd never suspect it. Even the rascals of the family, Miss Lillian and Brother Billy, seem a bit bland, although he reveals that Miss Lillian once jocularly addressed the King of Morocco, as a "damn foreigner." Billy, for his part, "exercised bad judgment" and had a "drinking problem" which he faced "courageously."

There is nothing personal here about Hamilton Jordan and Jody Powell. Zbigniew Brzezinski is, next to his family, "my preferred seatmate on a long trip...we might argue (about what, Carter doesn't say), but I would never be bored." Warren Christopher is "the best public servant I ever knew"; Helmut Schmidt is excitable, Deng "tough," Sadat and Ohira of Japan "special friends" among foreign statesmen.

What one misses, except in the case of John Anderson, the spoiler, and William Sullivan, the insubordinate ambassador in Iran, both of whom get trips to the woodshed, is an occasional splash of vinegar. Not even Ted Kennedy is roughly handled. Generally, Carter seems to view others, however vexing they may be, as mirrors of his own guileless character, errant sometimes but not malicious. If there is what Jungians would call a shadow side of Carter, it is well suppressed.

Carter's presidential purposes, measured by the space he gives them, are equally unsurprising. Often for reasons not of his choosing, Carter became overwhelmingly a foreign policy president. The pages assigned to distant imbroglios—Mideastern negotiations through Camp David (substantially more than a fourth of the book), the negotiation of SALT II and the ratification of the Panama Canal treaty, the Iranian revolution and the hostage crisis—all but overwhelm the agenda.

Accordingly, the domestic scene is scanted. There is a short chapter on the Bert Lance affair, interpreted as a press escapade, in which Carter skirts the issues that absorbed the U.S. comptroller general in two large volumes and the Senate Government Operations Committee for weeks. There are sporadic, often cursory, discussions of energy, budget policy, health planning, the Kennedy political challenge. There is a running motif of sidelong and baleful comment on the (usually unsatisfactory) performance of the press.

The latter, incidentally, will be of interest in media-haunted

Washington. *Keeping Faith* suggests that Carter, maybe wisely, paid as little attention to press notices as any president ever has—his must be the first presidential book in decades that omits even Scotty Reston and Walter Cronkite from the index. But some of Carter's suppositions—e.g., that former senator Frank Church, source of an untimely leak about the Soviet brigade in Cuba, was "a favorite of the Washington press"—are ludicrous. Others—e.g., that the Kennedy forces' transparently phony plan for an "open" convention in 1980 was generally approved by the press—are simply misinformed.

The thin coverage of domestic matters means that such highly advertised Carter causes as deregulation, price stability and the long-forgotten "zero-based budgeting" are all but ignored, perhaps for the natural reason that many such hopes were disappointed. Still, a president's frustrations can be instructive, and Carter's, at least in home politics, are muted. For example, he makes his relationship with the congressional leadership sound considerably more cordial than it was reputed to be.

For a variety of reasons, the account of what Carter clearly sees as the signal success of his presidency—the Camp David accords—is the liveliest, as it is the longest, of the book. Camp David showed Carter at the top of his form: patient, well-briefed, resourceful, meticulous, willing to wager presidential prestige on thin hopes and prevail, and compassionately attentive to the foibles and sticking points of his prickly negotiating partners, Begin and Sadat.

From extensive personal notes, Carter reconstructs an absorbing account of the rollercoaster search for agreement in the Maryland hills. He recounts how he refereed, in a small study at Laurel Lodge, two lengthy and acrimonious arguments between Sadat and Begin; how their passionate altercation was oddly punctuated by occasional bursts of laughter, as when "during an argument about which one of them was responsible for the hashish trade through the Sinai." Carter himself drafted or vetted every line of the final texts of the Camp David accords.

Winston Churchill once called Neville Chamberlain "a good lord mayor of Birmingham in a lean year." On the strength of the Camp David narrative alone, Carter must be pronounced at least a superb secretary of state in a good year.

Was he more? Or perhaps less? That was the question that lingered when Jimmy Carter left Washington, shadowed by a stinging repudiation at the polls. The repudiation shocked him. Carter characteristically believed that when American voters compared his careful, rational and moderate positions with what he viewed as Ronald Reagan's rash hip-shooting, their verdict would be foreordained. But *Crisis*, the recent (and more vivid) memoir of Hamilton Jordan, is far more revealing about the political adversities of 1980. Jordan, among other things, grasps perversity and paradox more readily than his chief.

In Washington, through which Carter passed almost as a stranger, a feeling persists that some critical "presidential" trait was lacking in the unusual Georgian from Plains. Part of this is undoubtedly Washington vanity, sharpened in Carter's case by his having snatched the presidency from under the noses of its gatekeepers.

Neither the question of Carter's capacity, nor the ultimate significance of his presidency, can be settled now. American presidencies do not lend themselves to shortrange assessment. The final verdict depends on time and events still to come, including the performance of successors and the durability of the issues he thought important. Certainly Carter's presidency cannot be measured, though it will not be diminished, by this rather curious book.

With the exceptions of the Camp David account, and a few unintended glimpses of self-disclosure, *Keeping Faith* is the work of a worthy. It reads at times like a prospectus for a presidency, not a retrospective upon one.

But while it is neither intimate or consistently revealing, Carter's memoir does correct some misconceptions. Carter is convincingly shown to have suffered, within his divided party, for recognizing candidly that "sense of limits" of which he spoke on inaguration day: limits on American power abroad, limits on our ability to sustain a cornucopia of entitlements without bankruptcy. Already, Carter's presidency seems an interval, a pause, between the disintegrating hopes of the 1950s and 1960s and the stark reaction that came with Reagan.

As president, Carter suffered from an inability to dramatize and project himself or his goals. He was as short of theatrical talents as his successor is long on them. These memoirs suffer from the same defect. He was an intelligent, morally serious man of high purposes, almost, as said, a Victorian worthy. But he lacked the epic sense and the streak of naughtiness that may be essential to great public men. *Keeping Faith* is as wholesome as milk, unlaced by the acids that amuse or startle. Sober, responsible, truthful, intelligent, earnest, rational, purposeful. Thus the man: thus the book.

—October 31, 1982

Dr. Kissinger's Legacy

Dr. Henry Kissinger has been secretary of state in fact or name or both for eight years and suffers from the usual rule: Unless they are nonentities, secretaries of state last longer than most federal officials and, as the price of durability, collect more critics.

In Dr. Kissinger's case, a curious misimpression prevails. One Washington television critic touted a documentary about him the other day as an exception to the generally "adulatory" press he enjoys. *Adulatory*? It is not quite the word—not on those days when Anthony Lewis or William Safire, or even the sage George Will, flays him before our eyes as "the P.T. Barnum of diplomacy," the double-crosser of the unfortunate Kurds, or a dilettante in matters of national security.

I confess that while I have had occasional reservations, I am not relieved at his departure. I think of the famous cartoon, "Dropping the Pilot," that greeted Kaiser Wilhelm's abupt ouster of Otto von Bismarck in 1890, following which Bismarck's intricate structure of peace began to fall apart.

The European parallel is more than literary. Three things have distinguished Dr. Kissinger's stewardship of American foreign policy—that he is indelibly European; that he came to this country a refugee from a civilized nation plunged suddenly into barbarism; that he is a historian by both temperament and training.

The Europeanness has to do with a form of experience that most Americans are spared—or denied, if you consider it a defect. "Europeans," Dr. Kissinger has written, "live on a continent covered with ruins testifying to the fallibility of human foresight."

No 20th Century European has escaped those ruins, reminders of the contingency and cussedness of life, the *lacrimae rerum* of Virgil. The American, typically, believes that things can be fixed up and, if fixed up, will stay that way; especially, one might say, if he is a lawyer conducting diplomacy. The European watches the joints and seams in sober expectation that they may crack or unravel, especially if they are the joints and seams of treaties.

That Dr. Kissinger became a refugee at 15 must also have left its mark—not, as his psychobiographer Bruce Mazlish would have it, the mark of trauma, necessarily, but the mark of re-

134

flection. That the land of Bach and Goethe could have become the land of Hitler; that the idealism of the Weimar republic could slide into the brutality of the Third Reich; that democratic political institutions could become the seedbed of tyranny; that there could be a dark side of "national character": All are lessons Dr. Kissinger's early experience, and his reflections on it, must have taught him to bear in mind.

It is remarkable that this early conditioning did not promptly bend Dr. Kissinger to the profession of history. He planned, it seems, to be an accountant! Accidents of war and personal association intervened. They sent him belatedly to the history books, where in turn the great conceptualizers of history (e.g., Spengler) taught him to see the past as a process. History was not, as Americans often suppose, fixed and static but a changing fabric woven of many strands. National destinies could not be isolated from one another.

If one were searching our own political tradition for a foil to Kissinger he would have to be Woodrow Wilson, moralist and peacemaker. Wilson, we can only suppose, was more complex than "Wilsonism," the outlook that carries his name. But Wilsonism by any definition is the antithesis of Kissingerism.

Consider Wilson's curious but representative remark, in the winter of 1917, about the origins of World War I. "The obscure fountains from which its stupendous flood burst forth," said he, "we are not interested to search for or explore."

It was a remarkable and revealing confession. To describe the complicated but scarcely unintelligible causes of this cataclysmic event as "obscure fountains," to renounce careful historical inquiry as if the renunciation were virtuous: this was very Wilsonian and, in some ways, very American as well.

If Henry Kissinger had done little else during his years as the premier figure in American foreign policy—if there had been no opening to China, no Vietnam negotiations, no shuttle diplomacy in the Middle East or Africa, no detente, no SALT agreements—it would be of lasting significance that he had brought historical realism to U.S. foreign policy. He has introduced an un-Wilsonian complexity into our consideration of the world and our place in it. But in the process the manifestation of these three traits—Europeanism, the refugee's uncertainties, the historian's view of events—has not endeared him to those who cling to myths of American innocence and American exemption from the toils of history. In their hands, his press notices have been anything but "adulatory."

—January 20, 1977

135

III. Myth and Perspective

The Dixiefication of Dixie

...mute speculation, the patient curse
That stones the eyes, or like the jaguar leaps
For his own image in a jungle pool,
his victim.
—Allen Tate, "Ode to the Confederate Dead"

I SOMETIMES THINK with amazement how little my own children, who are of the modern suburban South, know of the region that existed only a few decades ago. If I told them about it—and if they listened, as I once listened to the family storytellers—they would surely think my South as strange and exotic as Xanadu. No sacred rivers ran through it (unless the Suwannee), and there were no measureless caverns. What was exotic about it was a texture of human experience now vanished.

It was, for those of us who were fortunate, a cozy and settled place of black servitude (to call it by its right name) and white paternalism, often generous and gentle but insensitive. That South, once so familiar to some of us over the age of forty, was probably closer in feature and spirit to the South of a century earlier than it would be to the present South. With the barest jog of memory, one can recall the rattle of mule-drawn wagons in which people came to plow the garden, unhitching the animal for the job, or returned the gleaming wicker basket of linens sent out the week before to be stewed, no doubt, in a distant iron pot in the country. One recalls the cry of street vendors in an old town on the Savannah River, melodically touting black-berries and garden vegetables still wet with dew; the early-morning whistle of the men who mowed and raked the yard; the nextdoor maid with the voice of operatic volume making the summer air ring with spirituals; the Georgia cousins mis-chievously teasing cooks in the kitchen about the razor blades that they allegedly hid in the folds of their stockings; the fetishes about doors and drinking glasses. It almost seems a caricature now.

This was, of course, a physical South—a South of props and roles dutifully played even by those who must have sensed in them the fragility of the theatrical. Anyway, the sets are long since stored and the script much revised. So the South that journalists, professors, and critics now tend to discuss at symposia—speaking, usually, as keepers of the flame—is not the experienced South but the South of memory and imagination, sometimes not less real. It is the South made present to us by Flannery O'Connor, Erskine Caldwell, Eudora Welty, and William Faulkner: a region of Tobacco Road and Yoknapatawpha. It is also the historical South of C. Vann Woodward and David Potter, the South portrayed or deduced from its past. All these Souths exist by a determined act of will, evocation, and self-consciousness. It is the South conceptualized, the flesh made word, the South that replenishes itself as, one by one, the solid stage props wear out.

It would be a daring student of that South who would say that it is finished. Yet few would, I think, deny that there is a certain burden and exertion in keeping it alive. I confess, in my own case, to a certain fatigue with this South of the imagination, in its more ghostly and disembodied forms. After seven years of absence from the region I find that my perspective has shifted in subtle ways. I still believe in *southerners*, for whose existence the evidence continues to be very real. But to believe in the larger abstraction called "the South" requires an increasing ingenuity and energy. The symposia continue. But how long has it been since we heard something genuinely novel said about the South or the southern experience?

As I review the influences that shaped my own regional consciousness—and of course all of us were southerners a long time before we began to think about it, as M. Jourdain had spoken prose a long time before he was told what it was—certain formative events stand out, events for which I find no recent parallels. The first, for me, after discovering W. J. Cash's *The Mind of the South* as a college sophomore (a fateful age to do so), was foreign travel, distancing the experience of growing up southern and suggesting that the assimilationist pressures of "Americanism" then (the early and mid-1950s) so much in the air might be eccentric to the larger world's experience: a point soon to be memorably made by C. Vann Woodward. In fact, the publication in 1959 of *The Burden of Southern History*, with its central essay "The Search for Southern Identity," was far the most important event for me after the Cash revival. Woodward's essays quickly became and remained a touchstone for defining (or refining) one's

139

regional imagination. Like a mineral trace they run in our blood and marrow now, carrying the notion that the southern experience of history had been touched with distinctiveness and was rather *un*American when it came to the point: that it involved guilt, not innocence; pessimism, not optimism; the experience of social tragedy and intractability, not easy progress; defeat, not victory; poverty, not riches. All of this made impressive sense to me at the time. The marks of it remain as indelible as the marks of Faulkner's great novels. The time and setting, moreover, were just right. The late 1950s and early 1960s—when so much of national importance was happening in and to the South —assured a cresting of interest in what it was like to be southern. We southerners were studied hard, everywhere, like savages brought in from a newly discovered continent in the Elizabethan Age.

Now, twenty years later, I sense that all this has changed. Where before there was a feeling that the South, guided through travail by its tragic bards to some deeper sense of guilt and gallantry, might become a fascinating showpiece of national destiny, there is now, I sense, a mood of boredom and impatience. As a theme for defining the national experience, regionalism has yielded to ethnicity. But despite some ingenious writing on the southerner-as-ethnic, it is not obvious what it adds to one's self-identification to imagine oneself a Pole or an Irishman with a difference.

Symptomatic, I believe, of this impatience was an amusing magazine article published four years ago by Norman Podhoretz, editor of *Commentary*: "How the North Was Won." Once a patron and publisher of literary southerners, Mr. Podhoretz is now weary of a style that he views in retrospect as deplorably subversive of Yankee character. He pictures for us an invasion of New York by cadres of southern literati: a small company of white southerners who intrigued their way into the editorial chairs of influential national magazines of the sixties, soon plunging the poor North into frenzies of racial guilt before it quite knew what was going on. The secret weapon of these neo-Confederate agents was the charm of their pens. They were, Mr. Podhoretz suggests, children of guilt atoned, compensating at the typewriter for the down-home bigotries that they grew up with. Worst of all, they identified the traditional ethnic enclaves of New York City (and other places) as ghettos, portraying an expression of affinity as an expression of racism. "The North," writes Mr. Podhoretz, "had no chance against the ascendant

Southerly analysis of those realities, with its simplistic diagnosis of racism as the prime cause of all the black man's woes."

I am less concerned here with analyzing this ingenious but fallacious theory than with noting its importance as a symptom. For surely it signaled the end of a submissive fascination with southern regionalism by our sometime collaborators among the New York ethnic intelligentsia. Not the least of Mr. Podhorctz's complaints, significantly, is that this southern literary coup heralded and foreshadowed the later election of James Earl Carter as president, with its populist tone and, as Mr. Podhoretz sees it, its scorn of middle-class urban values. No one is very happy today with that experience, although our own unhappiness must necessarily differ from Norman Podhoretz's. Mr. Carter was, after all, the first authentic southerner to become president in more than a century. Bearing Woodward's thesis in mind, we might have expected him to exhibit that sense of historical complexity and tragedy that the historian found to be close to the core of the southern experience. But the appearance, at least, was often to the contrary. So far as a sense of history was concerned, Mr. Carter traveled light.* It was not so much a sense of tragedy as of rationalism, optimism, excessive deference to popular vanity, the engineer's illusion of a manipulable world, that became the hallmarks of the Carter style. His claim to be a student of Reinhold Niebuhr, hence presumably a sort of historical pessimist, did not sustain exacting scrutiny. That recent foreign-policy failures reflected a larger failure to tap the innate "goodness" of people in the mass—one of Mr. Carter's early themes—was about the last thing one could imagine Niebuhr suggesting. Having ventured, as other southerners did, to hope that we could expect a subsidence of facile secularism and moralism under Mr. Carter, I was as disappointed as Mr. Podhoretz, though for very different reasons.

---

*See James Fallows, "The Passionless Presidency," *Atlantic Monthly* (May 1979): 33-48. Fallows, Mr. Carter's chief speechwriter, offers several interesting comments on the president's sense of history, e.g.: "It often seemed to me that 'history' for Carter and those closest to him, consisted of Vietnam and Watergate; if they could avoid the errors, as commonly understood, of those two episodes, they would score well. No military intervention, no dirty tricks, no tape recorders on the premises, and no 'isclation' of the president" (p. 38). "The first clue…was Carter's cast of mind: his view of problems as technical, not historical, his lack of curiosity about how the story turned out before…In two years, the only historical allusions I heard Carter use with any frequency were Harry Truman's rise from the depths of the polls and the effect of Roosevelt's New Deal on the southern farm…Carter occasionally read history—he loved David McCollough's book on the Panama Canal—but history had not become a part of him…Later I read that he had decided that history was important, and that he needed a better background for his job" (pp. 44-45).

The Carter experience (and I am offering here no sweeping judgment on his presidency, especially by comparison with the simplicities of judgment and optimism that now seem to have come after it) suggests, for one thing, the limits of the Woodward thesis. Indeed, it gives life to Richard King's suggestion that the insights provided by essays like "The Search for Southern Identity" are of more instructive than descriptive value. "The central problem with Woodward's eloquent essay," writes Richard King in *A Southern Renaissance*, "was that it was difficult to detect which southerners gave evidence of having learned from the region's unhappy history or at least of having learned what Woodward wanted them to learn. In this sense Woodward's essay was addressed as much to the South as it was to the rest of the nation, and expressed a hope for what Southerners might come to believe in the future as much as it described the present state of Southern historical consciousness." However the case might be, Jimmy Carter had possibly missed the point either way. One wondered, with King, how many other southerners had missed it also.

It was perhaps unreasonable to expect that the first southern president in a century or more would know, or school the nation in, those hard historical lessons of our imagining. The presidency remains a bully pulpit, but Carter found other matters to preach upon. Nor, perhaps, should we make too much of Norman Podhoretz's disillusionment with the "southerly analysis," since he is troubled about many things these days. But Mr. Carter's failure to act up to the historical role that we as southerners might have coveted for him, and the fatigue registered by Mr. Podhoretz, echo a certain impatience with southern myth, inside and outside the family.

This would not necessarily concern us, who deem it our role to keep the flame of regionalism alive, if we could be confident that our myths and preoccupations were grounded in a solid social reality. Are they? Might we be approaching a time when the southernizing enterprise flirts with obscurantism and self-caricature? When might it become a matter of, if you will, Dixiefying Dixie: putting a sort of stage-prop front on a mercurial reality? This has been, for southern intellectuals, a lurking worry all along.

In a piece I wrote for Willie Morris in 1964 about W. J. Cash, I spoke of "the tacit alliance that reaches down from the rarified meditations of professors, authors, and journalists to the inchoate consciousness of the leather-jacketed hot-rodder who sports a Confederate flag on the rear bumper." There was, I suggested,

142

"little doubt that if the South lacked working mythologists to go on holding up a mirror to 'the mind of the South' this mind would vanish as a distinctive study in self-consciousness." I was still disconcerted by the possibility even some years later when I introduced John Shelton Reed's *The Enduring South* and admitted that in the dark of night those of us who traffic in southern "differences" contemplate our profession in terror: "Is [one] dealing in tomfoolery, or raising ancient spirits better left sleeping? Is [one] a cotton-patch Spengler, a Lysenko of the magnolia groves?"

I assumed then that those questions were rhetorical and that negative answers might safely be expected. I still think so, but with less assurance. The continuing exercise in regional self-consciousness, when it is all that stands between "the South" and its disappearance, was assuredly worth the candle when we could plausibly suppose that a distinctive historical experience was at stake, when that experience had direct political consequences in a nation given to utopianism, or when the point was to repel facile cant about a national "mainstream" in which the South should, for its sins, immediately immerse itself. (Happily, as George B. Tindall has observed, "it is not the South that has vanished but the mainstream, like one of those desert rivers that run out into the sand, consumed by the heat.") Our somewhat narcissistic enterprise could be indulged to constructive purpose so long as we were confident of a special sensibility, of a literature demonstrably richer and more searching than any other in America, and even when we could suggest with a straight face that our statecraft was something quite special.

But what now? What do we do when we begin to suspect that there may be more smoke than fire? Is it really for slick country music, or franchise fried chicken, or a resurgent Ku Klux Klan, or for grotesquely reactionary politicians that so much ink is spilled? Is the nourishing of these things, *faute de mieux*, not the essence of what I call Dixiefying Dixie? I know the pitfalls of all this, even as I write it. The South of imagination and memory has shown great tenacity in the face of physical, political, economic, social, and maybe even psychological change. But new times demand new themes. And the discovery of new themes might mean, incidentally, facing up to our own ambivalence about change. Was it facile to believe, as some of us did as recently as ten or fifteen years ago, that what was good and valuable in southern custom, experience, myth, and manners could be preserved, while the dross of evil was slowly refined away? Was the dross actually consumed, or has it now merely reached its rococo stage?

Of course, even in our willingness to part with the South of memory and imagination, along with the physical South of which I spoke briefly at the outset, we would often be offended by the tawdriness of what was left. We might find ourselves exclaiming, with Ophelia, "O, what a falling-off was here!" and seeking mental refuge in a sullen sense that we had lived before the revolution and had known the gentleness of life. But even this sullen sense of loss might be preferable to a merely antiquarian regionalism, a fly-in-amber quaintness. I do not know, and would not venture to predict, whether it would or not. All I know is that *my* South is fading and that I find it difficult to muster the will or imagination to revive or restore it. Nonetheless I must close with the usual disclaimer. I would like to be shown to be another, neither the first nor yet perhaps the last, who prematurely consigned the South to the boneyard. Maybe Dixie can be Dixiefied yet again. It is a rash man who dismisses the possibility.

—*Fall, 1980*

First Bloom of Activism

It has been 115 years since Chief Justice Roger B. Taney died in Washington, unmourned, amid the great Civil War some blamed him for helping start. "The temple of the man-stealers has been rent from foundation to roof," gloated the *Chicago Tribune*, "and the ancient High Priest lies cold at the altar."

High priest of the man-stealers? The *Tribune's* harsh allusion was to Justice Taney's astonishing decision seven years earlier in *Dred Scott v. Sanford,** a decision to which historians customarily assign a pivotal role in blasting the Union asunder. All future discussion of the case and its effects must now begin with Don E. Fehrenbacher's magisterial book. Mr. Fehrenbacher, who teaches at Stanford, won my admiration some years ago with a splendid little book on the early political career of Abraham Lincoln. He has renewed it here.

The Dred Scott Case: Its Significance in American Law & Politics, By Don E. Fehrenbacher (Oxford University Press, 1979)

This study is assured the admiring attention of scholars, but it deserves a larger readership. Slaveholding in the U.S. territories, the issue in *Dred Scott*, is long settled, for what Taney ordained one March day in 1857, the blood and iron of civil war soon shattered forever. But the case remains a window on an era. It is also of continuing interest to all students of the quirkiness of human fate.

Dred Scott, the most famous slave in American history, was born in Virginia. Eventually, in Missouri, he was sold to an itinerant army surgeon, Dr. Emerson, who took him to various outposts in Illinois and the Wisconsin Territory. When Scott and his wife first sued for freedom, in 1846, their case seemed to be a cinch under Missouri law. Slave status, the legal theory was, could not survive residence in a free territory. This indeed was the finding of the first court: Dred Scott and his wife were free.

But between that verdict and the first appeal, circumstances freakishly contrived to make Scott's case the focus of a great and intensifying controversy over the status of territory acquired in the Mexican War. The issue was Congress' authority to regulate slaveholding in U.S. territories. When the *Dred Scott* case came before the Taney Court in Washington, after a decade, it was expected—nay, insisted—that the Court should "settle" the issue forever.

We see clearly in retrospect that this was far too much to expect of any court, even if its sectional bias had not predisposed it to a partisan conclusion. Chief Justice Taney, then nearly eighty years old, was no firebrand of slavery. But he believed that, denied its "peculiar institution," the Southern way of life was doomed. It thus fell to a jurist of fervent Southern loyalties (Mr. Fehrenbacher leaves no doubt on this oft-disputed point) to decide the case, and he wound up writing the most explosive opinion ever delivered by the U.S. Supreme Court.

Negroes, the Chief Justice argued, were not U.S. citizens and never had been or could be. Indeed (he observed in a tone of regret), at the time when the Constitution of 1787 was framed, they had been regarded generally as "beings of an inferior order...and so far inferior, that they had no rights which the white man was bound to respect." Congress, moreover, had never had constitutional authority to restrict slavery in the territories. The territories, he argued, had not belonged to the nation formed in 1787, but were the "joint property" of the sovereign states, tendered only conditionally to the Union.

From the first proposition it followed that Dred Scott had no standing in the federal courts; from the second, that all

145

congressional legislation in any way confining territorial slavery (even the great "compromises" of 1820 and 1850) was null and void. It was dubious history—how dubious, Mr. Fehrenbacher easily shows. And even if the history had been sounder, the degree of what we call "judicial activism" would have been no less, though of course the political arms of government had invited it by leaving the Court to settle their great quarrel for them.

The *Constitutionalist*, an Augusta, Ga., newspaper, spoke for the Southern ultras when it observed that, given Justice Taney's decision, "Southern opinion on the subject of Southern slavery...is now the supreme law of the land...and opposition to Southern opinion upon this subject is now opposition to the Constitution, and morally treasonable against the government." On the apparent meaning of Taney's judgment, if not on the *Constitutionalist's* daring inference, the Northern antislavery ultras completely agreed.

Now, the irony of all this was that the constitutional issue was mostly illusory. Few slaves had entered the new territories of the West. Not even "bleeding Kansas," over whose status as slave or free an unseemly battle raged, counted more than two hundred slaves. The antislavery majority was sure to win out in due course. Moreover, as Stephen A. Douglas was arguing— he was bent on being President and working to avert a Democratic Party split—slavery could not flourish where local residents denied it those "police regulations" needed to hold slaves.

Why, then, did the fury over territorial slavery engulf the nation within four years? Essentially, as Mr. Fehrenbacher tells us, because the slavery quarrel, which had once been political and manageable, had become a "constitutionalized" quarrel over the American future. The Southern ultras saw their way of life as being impudently challenged; the Northern ultras saw their liberties as being besieged by a monstrous, conspiratorial "slave power." Thus Mr. Fehrenbacher's book really is a study of passion in politics and how hard it is to temper passions judicially. Roger B. Taney believed, with an intensity that lured him into historical casuistry, that right and law lay on the side of slaveholding. His personal commitment was not to slavery itself— he had manumitted his own slaves years before 1857—"but rather to Southern life and values, which seemed organically linked to the peculiar institution and unpreservable without it."

Although the focus of this masterly book is on the politics and law of the territorial question, and necessarily so, it might perhaps have explored the human dimension more thor-

146

oughly—since, after all, it is the folly and passion with which men believed and acted, more than *what* they believed, that make the dreadful uproar of the late 1850s intelligible. Mr. Fehrenbacher's book does, however, clear up a number of misconceptions (for instance, that the case was faked or contrived, or that Roger Taney really didn't mean what he wrote in the opinion, or that it's easy to trace the secessionist fever of 1861 in a straight line to the *Dred Scott* case). Many errant textbook accounts will need updating in the light of his splendid scholarship and writing.

—*From* National Review, *March 2, 1979*

Reparation for All?

In a long three-decker editorial, fittingly called "Reparation, American Style," *The New York Times* pronounced last Sunday that "it is in the national interest" for Allan Bakke to lose his case against the University of California regents.

Mr. Bakke, you recall, is the engineer who desperately wants to study medicine, but was twice refused admission to the new University of California medical school at Davis—while, under relaxed standards, 16 less qualified "minority" applicants were admitted.

I can see the *Times* editorial vanishing into files all over the country. It deserves a better fate. *The Times* puts the case for "benign" discrimination as thoughtfully as a case so wrongheaded can be put.

Bakke's personal story is full of interesting details—how, for instance, at the age of 33, while working at a NASA lab, he conceived a passion for the healing arts. But the crucial fact is that he is a white male of exceptional academic ability and believes himself the victim of an "experiment, noble in purpose."

The noble experiment was this: In the years when Bakke was an applicant, California's Davis medical school allotted 16 of 100 openings in every entering class to "applicants from economically and educationally disadvantaged backgrounds," screened by a special admissions committee applying lower standards. Race is not mentioned, but being a member of a minority race was obviously an asset. Bakke, feeling discrimi-

147

nated against, has won two rounds in the California courts. The state has appealed; and the U.S. Supreme Court has agreed to hear the case next fall.

The Bakke case raises two crucial issues: Was Bakke, as a white male, in fact injured by reverse discrimination in the admissions process? Even if he was, might such an injury be tolerated out of larger social and historical considerations? The first may be an issue that can be settled by factual argument; the second and weightier issue is philosophical, social and legal. It is the issue *The Times* addresses.

"Major educational, vocational and social goals," in its view, cannot be realized unless some "benign" discrimination is permitted under law. Its argument against Mr. Bakke, then, is pinned to the need for "more black medical students and doctors," an indisputable and worthy need.

"If the problem is racial," *The Times* continues, "the solution must be too, in some degree…Those who recognize the racial and ethnic ingredient of deprivation in our society must hope that many *temporarily race-conscious remedies* (my emphasis) will be admitted to the American legal and philosophical tradition. The sooner they are, the sooner they will become unnecessary."

That view carries a powerful emotional appeal, for those who believe, as I do, that historical reparations are sometimes in order. I share William Faulkner's obvious admiration for the members of his McCaslin clan (see *Go Down, Moses*) who took a redemptive view of the legacy of slavery, and acted upon it. But the McCaslins' sacrifice was personal and voluntary and injured no one else. It was not a levy upon the legal and philosophical custom of their society. It is important to understand the distinction. It is important to understand what elements of "the American legal and philosophical tradition" could be compromised, or even lost, if Mr. Bakke lost his case.

It would be established, for instance, that what counts as the basic unit in the eyes of the law is not the person, but the group he belongs to. Ironically, we are only now recovering from an era in which blacks were classified, even stereotyped by group, to the grievous injury of countless individuals.

Constitutional sanction for the California special admissions policy would introduce yet another form of group stereotyping—a sort of "enclave" theory, highly deterministic, that certain groups simply can't compete and must be favored.

There might be nothing wrong with this, perhaps, except that "benign" preference for one person might mean malign dis-

crimination against still another. The major defect of "temporarily race-conscious remedies" will be found just here, I think.
When the group replaces the person, when group membership
becomes a badge of preference, the spiral of inequity simply
continues.

"In a country of many minority groups," asks John Bunzel
in a recent *Commentary* article on the Bakke case, "is it possible
to discriminate in favor of a minority without discriminating
against another minority (let alone the majority)? Who is to decide which groups are to receive special treatment, and whether
that special treatment is to be temporary or permanent, and
what guidelines will be used to make these determinations?"

Good questions all. Today Spanish-surname Americans, or
blacks, or Indians, await "reparation." But if the merits of groups
are weighed, who shall be denied it? Most Americans descend
from put-upon groups of one sort or another, and with the new
ethnic consciousness the queue at the reparations window may
lengthen uncontrollably.

Into such a tangle of legal and philosophical heresies would
a decision unfavorable to Mr. Bakke drag us. I cannot believe
that course would really be "in the national interest." And I cannot believe, accordingly, that the Supreme Court will follow the
magisterial advice of *The New York Times*.

—*June 23, 1977*

An Irrepressible Conflict?

On the eve of the American entry into World War II, the
distinguished historian and Lincoln biographer J. G. Randall
delivered a jolting presidential address to the Mississippi Valley
Historical Association. He charged that the men of Lincoln's
"blundering" generation had "stumbled" into the Civil War.*

Many historians, notably Pieter Geyl and the late Bernard
de Voto, have challenged the "blundering generation" thesis,
historians somewhat more pessimistic than Randall about the
capacity of conscious statecraft to calm the storms of politics.
But Randall's essay established the theme for a great debate on

---

*Crisis of Fear: Secession in South Carolina, By Steve A. Channing. (Simon &
Schuster, 1971).

the eternal question of how and why the processes of democracy seem at times to go sour, immobilizing temperate men, setting foolish men and foolish measures in their place.

The question is always pertinent, as to both past and present "crises of fear." Steven Channing is a young historian, recently trained at Chapel Hill, whose study of secessionism in South Carolina has much to say to us. Like Randall's critics, he is on the whole a pessimist—or fatalist. His is a study, and a depressing one, in the potency of political irrationality.

Channing believes that it was South Carolina's hotheaded and headlong bolt from the Union in December, 1860, following the election of Lincoln, that led the nation into Civil War—although, as everyone knows, the powder keg had been packed, the fuse shortened, by events stretching well back into the previous decades. Indeed, one really can't trace its origins with depth and balance without almost infinite regress. Were the seeds of bloody civil conflict sown when the first slave ship landed its cargo? With the framing of the Constitution? With the temporizing compromises of the Whig era? With (as I believe) the Mexican War? Emotionally, however, there is no question but that the war sprang from a shared feeling, North and South, that the U.S. must some day choose between slave labor and free labor: There was profound truth in Lincoln's observation that the nation could not exist half slave and half free. As the years wore on, the means of choice narrowed.

Yet it is a curious fact that if you put aside the irreconcileables on both sides—the Southern fire-eaters who deemed slavery more vital than union; the abolitionists who deemed the Constitution less vital than a "higher law" of divine command— there was in both North and South a moderate majority who believed that the extremists must not prevail, that the slavery issue must be settled in the best interest of national unity.

How, then, did the zealots gain the upper hand? This is Channing's timely theme.

For South Carolinians, whose impulsive departure from the union set the stage for war, the decisive event came, Channing believes, with John Brown's raid on the federal armory at Harper's Ferry, Virginia, in October, 1859. This crazed fanatic, a murderer and horse-thief for God, had an eye on stirring slave rebellion. In his effects were found maps of the slave states marked, it was supposed, for slave rebellions. "The fear and rage he aroused," writes Channing, "were at the heart of the secession movement...the white community was pervaded with a sense of loss of mastery over the blacks." Southern emotions revolved

150

between two contradictory notions—that the slaves were happy and fortunate, but liable to be "tampered with," as the phrase had it, and made rebellious.

This is not a new theory, of course. Vann Woodward examined the panic and its irrationalizing effect several years ago in a masterly essay, "John Brown's Private War." Channing shows why it had such devastating effect in South Carolina. That state's plantations and farms were on average the largest in the nation; its slaveholdings among the densest. Its slaveholders, isolated in their sea of chattels, saw in Brown's raid (and in the applause for it that rang out in the North) a dire threat to their purses and their very lives. (They had long since learned to suppress the terrible and haunting issues of justice raised by slaveholding.)

In their alarm, the South Carolinians, or most of them, did not pause to note that the men who led the Republican Party, Lincoln and Seward, condemned Brown's raid for the outrage it was and declared that in hanging he received all he deserved. No; the fire-eaters immediately, and the moderate unionists eventually, were caught up in a "psychological set" of gloom and fright: Brown's raid was Republicanism in action; therefore the election in 1860 of a Republican President would write abolitionism into national policy. It was, among other things, a self-fulfilling prophecy. And alas, the one national politician offering realistic prospect of escape from this set of mind, Democratic Senator Stephen A. Douglas of Illinois, merely confirmed it when he told the U.S. Senate that Brown's raid was the "natural, logical, inevitable result of the doctrines and teachings of the Republican Party."

One lacks space to trace, as Channing does so skillfully, how such alarming misapprehensions were at once bravely contested by South Carolina unionists like Representative James Orr and the Edgefield newspaper editor, Arthur Simkins, and cynically exploited by "radical" Southern nationalists like Robert Barnwell Rhett, who used them as a wedge to split the Democratic Party. (Or to dwell upon the presence in the White House, in these anguished months, of a president whose "Southern strategy" it was to appease secession and thus feed the illusion that it would be accepted peacefully.)

The pattern of runaway political irrationality, feeding on fear, offers unsettling parallels to our day: Vigilante panics in which constitutional niceties are swept aside for security's sake; rhetorical exaggeration of matters already sufficiently serious; the bearing of false witness against political opponents; the whole grim tissue, in short, of a society choked with fear of its own shadow.

I rather share with Channing and other "fatalists" the feeling that conflict over slavery was, in the catchword of the time, "irrepressible." Certainly it could not be resolved by more half measures. But that is not to say that Randall was altogether wrong about "the blundering generation"—that sane and timely statecraft might not have softened the explosion. But where was it? The statesmen were eclipsed. And the everlasting shame is that even in the election of 1860 the moderate presidential candidates among them polled 124,000 more *Southern* votes than the "radical" Breckinridge-Lane ticket: evidence based on the paralysis of a moderate majority that no one could rally to save the Union without bloodshed.

—*January 31, 1971*

Mr. Wicker and the Confederacy

Tom Wicker of the New York Times, whose comments are rarely less than provocative, introduces a curious historical parallel into his otherwise persuasive analysis of South Vietnam's agony.

Mr. Wicker tells us that he has been reading the last volume of Shelby Foote's narrative history of the American Civil War, "the closing chapters of which describe the crumbling of another artificial nation which never had much chance to survive."

If the Confederacy was an "artificial nation," it was an artifice to which a lot of plain people paid the tribute of blood and financial sacrifice, not so much out of personal or economic interest as in spite of it.

In fact, close readers of Mr. Wicker's column who know something of Civil War history may wonder why this parallel sprang to mind, apart from the mere coincidence that Mr. Wicker was reading Shelby Foote as South Vietnam began to fall apart. Certainly, "the internal weakness of Thieu's position and leadership...American acquiescence in repressive tactics...corrupt and inept officers"—the factors he cites in support of this curious comparison—find no answering parallels in the history of the Confederacy.

Let us concede that historians have long debated the character and leadership of Jefferson Davis—the Thieu of our Civil War as Mr. Wicker would have it. But none, to my knowledge, has suggested that he lacked stamina, dedication or ability. One historian, the late David Potter of Stanford, did find in Davis a certain rigidity of mind, in that he "always thought in terms of what was right, rather than in terms of how to win. There is no evidence in all the literature," Potter continues, "that Davis ever at any time gave extended consideration to the basic question of what the South would have to do to win the war."

If Potter's evaluation of Davis is correct, it throws further doubt on the Wicker thesis. No one would argue that the Confederacy failed out of "repressive tactics" or "corrupt and inept officers" (Lee and Jackson?); quite the contrary.

A comprehensive reply to the Wicker parallel need not be written anew, here and now, because it has been in print for years. That answer is Prof. David Donald's famous essay, "Died of Democracy," in which he argues that "the real weakness of the Confederacy was that the Southern people insisted upon retaining their democratic liberties in wartime. If they were fighting for freedom, they asked, why should they start abridging it?"

As evidence of this stubborn, possibly self-defeating insistence on the courage of Confederate political conviction, Donald offers a number of contrasts. There was, first, the election of officers, "a carry-over from the old peacetime militia." There was, in the political realm, the fact that "at least 15,000 civilians were imprisoned in the North for alleged disloyalty or sedition, while over 300 Northern newspapers were suppressed for varying periods because they opposed the administration's policies." There was no comparable repression within the Confederacy, although arrests and newspaper suppressions have indeed been common under President Thieu in South Vietnam.

It was, as Civil War historians know, an accident of events alone that barely averted European intervention—an intervention that might in itself have assured Confederate independence. If England, whose government was pro-Confederate, had poured into the South the same resources the U.S. has poured into South Vietnam, that "artificial nation" might have established itself.

The point of saying all this is not to argue that the Confed-

153

eracy should have prevailed, but to suggest that Tom Wicker's is a kind of moral judgment, not an historical one: a judgment of righteous merit barely disguised as political and military analysis. One can say that whatever loyal Confederates thought they were fighting for, they were fighting, in fact, for the survival of a moral evil—human slavery—that should not have prevailed in a just world. But it is difficult to see any such flaw in what Mr. Wicker calls "the Job-like suffering" of South Vietnam.

The best that can be said of any imaginable parallel between South Vietnam and the Southern Confederacy was said by Abraham Lincoln, the supreme spirit of that struggle. He said more than once that if the war represented a visitation of divine judgment and wrath on the land, it was a judgment impartially visited on both sides, whose ultimate purposes elude human grasp. Mr. Lincoln had well understood the Book of Job. Tom Wicker, in his casual dismissal of two "artificial nations," seems to have understood neither the Book of Job nor Shelby Foote's account of the Confederacy's collapse.

—*April 2, 1975*

Saint Robert

The rediscovery of General Lee's lost oath of renewed allegiance to the United States, signed in October 1865, reminds us that he was first and last a unionist at heart. It is one of the inconvenient facts about Marse Robert that the cultists of the Lost Cause tended to ignore.

The formal restoration of citizenship that Senator Harry Byrd Jr. of Virginia has urged upon Congress may indeed prompt the general's demotion from sainthood to mere humanity too, which would be well. But there is no way of predicting how Congress will react. When the elder Senator Byrd proposed a similar resolution 14 years ago, generous men of every region, men with a sense of history, joined him—Hubert Humphrey and John F. Kennedy among them. Yet the resolution failed.

How could such a resolution fail? It failed, I suppose, because it is difficult for some non-southerners to grasp the difference between admiration and a cult. I think back, with amusement, to a personal experience.

154

My wife and I had arranged, some years ago, to meet two old friends then living in Washington—a couple, he from Massachusetts and she from New York. Lexington, Va., was a convenient halfway point for a rendezvous.

We proposed a tour of the Washington and Lee University campus, with appropriate stops at the Lee Chapel (where, in the East window, General and Mrs. Lee are "gathered with thy saints, in glory everlasting") and in the curious little library/museum where Traveler, stuffed, then still stood on a wheeled pedestal. (Traveler, I am told by a friend at the college, has since disappeared—"It is said that he was assumed.")

We were slow to surmise, much later, that this little pilgrimage had made our Northern friends uncomfortable. Not that they were scornful or indifferent, not that they could suspect our secretly pining after the Lost Cause; rather, they could not grasp in just what spirit we approached these shrines.

It was a kind of Henry James situation, everyone's imagination working at cross-purposes, and all too polite to compare notes. I suppose our friends would not have been altogether shocked if one had genuflected before either Traveler or the altar window. They felt, I suppose, like two infidels touring the shrines of Mecca with two Muslims. I would have told them, had they asked, that I felt only the most mundane and secular curiosity, little else.

I would have told them, moreover, that despite almost a century of the cult Marse Robert was too interesting to be a saint. To be sure, his character after the War was formidable to the point of—dare one say it?—priggishness. One thinks, for instance, of his refusal to write war memoirs, as so many lesser generals did, with the explanation that he would not trade in the blood of his men—by implication a drastic judgment upon those who did so, although I doubt that Lee saw it in that light.

I would have told them that, from a modern viewpoint, the most interesting and salutary thing about General Lee is that his career so perfectly mirrored the travail of the border South. He was a man of torn loyalties. His career forms a vivid contrast to unexamined nationalist loyalties—the purely abstract conceptions of "patriotism"—so much exalted today.

That Lee, like so many Virginians and North Carolinians, Kentuckians and Tennesseans, of his time hated secession we know. Educated at West Point, he maintained strict unionist loyalty to the eleventh hour; and sent his son Rooney not to some good sectionalist school but to Harvard, where he emerged, like his father, as a natural leader.

In March 1861, with the fire-eaters in full cry against Lincoln's election, and Lincoln's inaugural declaration that "in contemplation of universal law and the Constitution...no state on its own mere action can lawfully get out of the union," Lee stood fast. He agreed. Indeed, he considered that Lincoln's policy was all the South could ask, or reasonably expect. Only Virginia's secession, which he counseled almost desperately against, finally prompted his resignation from the U.S. Army. "I have been unable," he explained, "to make up my mind to raise my hand against my native state, my relatives, my children and my home."

Here was a decisive complexity of character, so much more interesting, knowing what we know today of the hazards of unfeeling submission to political abstractions and "orders"; and far worthier of contemplation than the plaster saint set before us for so long by the cultists. Lee's first loyalties were intimate, concrete, humane. In that he was ahead of his time, and perhaps of ours as well.

—March 12, 1971

The Reconstruction Myth

Like most Southerners of my generation—and certainly of earlier ones—I was brought up on the view that Lincoln's untimely death, far more than the sad April proceeding at Appomattox, was the greatest of the tragedies of 1865.

I don't recall ever hearing slavery defended—although the history books we studied sometimes reflected the familiar plaint that slaves had been less crudely treated than Yankees thought. We were well rid of slavery, it was said, and in due course probably would have ended it for ourselves.

No, the supreme misfortune was that John Wilkes Booth's bullet had ended Lincoln's life, and that act had prepared the way for a vengeful and devastating Reconstruction. And of it there was nothing, and I mean *nothing*, good to be said.

It is always hazardous to generalize from personal experience. But the universal, unsparing condemnation of Reconstruction and all its works suggests that the Reconstruction period left a deeper mark on the Southern mind than did the war itself. To be sure, General Sherman's wartime visits were remembered. But so was Winston Churchill's gallant remark that it had been the last war between gentlemen, and that was the prevailing and pleasant judgment. The scars and bitterness sprang not from the war, but from what was universally thought by Southerners a hard, Carthaginian peace.

Those of us who have heeded the historical debate of the last quarter century know, of course, that there was much to be said on the other side of the question. Yet, it wasn't said—or at least it wasn't said within the earshot of sentient Southerners. That fact is itself mysterious. If you go back to the writings of Professor Dunning, you find that his own judgments about Reconstruction, at least as a policy, are more measured and balanced than the reputation of the "Dunning school" would lead one to believe. Yet this measure and balance did not percolate down to the popular level. Perhaps there were too many Confederate grandfathers, with memories as long as their goatees, contending with the historians.

Few would deny, I suppose, that the flowering of "revisionism" in Reconstruction history was vitally related to what Vann Woodward has called "the second reconstruction," the civil rights movement. Our perspective on Reconstruction was bound to shift dramatically as current experience made it possible to see long-vilified figures like Sumner and Stevens as precursors of modern attitudes. What is odd to recall—I believe my memory is reliable on this—is that until the onset of revisionism, and even after it, there remained no logical connection between a given Southerner's view of Reconstruction and his political outlook. A Southern liberal, a Ralph McGill for instance, might uncritically accept the conventional view that Reconstruction was the "saturnalia of robbery and jobbery" Lord Bryce said it was; while a conservative—one thinks of the redoubtable Francis Butler Simkins—might see hidden virtues in it.

What the foregoing suggests to me is that if we are to grasp the impact of Reconstruction on the 20th Century Southern mind, we first need to refine the terms. Obviously, we don't mean its impact on selected Southern *minds,* individually considered; in that sense there can be no substitute for case-by-case analysis. I am assuming that we mean, for present purposes, its impact on the regional "mind" considered as collective memory or sensibility.

We are dealing, in other words, with the familiar power of historical myth: something not false or fanciful, necessarily, but

157

whose grip is independent of whether it is true or not: a fixture of the collective imagination.

History as a discipline aspires to understand "the past as it happened"—or at least the 19th Century Germans thought so. But history must deal, too, with what people *think* has happened. As a memory, of course, Reconstruction was a different thing for a North Carolinian than for a South Carolinian, for a Georgian than for a Virginian. Indeed, it was yet a third thing for states that fell, as did Louisiana and Mississippi, under the disputed sway of "carpetbagger" governors. You may elsewhere gain some solid notion of "what happened" insofar as it can be stipulated or at least debated in an orderly way. My subject is what was *recalled*—a very different thing.

The South's view—its mythic view—was that with Lincoln's assassination the scourges of the South took over. The South being prostrate, they vetoed President Johnson's attempt to knit up the wounds of war quickly by readmitting the vanquished on easy terms, and instead sent southward a swarm of ambitious politicians, unemployed military officers, economic adventurers, and mad dreamers who insinuated strange notions of political equality into the freedman's head. (Such strictly historical episodes as the critical election of 1866 tended to be forgotten). With the collaboration of a "disloyal" caste of natives, the "Scalawags," these invaders rewrote state constitutions, plundered state treasuries, helped themselves to jobs, issued worthless bonds, and all the while enforced the new order with swaggering black militias. The image was that of Russia in Poland or England in Ireland—or at least of the sway of Cromwell's puritan colonels over the ruined cavaliers of 1649.

Do you doubt this? Consider the case of Wilbur J. Cash. When Cash came to deal with Reconstruction in *The Mind of the South,* he turned to the glossary of the English civil war. He chose the word "Thorough," a revealing if anachronistic choice. Thorough was, of course, the impractical policy of the high-minded Archbishop Laud, in his attempt to extirpate puritanism in the Church of England. The connotations of the word are, in terms of the Southern mythology I describe, utterly appropriate. Both "thoroughs" were disasters.

The outcome was, in the view of most Southerners, and until quite recently at that, just as Cash describes it in *The Mind of The South:*

"And so inevitably the Yankee…came back. Came back in towering rage and hate, and shorn of all the

158

fine notions of chivalry, the remembrance that he was after all a Christian, with which he had hitherto occasionally toyed. Came back to sit down for 30 years this time, to harry the South first with the plan called Thorough and the bayonet, and afterward with the scarcely less effective devices of political machination and perpetually impending threats...To rob, to loot, to waste the pitiful remaining substance of this people in riot. To subvert the Southern world again and hold it subverted. Not only to strip the Southern white man of mastery...but also to hand over at least the seeming of that mastery to the black man."

One who looks to measure the strange phenomenon I describe need, then, only stir together two parts Cash with one of *Gone With The Wind*. That is the authentic concoction, the mythology that explains Reconstruction's "impact" on the 20th Century Southern mind. That Wilbur Cash, who was in so many ways an iconoclast and a challenger of magnolia and moonshine Southern romance, should write in this hectic vein of Reconstruction is revealing. What counted was not what happened but what even the most enlightened Southerner thought had happened.

Indeed, Cash's account of Reconstruction and its effects is of a full-throated rhetorical intensity uncommon even for him. It is as if Cash had harbored secret doubts about the conventional view of Reconstruction, yet had no solid ground to challenge it, and by a familiar device was the more insistent upon what he half doubted.

It is, of course, a mixed bag: the picture Cash gives. No doubt, as he says, Reconstruction intensified the sense of "Southernness" and distinctiveness. Perhaps it also brought about a kind of social equalization, at least among whites, varied only by the gentry's shabby tailcoats and their "tired old carriages, drawn by sad-eyed, introspective nags." No doubt it stirred nostalgia for the Eden-like "Old South," and thereby rendered Southerners, as Cash says, "the most sentimental people in history."

But that Reconstruction itself had as much to do as Cash insists with the "rape complex," with the resurgence of religious fundamentalism, with the impairment of Southern faith in formal justice, with the spirit of regimentation in values which he calls "the savage ideal," may be doubted. Especially so, when we stop, amid the rhetoric, to recall that the affair was essentially over and done with throughout the South by 1877, and in most

159

places earlier. It was, to recall a vivid image of the late Walter Lippmann, the splashing of a hand upon a large and placid surface of water. The South remembered the splash, the noise, the spreading ripples, but not how soon the calm returned.

In this the Southern memory differed from that of the hero of Judge Albion Tourgee's novel of Reconstruction in North Carolina, *A Fool's Errand,* who mused on the dashed hopes of a well-meaning Carpetbagger:

> "...that the social conditions of three hundred years are not to be overthrown in a moment, and that the differences which have outlasted generations, and finally ripened into war, are never healed by simple victory,—that the broken link cannot be securely joined by mere juxtaposition of the fragments, but must be fused and hammered before its fibers will really unite."

Again, what had happened was far less important, to the Southern mind, than what was thought to have happened. If Cash could present the unvarnished myth as late as 1941— 64 years after the last Yankee bayonet was sheathed and the last meddlesome Yankee schoolma'am had run for cover—one is tempted to think that as the years receded fact steadily lost ground to fancy. The Carpetbaggers had retired or melted into the local scenery; the "Scalawags" sought respectability in conformity; but the Confederate grandfathers lingered on their verandas, rationalizing the Southern order of things as a response to Yankee intrusion and vengefulness.

This, I believe, was Reconstruction's legacy—and burden— for the 20th Century Southern mind. Even for many otherwise sensible Southerners, it quieted for too long all suspicion that Reconstruction had had to do with the enforcement of the 14th cr 15th Amendments. It left the Southerner skeptical of large-scale political enterprises having reform as their purpose, even possibly beneficial reform. It left the Southerner complacently believing that if the South was, as some constantly alleged, economically and socially frozen, the fault was the Yankee's. There had been, you see, a madcap experiment in rash equalization and this was the primal fault.

I do not disparage these reactions—I was more comfortable with "the South," for all its faults, than I am with the "Sunbelt," for all its vulgar energy; I only notice the questionable relation of these memories to fact, and marvel at their durability.

160

More damaging, perhaps, the memory of Reconstruction made unworthy heroes of the "redeemers" who were thought to have salvaged hearth and home from social revolutionaries and mob rule. It left the Southern mind permanently—I do not say unhealthily—suspicious of Yankee purposes, and permanently rather paranoid about the reception that Southern values, institutions, statesmen and products might expect to enjoy elsewhere in the nation.

Like most political reactions, most Thermidors if you will, this reaction had saving virtues. But for the Southern mind the memory of Reconstruction was a paralyzing force, a powerful shot of political curare, and it left the South ill-prepared for the monumental changes and challenges that came with the postwar world.

—April 24, 1977

Strange Propitiation of Racial Guilt

With Charles Collingwood at the anchor spot, CBS News last Friday evening did the best television reporting I have seen on the "busing" controversy, deftly exploring both the pluses and the minuses—and there are both.

Above all, it rang true. There is, I think, a kind of snobbery among those who as parents have experienced this "experiment noble in purpose." Let me try to explain it. My own son entered the first grade of a neighborhood elementary school in a medium-sized Southern city—a typical school serving an affluent clientele, excellently staffed and academically demanding. It was not a segregated school; but under the "freedom of choice" plan, the black children who came there came of their own choice. Test scores averaged about a year above national grade levels.

After the Swann decision, all this changed drastically. My son became one of a minority of six in a class of 24. Some of the better teachers began retiring early, others moved to private schools, everyone began to mark time academically. That remained the case in the ensuing elementary years, during two

161

of which my son arose well before sunrise to be bused across town to a school with which his own neighborhood school had been "clustered."

Two broad results flowed from the cross-busing: My son and his neighborhood friends heartily disliked "busing" but got on well enough with their new classmates from across town, learning to evaluate them as people rather than as racial stereotypes. They suffer from none of the marks of the old paternalism under which I grew up: rule-ridden, polite and inhibited.

Yet for many of them, including my son, the educational results were largely negative. There was, for one thing, no homework: the schoolbooks, once allowed from the building, did not invariably reappear. There was no discipline of the old stay-after-school variety—most of the children were too far from home to walk or to be picked up by parents. To call the situation academically undemanding is to overstate its educational possibilities.

This was not the first instance, and I guess it won't be the last, when American public schools—ours were fairly typical— have been summoned to perform tasks of democratic socialization at the expense of scholastic seriousness. I was interested, in watching Mr. Collingwood's report, that the counsel of the NAACP candidly admitted that in his view this socialization— this mingling of the races—is more important than the strictly educational claims once but no longer seriously made for "busing." (The first Coleman Report, you recall, advanced fairly specific if limited educational claims: particularly that when black children were exposed to the educational standards of white middle-class schools their performance would improve, without injury to those standards.)

Unfortunately, those claims could not be conclusively tested. No cross-busing plan could work, could gain even a minimum of grudging approval, unless every school in the system were required to undergo more or less the same degree of racial mixing.

This, not some imaginary "quota" system, was the actuality underlying "racial balancing," as it came to be called—meaning that every school was to have more or less the same black-white ratio as the system and the city. The point is not well understood: To try wholesale integration on any other plan was to ensure a frantic effort on the part of mobile white parents to move to neighborhoods and schools exempt from the general pattern.

I suppose that if one accepts the priorities of the NAACP— if one accepts the proposition that the strictly academic functions of the schools should be subordinated to the function of

162

socializing the races—there are places, mostly in the South, where busing may be described as working—after a fashion.

But a lot of parents, black as well as white, do not accept these priorities, do not accept the slovenly theory that the public schools are enclaves for learning social values which the society at large refuses to practice. Indeed, in larger Northern cities (as in Washington) the strongest theoretical support for "busing" seems to come from affluent parents whose children are safely lodged in expensive private schools, learning the basic English grammar, math, and foreign languages that they must master in order to enjoy, in their turn, the privileged jobs and incomes their parents enjoy.

So far as I can see, the Boston experience has been a disaster. It has selected as subjects the children of black neighborhoods and ethnic white enclaves for a noble experiment from which the suburbs are exempt—the suburbs offering a caste refuge unavailable in most Southern cities.

Nothing is more infuriating to those who are acquainted with the actualities of "busing"—busing snobs, if you will—than to hear the apprehensions of its victims called "racist." So in some instances they undoubtedly are, alas. But the main apprehensions are educational when they do not have to do, as they do in all too many cases, with the physical safety of children whose parents nervously watch them shipped off every morning to strange and distant neighborhoods. Such apprehensions are not peculiar to any race or caste.

What any reasoning veteran of "busing" sees in it, as Mr. Collingwood discovered, is a mixture of pluses and minuses, to be sure; but beyond that one of our stranger American propitiations of racial guilt.   —*June 3, 1976*

The South's
Dream of Uniqueness

I had a friend, a newspaperman who later entered government service, who used to tear his hair over what he called "the South, South, South syndrome," that is, the eternal nattering of fellow Southern liberals about the South's destiny.

As I watched last Friday's PBS documentary, "About Us: A Deep South Portrait," I thought with amusement how he would have loathed it. The film, made by two Auburn University professors and introduced by Julian Bond, had its moments of unstudied originality. My own favorite was when a jackleg fundamentalist preacher, full of biblical boosterism, was shown instructing his gaping flock in the Old Testament's lessons for modern life. "Now where Lot made his mistake as a Christian...," he was saying.

In the main, however, these "South, South, South" films are as cliche-ridden and predictable as Saturday afternoon horse opera. There is not only the familiar old rhetoric of speech—the standard reiteration of the South's well-known vices and virtues; there has now developed, as well, a sort of rhetoric of the camera. There is the predictable footage of lonely dirt roads winding along to rural churches, tar paper shacks, revival services, Atlanta skyscrapers, crackers talking about being beaned with Coke bottles (violence, you know), crop-dusting airplanes, and of course the university seminar where savants gather on a foundation grant to muse on the nationalization of Dixie and the dixiefication of the nation.

I don't mean to be waspish. But it ocurs to me, as it did to my friend, that it is the genius of Southerners to discover a new talking point as every old one is abandoned.

One is told—and it is true—that race relations are healthier today in the South, as a rule, than they are outside the region. The South has made its peace with the 14th Amendment more gracefully than Boston, that seat of puritanical scorn and hypocrisy. That is what one hears.

What one more rarely hears, however, is why this is true. I myself think it is true because race relations were, in a fundamental human sense, *always* better in the South, even in the evil old days of Jim Crow, than in the cities that then and now caught the spill-over of blacks and mountain whites in flight. Within the code of Southern paternalism, for all its blindness to brute fact, white and black southerners could know and like or dislike—sometimes even love— each other as people. When the constitutional crisis came, it was a psychological and social barrier, not a physical one, that had to be crossed. Southerners might be adversaries; they were not strangers.

Barriers have been crossed, but at the price of growing impersonality. Some such exchange is inevitable. Vices and virtues tend, I think, to interlock. There is a social ecology, as there is a natural one; and as the South becomes more industrialized

164

and suburbanized and democratic the old human contacts are probably breaking down as rapidly as the new ones are succeeding, at least where racial lines are concerned. The selective surrender of values is a trick that few organized societies have managed to bring off.

Which brings me to the main point. The conundrum with which the South's savants are wrestling today, as the PBS film showed, is this: Can the South's cozy human qualities, from its whacky and colorful religions to its habits of ease and leisure, survive prosperity? This is the issue to which a body called the Lucius Quintus Cincinnatus Lamar Society hopefully addressed itself a few years ago. It remains, I gather from "About Us," an absorbing preoccupation.

It has become an article of faith among Southern intellectuals—and more power to those who believe it—that the South can glide painlessly into the age of machinery, computers and fast-food strips—prosperity, American style—without paying the usual price of admission. The usual price, as we know, is a terrifying de-personalization of relationships, the replacement of paternalistic values by the cash nexus.

That is really what the battle over unionization in the South is about, in part. Southern textile entrepreneurs are not lacking in the usual quotient of greed; but some of them really believe that their workers fare better under a benevolent paternalism than they will fare if the repeal of 14-B brings the union shop to the South. They may be right.

That is only one manifestation of the problem, alas. It is easy enough if you own a newspaper (like my wise friend Brandt Ayers of Anniston, Ala.), or a textile mill, or hold down a lucrative teaching or research post, to embrace the old values as now modified and to believe that they can survive and serve to the benefit of all. It is the everyday Southerners I wonder about. They are not given to self-scrutiny of the "South, South, South" variety. Yet on their attitudes will hinge the success of the South's latest, and most extravagant, dream of uniqueness.

—*August 18, 1977*

"Roots" as History

The visceral response to the televised version of Alex Haley's "Roots" reminds me of a friend's reaction some years ago to the movie "Exodus." "I went in vaguely anti-Semitic," he explained, "and came out a raving Zionist."

Well, second births of new vision are the order of the day. If it takes the broad brush and splashy palette of television to set this historyless generation thinking about slavery let us make the best of it.

But I would be sorry if the millions who found themselves imaginatively engaged in slavery, many for the first time, made do with "Roots" and its inspiring mixture of truth, half truth and sheer historical nonsense.

For one thing, the past two decades have been a golden age in the study of slavery. The writing of Stanley Elkins, Kenneth Stampp, Eugene Genovese, David Brion Davis, David Donald, Winthrop Jordan, Peter Wood and many others have made ignorance unnecessary, even unpardonable.

For another thing, melodrama—even good melodrama—is a poor guide to understanding. Don't mistake me. One always concedes a writer's right to reconstruct the past in fiction with imaginative license—Alex Haley as well as Margaret Mitchell or Thomas Nelson Page. The parts of "Roots" that reflect Mr. Haley's dogged and successful search for his African heritage and his family's heroic resistance to Samboism, are wholly admirable.

But those with a long memory know that the dramatic mode can be tricky and its changing fashions ironic. During the brutal scenes of night-riding and whipping by the Ku Kluxers, I found myself remembering that as recently as 1938, in "Gone With The Wind," Hollywood unblushingly romanticized the "valiant" struggle of Southern night-riders against "Negro rule." And before that, one of the most popular American films ever made, "Birth of a Nation," depicted the Klan as almost a reembodiment of King Arthur's Knights.

Viewing the unrelieved viciousness of the whites in Mr. Haley's story, I recalled what David Donald had written about Mr. Haley's book in a recent *Commentary:* No one, said Mr. Donald, had written black dialogue quite that way since Joel Chandler Harris and Thomas Nelson Page, "late 19th Century Southern historical romancers...*Roots* should be read as a continuation of this hoary tradition—but with the racial signs reversed. In Haley's novel it is a black family of noble lineage, rather than a white one, that is spirited off to adventures in America….It is the blacks who exhibit diligence, loyalty, truth, honor, and a fierce spirit of stubborn independence, even though they are surrounded by degraded, disgusting whites." And as they wrote of "darkeys," observes Mr. Donald, "so Haley can hardly bring himself to speak of whites but refers to them as 'tou-bob'—presumably a word of African origin."

Turn about is fair play, I suppose; but it is as if William Faulkner—or William Styron—had never lifted a pen. To be sure, the gratuitous cruelty of the white world is slightly redeemed by two whites, a boyish war refugee from up country South Carolina and his wife—a pleasingly mischievous twist on historical convention, since it is usually assumed that racism was at its most virulent among the white yeomanry rather than the master class.

The deficiency of "Roots" that most needs correcting is, I think, that it all but ignores the institutional complexities of slavery. To say that slavery was, after all, an institution (a peculiar one, as its Southern apologists said) is not to defend it—only to say that it does not yield its deepest secrets to the moralist viewing it as a unambiguous contest of good against evil.

Slavery, as "Roots" emphasized, did license the tyrannical passions of wicked men (of whom there were many) but it did not altogether defeat the persistent effort of good men to soften its rigors.

As early as his Notes on Virginia, in 1781, Thomas Jefferson was clearsighted about its corruption of morals and manners: "The whole commerce between master and slave is a perpetual exercise of the most boisterous passions, the most unremitting despotism on the one part, and degrading submissions on the other." Yet Jefferson, as we know, kept slaves—many of them—in spite of his moral revulsion. His own ambivalence, we must suppose, did not become extinct in after generations. Here is the stuff of artistry and history—not the spectacle of stick-figure sadists degrading their slaves, but of a people of reasonable impulses trapped in the clutches of an institution whose evils many of them deplored. I wish "Roots" had dwelt as much on the tragedy as on the mean-mindedness of the peculiar institution; for thus might heroic melodrama have been deepened to history.

In saying this, I suppose I should confess a historic interest. I am by birth and heritage a Southern white whose ancestors on one side were slaveholders. The last of them, my great-grandfather, met his end at Cold Harbor. I like to think that he was not an evil man and that if he could have lived to share in Mr. Haley's exploration of "roots" he too would have applauded the developments over a century that emancipated both races, together, from their common curse.

—*February 3, 1977*

Demythologizing Dixie

The South loves a myth. "The infinite variety of Southern mythology," as one historian has written, "could be catalogued and analyzed endlessly. A suggestive list would include the pro-slavery South, the Confederate South, the demagogic South, the states rights South, the fighting South, the lazy South, the folklore South, the South of jazz and the blues."

In the same tradition, Prof. Vann Woodward of Yale delivered a provocative talk at Chapel Hill the other day, designating as myth—and vicious myth at that—nearly the whole Southern understanding of the slavery question. The effect of Mr. Woodward's expose is, if valid, to leave the South a shorn lamb without so much as a barrel to temper the historical chill.

I cannot brief here the richness and sly wit of this talk, nor would I dispute the underlying argument—that in the construction of its version of the past the white South has for its own convenience and exculpation relegated the Negro, who shared it as bondsman or underling, to a position of strange irrelevance.

What Mr. Woodward asserts—I find it highly debatable—is that certain historical accounts leading the southerner to believe that his ancestors were in a measure victimized by "outsiders" and forces beyond his immediate control are "myths" in the sense of being false.

Thus, he says, it is a myth that Yankee slave-traders had much to do with fastening the slave system on the pre-Civil War South; a myth that Eli Whitney's cotton gin gave a fillip to slavery just as the exhaustion of the old croplands of the Upper South was rendering it unprofitable; a myth that William Lloyd Garrison and his fellow abolitionists did much more than "aggravate" the quarrel over the constitutionality of slavery.

He declares—it is a masterpiece of paradox—that the cot-

168

ton gin, far from giving new life to the slave system, may ultimately have isolated and doomed it by diverting the slavers of the Old South (chiefly Virginia) "from the Ohio Valley, their normal line of migration, down to the cotton belt of the Lower South."

And just, it would seem, for the insult, Professor Woodward reminds those who venerate Thomas Jefferson that he and his party, while condemning slavery in theory, "flung open the vast territories of the Southwest and the Gulf states to the cotton kingdom of slavery, grasped the Louisiana territory, the Floridas and secured the vital port of New Orleans...and (thus) cleared the way for the greatest of all American expansions of the Peculiar Institution."

I doubt that most southerners now are vitally concerned with these large chunks of accepted history which Mr. Woodward calls "myths." But is seems to me wicked of him to bulldoze away so much of the historical landscape at one time; and indeed it is possible that in his zeal to prune away illegitimate excuses he has performed butchery rather than surgery.

Let us begin with slavery extension. Surely it defies common sense, as well as the evidence, to believe that the Ohio Valley was or could have become—cotton gin or no—a hospitable area for slavery. That was what all the shouting centered on from the Missouri Compromise in 1820 to the Civil War. It was a real quarrel over largely imaginary economic fears.

To reckon that the migrant planters—even if they'd had a crop to plant out there in the snowy Midwest—could have beat the surging homesteaders to the territories is in itself to erect a historical myth.

And what of taxing the Jeffersonians with the "guilt" of having snatched Louisiana, the Floridas and New Orleans? One might as usefully argue that James Knox Polk is responsible for the prosperity of the John Birch Society because he confirmed the independence of Texas and snatched California from the Mexicans. Jefferson suffered pangs of conscience over the Louisiana Purchase, not because its northern reaches offered *lebensraum* for plantation slavery, but because the Constitution did not authorize so sweeping an act of executive power.

Moreover, Jefferson was actually the father of Western anti-slavery free-soilism, by virtue of this authorship of the Northwest Ordinance; and when the anti-slavery people sought a name for this new party in the 1850s, whom did they name it for? The old party of that dupe of Southern aggression, Thomas Jefferson!

It seems to me pointless to quibble over when or how the South might have emancipated the slaves. But I suspect that

169

clues lie less in the temper of the Old South than in the eventual impact of industrialization—which by 1861 had led to the emancipation of Russia's serfs. To my mind, however, there is no doubt that the abolitionists, by the operation of familiar laws of provocation and response, made slave manumission unthinkable—as there is really no question that the cotton gin gave new economic point to slavery.

Perhaps Professor Woodward, whom I admire extravagantly, has consulted too many Yankees during his recent sojourn in the history department at Yale. The point of this modest rejoinder is to try to salvage some historical landscape whose chief value, for me, lies less in regional self-defense than its simply being there—enriching memory and imagination. I trust that Mr. Woodward's infidelity to the old verities is merely temporary.

—May 2, 1966

Jefferson's Troublesome Pen

Many years after he wrote the Declaration of Independence, whose 199th year we observe tomorrow, Thomas Jefferson hoped that it would arouse all men everywhere "to burst the chains under which monkish ignorance and superstition have persuaded them to bind themselves."

Like the Declaration—like so many of the glittering tropes that tripped from Jefferson's pen—the line about "monkish" ignorance is elusive. What, exactly, did he mean by it? He had been to Paris, where anti-clerical rhetoric was in vogue, although one doubts that Mr. Jefferson knew or cared very much about monasticism. And if he did he must have known that the Celtic monks of Iona had once saved the culture of Western Christendom from extinction. Monkishness was not of a piece.

We need not linger over this all too typical Jeffersonian flourish, for as Carl Becker said, Jefferson often "thought with the heart as some people feel with the head." It was Jefferson, after all, who once wrote to a friend that "the tree of liberty requires to be watered from time to time by the blood of patriots and tyrants...its natural manure." One imagines that this sanguinary sentiment was meant to impart a mild shock, but only

170

a mild one. It sounds more like a lost line from a pastoral ode than a political dictum.

Even members of the Jefferson Mafia—and I am a devoted one—must concede that Mr. Jefferson had some of the marks of the parlor revolutionary. Not that his politics were frivolous. But he loved the play of language so well that he often played with words when speaking of somber subjects.

When the Continental Congress chose him as the principal draftsman of the Declaration (he was joined on the drafting committee by John Adams and Benjamin Franklin, who deferred to him) he was known to be perhaps the best writer in the colonies. He understood the techniques of rhetoric; he nursed and burnished his sentences. But as the splendid phrases flooded from him one wonders how carefully he weighed their effect. He later said he had tried to capture "the common sense of the subject" of American independence. But some of the Declaration's notable phrases are anything but "common sense," if by that one means obvious to the ordinary sensibility.

There is, for instance, the troublesome notion that "all men are created equal and endowed by their Creator with certain unalienable rights." It is a mystic's notion, more contradicted than confirmed by plodding observation. If there was, indeed, a common endowment of rights, why was inequality so prevalent? Natural rights were orthodox English whig doctrine, up to a point. But Locke had included "property" among the natural rights, and Jefferson typically substituted the more ethereal "pursuit of happiness." What is an "unalienable right" to the pursuit of happiness? Whatever Mr. Jefferson meant by this endowment of natural right, he couldn't have had in mind the crazy egalitarianism that was to sweep France within two decades. Nor did he include within this special endowment the slaves of Virginia—a paradox that prompted Dr. Samuel Johnson to demand impatiently: "why it is that we hear the loudest yelps for liberty from the drivers of Negroes?"

Mr. Jefferson's Declaration, so radical and so mysterious, was the work of a young man of 33 who represented the best of a settled society, and this was curious. But no more curious than anything else about him. He was to be, later, the strict constructionist of the presidency who bought Louisiana, the civil libertarian who cut corners to get at Aaron Burr, the Francophile who urged "marriage to the British fleet and nation" when Napoleon showed signs of colonial ambition in America. No wonder that the Declaration remains a curious, a vexatious, a troublesome legacy for this nation and the world. One sometimes won-

171

ders where it will lead us. Certainly it has not yet led all mankind to burst the chains of "monkish ignorance and superstition"—not yet anyway.

—July 3, 1975

From Bloody Shirt
to Damp Hanky

According to President Nixon, last Wednesday may go down in history as the day they drove ol' Dixie down—"they" being the 51 U.S. senators who ganged up to reject his Supreme Court nominee Judge Harrold Carswell "because he had the misfortune to be born in the South."

It was only after a cruise on the Potomac with his political advisors that Mr. Nixon proclaimed this theory of the Carswell defeat, in a skillful display of calculated bitterness. "I understand," he said, "the bitter feeling of millions of Americans who live in the South about the act of regional discrimination that took place in the Senate."

There is, perhaps, the tiniest grain of truth in what Mr. Nixon said. But there is little evidence that the Senate ganged up on Dixie. As the historian Henry Steele Commager has observed, the only identifiable sectional vote was that every Democrat who voted for Judge Carswell, save one, was from the South. But that is far from suggesting that every senator who voted against him voted a sectional point of view.

Let us look beneath the surface of this matter. For what we are dealing with here is a familiar phenomenon—the feeling southerners have that they are, as Robert Penn Warren once said, "damned special."

Historically, it has been the Republicans who nurtured the feeling of damned specialness. From the end of the Civil War to the election of Grover Cleveland, and beyond, the Grand Old Party commanded a solid national majority by "waving the bloody shirt"—that is, by intimating that the Democrats were the party of the South, ergo the party of the Rebellion. Rum (the temperance question); Romanism (the Irish immigration question); and

172

Rebellion (the Southern question) summed up GOP political strategy from Grant to Mark Hanna.

Accordingly, it was natural that the South should develop a severe case of political paranoia—a sense that it was being denied a place in the national sun by the Republican tariff, or by freight-rate differentials (established for the benefit of railway magnates who bankrolled Republican campaigns). The South, that is, felt that it was being bled at bargain rates.

If the actuality was more complicated, there was enough truth in the theory to keep a patriotic southerner in a pout of self-pity.

How ironic that just as the South is beginning to emerge from its cocoon, to be weaned from paranoia, the party that once waved the bloody shirt is now waving the damp hanky. Mr. Nixon is waving the damp hanky when he suggests that southerners are being persecuted in "acts of regional discrimination" by the Senate. It is Mr. Nixon's right, as it is probably his aim, to try to recruit Southern votes by playing on these tender sensibilities. The issue is whether this neo-sectionalism is as good for the South as it may be for the Republican Party.

The waving of the damp hanky is infinitely patronizing. The chief architect of Mr. Nixon's "Southern strategy" is Kevin Phillips, who has written a book called *The Emerging Republican Majority*. His central theory is that an anti-liberal, anti-Democratic presidential majority is emerging, with the white South as its keystone. Phillips describes it as "the great, ordinary Lawrence Welkish mass of Americans from Maine to Hawaii"; and he calls the Southern contingent "the Yahoo belt," the place where John Wayne goes over big among the "schmucks."

That Richard Nixon, who went to law school in the South, takes Kevin Phillips' colorful and condescending rhetoric at face value one must, in all fairness, doubt. But his carefully staged reaction to the Carswell defeat makes one wonder. Any southerner who knows anything knows that the U.S. Senate is a bastion, if there is one, of Southern sympathies; yet we are treated to intimations of senatorial malice.

A South bursting with new energies and new social attitudes is to be invited to sulk in revivified sectionalism and lick imaginary wounds. Maybe Mr. Nixon can talk the South into a persecuted mood. Imaginary wounds can hurt as much as real ones. But that mood will only retard the South's emergence into the modern age, whether or not we vote Republican with that "great, ordinary Lawrence Welkish mass" this year, or in years to come.

—April 16, 1970

Cartoon Politics

I am told, though I can't vouch for the fact, that an admiring cover review in the Sunday books section of the New York *Times* is the best fate that can befall a book on these shores. To my astonishment, that fate last Sunday befell Kirkpatrick Sale's trendy caricature of American politics, *Power Shift*, whose theme is that the sun-drenched, scheming, wicked, avaricious, new-rich racists of the "Southern Rim" are seizing control of the country from the "Eastern establishment." The "cowboys" have dished the "yankees."

An admiring notice of this book, whoever the reviewer, would be astonishing for reasons to be explored below. It is doubly so when the reviewer is Prof. Robert Lekachman, the NYU economist, who in soberer moments has written excellent books on Keynes and inflation. Mr. Lekachman quibbled a bit, as reviewers will. He found himself annoyed by "inaccuracies of detail" and "a tendency to strain argument beyond evidence." The book wowed him all the same. It is "striking...important...successful...generally impressive...the most serious investigation available into the implications of a genuine power shift...powerful and persuasive"—one can picture the publicity brigade at Random House rushing to pluck these juicy adjectives from the lush foliage of Mr. Lekachman's prose.

I do not propose to dispute Mr. Sale's central theme, that the South has riz again. Like most grandiose politico-historical themes it is vitiated by countless exceptions. Further, it is no novelty. The burgeoning power of the Southern "sun belt" was quite recently the hobby-horse of Kevin Phillips, who once aspired to be John Mitchell's Mitchell. Phillips' theories, smacking of the demographer's study and the inkhorn far more than of the smoke-filled room, always seemed too rigidly schematic: just the sort of speculation a city boy from the Bronx might make in Southern political futures. But by comparison with Mr. Sale,

174

Kevin Phillips has the theoretical subtlety of a Montesquieu and the practical shrewdness of a Huey Long.

One is reminded, as one turns the pages of *Power Shift*, of the vogue once enjoyed by Vance Packard's costume-gems of sociology—*The Status Seekers* and suchlike—although even in his wildest pages Mr. Packard remained a diligent researcher with wit enough to wink occasionally at the reader. Kirkpatrick Sale, by contrast, writes with an abandon and a solemnity worthy of Izvestia. It is to his purpose to argue, for instance, that as "Rim presidents" Lyndon Johnson and Richard Nixon were all but indistinguishable in character and outlook.

Both, presumably by dint of long basting in the Southern sunlight, were racists. This argument requires, in the *Izvestia* manner, a certain adjustment of fact. Thus, of LBJ, Sale writes that "his entire congressional service of 22 years was marked by its unanimity with the rest of the racist Southern delegations"—a charge that quite overlooks Johnson's role in the passage of every modern civil rights bill from 1957 on. Of Johnson's 1965 Voting Rights Act, which inconveniently stands in the way of the theory, Sale writes that it "merely reaffirmed a constitutional right, anyway" and "was enforced by Johnson in barely a tenth of the counties available..." That qualifying weasel word "merely," as well as Sale's failure to explain the trigger device that excluded the act from certain counties, are typical Sale talk. So is a sentence like: "The only member of the U.S. Supreme Court in its 200-year history ever to resign in the face of public scandal...was Abe Fortas, from Tennessee—appointed by Lyndon Johnson, from Texas."

Mr. Sale's world is a cartoon vision of geographical determinism, where villains grow wicked from overexposure to high temperatures (60 degrees or above, if you wonder about the danger point). Thus Sale becomes the first pundit to discover geographical—as distinguished, say, from psychological or political—significance in the Nixon enemies list: "On the actual enemies list...exactly 60 per cent of the targets were from the Northeast, only 30 per cent from the Southern Rim."

To return, however, to the central question: How is it that a book so sloppily researched, so grotesque in perception and perspective, is lauded as a "serious investigation" in what is said to be our most influential book review? Mr. Sale may have friends on the staff, but even so, the answer must lie deeper.

There is much evidence that Americans thirst today for political simplification and fantasy, and respond to political animationists who do for politicians what Walt Disney did for animals. Then, there is the great struggle between good and evil, cowboys and Indians, cops and robbers, which without having any notable counterpart in the real political world is the constant fare of televised news.

If you have been pickled in the evening news, or if you have noticed the Herblock cartoons in which swaggering cowboys wearing dark glasses and smoking long, vile-smelling cigars, oppress welfare mothers and flagellate ethnic minorities, you are well into the world Kirkpatrick Sale sets before us in *Power Shift*. That a reputable reviewer should hail it a "serious investigation" tells us much of the vacuity of political inquiry in this country today.

—December 4, 1975

A Grand Old Label

My colleague Thad Stem, the Oxford (North Carolina) Erasmus, is weary of seeing the "populist" label glibly affixed to every contemporary rascal. So am I, for reasons both historical and personal.

Mr. Stem recently denounced this tawdry practice; and that was before one of the slicker Yankee pundits, commenting on the Philadelphia mayor's election, introduced the Hon. Frank L. Rizzo (God save the mark) into a host including, but not limited to, George Wallace, Wright Patman, Lyndon B. Johnson, and even the late Sen. Joe McCarthy of Appleton, Wisconsin.

What is there about so mixed a bag of political figures that makes it virtually impossible to write about them without calling them "populists"? If you blipped the word from some journalistic vocabularies today, they would dry up. "Populist" has become one of those tic-words we fall back on when we are too lazy to say just what we mean.

"Populist," I surmise, can mean not only any political insurgent of popular appeal, but racist, anti-Semite, xenophobe, rabble-rouser, demagogue, utility-baiter, or rustic. When journalists use the term, they use it with an Alice-in-Wonderland abandon; it means just what they say, neither more nor less.

This journalistic malpractice, which some historians also commit with less excuse, needs to be halted. And North Caro-

176

linians, knowing something of the actual history and associations of the word, are especially obligated to call a halt to its abuse. For in the last decade of the 19th Century, and the first of the 20th, North Carolina became a stronghold of Populism—the genuine article.

In fact, if your family was North Carolinian in those years, the chances are better than 50-50 that a father, a grandfather, or a great uncle was a Populist (if he had guts enough) or a Populist sympathizer (if he kept his politics to himself).

Populism—the movement and the political party—was rooted in the agricultural depression that wracked the South and the plains states in those years. At Omaha, in 1892, the party advocated free coinage of silver, easier credit, the progressive income tax, the popular election of senators, railway nationalization, civil service reform and the eight-hour day.

The more appealing of their causes worked their way into the platforms of the two major parties, and thence into the law and the political consensus. In North Carolina, which produced some of the ablest populist leaders, notably U.S. Sen. Marion Butler, the party "fused" with Republicans to give the state some of its more progressive measures.

To my mind, the most offensive confusion about Populism is the vague but persistent association with racism. It is unhistorical. Alone of all the indigenous political movements in the post-Reconstruction South, the Populists formed biracial coalitions. As Mr. Stem writes, "If its ideals were resurrected today, a better spokesman than George Wallace could be found. Wallace's tenures in Alabama are the living refutation of Populist principles."

Quite right, as I have personal reason to know. My grandfather, Colin Monroe Yoder (1863-1953) of Catawba County, suffered, as I do, from the foible of not being able to keep his political views to himself. He was an arch-Populist and a follower of William Jennings Bryan, the first to join and the last to leave. I remember him well. He was a very old man when I was a boy: a magnificent figure with frosty blue eyes, a great thatch of silvery hair, and the most splendid Roman nose I have ever seen outside the statuary at the Louvre.

In the family history, his eldest son, Fred R. Yoder, writes: "(As) county chairman of the Fusionist executive committee...he persisted in his efforts to retain and gain adherents to the Populist Party until 1910...Finally, in the early spring of 1910, he announced...that he was giving up Populism and returning to the Democratic Party. The Charlotte Observer, tak-

177

ing note of the announcement, wrote an editorial calling him 'The Last Wheelhorse of Populism in North Carolina.'"

I cite this personal interest only to vouch, of certain knowledge, that North Carolina populism of my grandfather's strain was none of the things (save utility-baiting, which was probably justified) today's glib urban journalists think. It sprang largely from the desperate state of farm prices—5 cent cotton, corn and wheat at 20 and 25 cents per bushel, by my uncle's account.

It was not racist, moreover, but the contrary. "In 1900," my uncle continues, "when the disenfranchising suffrage amendment, with its famous grandfather clause, was the red-hot issue in the campaign, he spoke and voted against the amendment... holding that it was not fair to disfranchise a man, black or white, because he had not had the opportunity to learn to read and write."

Like my friend Thad Stem, I take some satisfaction in North Carolina's populist heritage, which was in many ways both constructive and prophetic. I despise the sullying of a grand old label by glib association with figures for whom my grandfather and his allies would feel contempt, and with repressive causes they would have contested to the bitter end.

—*May 23, 1971*

Senator Dole's Impressionistic History

Several of my friends, not all of them partisan Democrats, are outraged by Sen. Robert Dole's liberties with history—his revival of the canard that the wars the U.S. has fought since 1917 are, as he put it in the televised debate with Senator Mondale, "Democrat wars."

Their anger may be wasted. Senator Dole's history tends to be impressionistic at best, and he has a new version almost hourly. "Four times in this century we have gone to war," he told a Veterans Day audience at Providence, R.I., this week. "Each time the harsh light of history reveals that war rarely began for reasons that were self-justifying—but rather because of weakness, wishful thinking and bad leadership."

178

When he considers his own disabilities—severe wounds in World War II left him partially handicapped—the senator "begin(s) to think about how it happened." But he couldn't be thinking very hard.

Senator Dole's line on the wars is roughly the political equivalent of the old Democratic practice of blaming the Great Depression on Herbert Hoover, which most Democrats have discarded in embarrassment. It argues a certain gross ignorance of "how it happened." The harsh light of history leaves Senator Dole in need of sunglasses.

There is, if anyone wanted to look into the question, no great mystery about the route to American involvement in World War I. "Weakness" cannot be among the charges against Woodrow Wilson, who reluctantly led us into that war—except, oddly enough, in the view of his vociferous Republican critic, Theodore Roosevelt. TR found Wilson's response to German submarine warfare insufferably timid, and clamored for a fight. Yet considering the murky international law bearing on the issue, President Wilson had by 1917 evolved quite a bold American policy. Its rock-bottom claim was that the citizens of a neutral nation enjoyed the right to travel unscathed on Allied merchant ships. When the German government launched unrestricted submarine warfare in the spring of 1917 it was fully aware that the step would leave the U.S. no honorable choice but to back up its position on "freedom of the seas" with a declaration of war. But freedom of the seas was not a Democratic position; it was historic American doctrine.

If one were next to join Senator Dole in the ridiculous search for partisan responsibility for World War II, he would find enough to go around. At the simplest level, it would have to be noted that the U.S. attacked no one but was itself attacked—by the Japanese at Pearl Harbor. But again, insofar as Americans could be held accountable for the trouble, it really began with our drawing of lines that Far Eastern aggressors could cross only at their peril—specifically the promulgation of the "Stimson Doctrine" in which the U.S. declined to recognize Japanese territorial acquistions at China's expense.

The interesting thing about the Stimson Doctrine, from Senator Dole's perspective, is that its architects were Republicans, not Democrats. Henry L. Stimson's policy accorded with traditional Republican views in the Pacific, always a Republican lake. Like freedom of the seas, the American non-recognition policy, albeit provocative to the Japanese, was neither

179

unreasonable nor dishonorable. But it did lead to more than a decade of aggravated conflict, culminating at Pearl Harbor.

It is likewise an embarrassment to Senator Dole's theory of "Democrat wars" that Adolf Hitler was so churlish as to declare war on the U.S. within hours of Pearl Harbor—a step eventually as disastrous for him as the attack on Russia earlier in 1941.

Of course, U.S. policy under the Democratic presidency of Franklin D. Roosevelt had provoked Hitler's enmity and had, indeed, divided American opinion—not on party but on geographic and ideological lines. Republicans of the Henry Stimson-Frank Knox-William Allen White stamp were sympathetic with Mr. Roosevelt's pro-Allied stance. Democrats of the old-line Progressive stamp, as well as Midwestern Republicans, were not. Kansas, Senator Dole's home state, was then as ever a crossroads and battleground of opinion—at once a hotbed of anti-interventionism (miscalled "isolationism") and the home state of William Allen White, one of the organizers of the Committee to Defend America by Aiding the Allies.

Perhaps all that Senator Dole is struggling to tell us, in his imprecise and waffling way, is that had he been old enough to engage in the great debate before 1941 he would have sided with the anti-interventionists or "isolationists." To confess it would be fair enough. But if he is going to argue about the origins of American involvement in wars—"how it happened"—he ought to brush up on the history books as well as the briefing books of the Republican National Committee. He ought to consider the bellicosity of Teddy Roosevelt and the Far East policies of Henry L. Stimson. And along the way, going on to still a third war, it would be candid of him to recall that the President he served as chairman of the party, Richard Nixon, was calling as far back as 1954 for intervention in Indochina when Democrats like Lyndon Johnson were still trying to prevent it.

The point of saying which, of course, is that for those who take a historical view of the matter there are neither "Democrat wars" nor Republican wars—only American wars.

—*October 28, 1976*

180

The South Goes On

In Sir Isaiah Berlin's now famous distinction between the hedgehogs and the foxes, Professor George B. Tindall is a fox—a Southern historian for whom the sheer multiplicity of the region's life and lore defy shaping into a single pattern or theme. In that respect, his encyclopaedic "The Emergence of the New South" is a refreshing departure from current fashions in South-explaining; indeed, as I write this my eye falls upon a shelf of recent titles—"The Everlasting South," "The Angry South," "The Lazy South," "The Southern Mystique"—suggesting that the hedgehogs are always at work. Professor Tindall is even less the hedgehog than Professor C. Vann Woodward, who in a classic preceding volume of this distinguished series produced *histoire à thèse* at its best.

Of course, this thick, lushly detailed volume would be easier to evaluate in brief if, after 725 pages, Mr. Tindall had finally with ruffles and flourishes drawn a curtain and disclosed *the* theme of Southern history from 1913 to 1945. Yet the price would conceivably have been a less faithful, perhaps a less durable, picture of the period.

The writing of fox-eye view regional history is not, to be sure, without its hazard. For unless the region described is peculiar, regional history is at best a convenience, at worst a caprice—the most hedgehoggish trick of all. The Southern historian is by definition, then, an historian of difference—or he is no Southern historian.

As a Southerner, Mr. Tindall suffers the nearsightedness of all of us similarly situated: In his bones he knows the South is distinctive—that quite beyond its merely measurable aberrations from the Great American Norm, it merits and repays separate study. Yet the historical fox is always intimidated by the region's sheer contradictoriness—that as the late William T. Polk used to say, it contains "not only Uncle Remus but Oak Ridge," and sometimes he must struggle to pinpoint the difference. Is the South still, as W. J. Cash perversely intimated, "another Kansas" plus Negroes plus heat and humidity? The predestined offshoot of a random mix of genes or economic patterns? Or is it, as Professor Woodward has argued, the product of an experience, unique to this land, of tragedy, thwarted will, and defeat?

Close readers of "The Emergence of the New South" may

find such hedgehoggish questions mutely answered; on the whole Mr. Tindall leaves us to draw our own conclusions.

Despite a certain failure to differentiate between what is vital and what merely colorful or measurable, Mr. Tindall's book is stout, rib-sticking food for conclusions. It so thoroughly covers the assigned territory, from the beginning of one world war to the end of another, that even if reluctant in judgment the book is likely for all foreseeable time to define this period for us. I can think of no important episode, doctrine, character, or statistic that is ignored. Does the reader seek to know what New Deal or New Freedom legislation owed to Southerners in Congress? An exhaustive survey of the trend toward crop control? An exposé of ticks, or pellagra, or poets? Does he seek the facts about unionism, demagoguery, or welfare legislation? A responsible assessment of the significance of Miss Ellen Glasgow, or the ineffable Mr. William Simmons? He need look no longer.

Looking at the book as a whole, however, I suppose that its great implicit truth is that in the years 1913-45 the South remained the only American region capable of being written about in terms of a distinctive imagination.

This imagination—I use the term in its broadest sense—transcends tidal changes of economic or social character, for no mistaking it, the South was changing. It was a dependency steadily assimilating itself, in all things statistically measurable save perhaps farm tenancy, to the union. It had more factories, fewer farmers; more money, fewer debts; more cities, less country life. King Cotton kept tottering, sometimes dramatically: At the outbreak of World War I, American cotton still served well over 60 per cent of the world market—it could deeply affect Southern attitudes towards the European struggle. By 1937, nearing the end of the period and nearing another European showdown, it served only 23 per cent of that market. In these years, industry came to stay, along with the "Atlanta spirit" of boosterism. Negroes left. The South in its lucid intervals emerged from progressivism, Mr. Tindall thinks, having accepted "the public service concept of the state." "The Babbitt warrens of the New South" made their mark; the dynamo, if not obtrusive, emitted a reassuring hum.

And yet, more visibly, the South in those years turned to the world above all a rich imagination—conceived in preindustrial ways of life; clothed, as always, in rich rhetoric. When Senator Carter Glass of Virginia endorsed Woodrow Wilson's League he did so, typically, in terms more reminiscent of the pulpit than the forum. It was, he said, "a covenant which contained the very essence of the Sermon on the Mount and was the consummation, so far as Christian nations could contrive, of the sacrifice on Calvary." The South was not only imaginative, it was in that imagination theatrical, Biblical, fervid—a stage where mountebanks and prophets pranced alike. It was also distinctly anti-modern.

Sometimes—as in William Faulkner's evocation in "Sartoris" of "a glamorous fatality, like silver pennons down-rushing at sunset, or a dying fall of horns along the road to Roncevaux"; as in the Nashville Agrarians' response to capitalism and the city; as in Miss Glasglow's doubts of "the twin curses of modern standardization and mass production"—sometimes the South's wistful rearward glance was subtle, even glorious.

At other times, in other guises, it was merely bumpkinish. The boll weevil could be seen as "a judgment of God"; cattle-dipping resisted, as if Ludd and his boys had returned, by dynamiting the vats. As late as 1920, "Tom Watson rode a wave of religious prejudice...into the Senate while Gov. Sidney J. Catts stood firm against the imminent transfer of the Holy See to Florida...On November 6, 1928, when the sovereign people of Arkansas delivered their electoral vote to Al Smith, they also voted Darwin out of their public schools..." Here, too, was the Southern imagination; sometimes the whole region seemed to pulse with outlandish visions and notions. "The Clansman" worked Georgians into a fit of xenophobia; the effusions of a Bilbo, a Vardaman, a Cole Blease, a Huey Long, as they vied for the plume of Southern statesmanship, were not to be believed somehow.

Yet as the works of imagination are ever more colorful and revealing than dryasdust statistics, it was in this still-riotous Southern imagination, wonderful and corrupt at once, that the South's true character yet resided. I think this is what Mr. Tindall's book tells us. That great Southern favorite William Jennings Bryan might intone about the Coral Gables commercial paradise and his tongue might be in it; but his heart still lay in the great war against modernist demons. Such could no doubt be said, perhaps as late as 1945, perhaps today, of most Southerners. And yet the proud corollary of this depressing fact, if such it is, is that during the period the South's literature—its imagination wrought to the finest pitch—became supreme in America. In the literary department, at least, Mencken's Sahara was no more.

On the whole, then, while there was barbarity and humbug in plenty, and while a great racial wrong slept undisturbed, the South, often disturbing but never dull, kept its identity. On paper it might be closer than at any time since 1828 to being a genuine part of the union. Yet, as Professor Tindall says, there remained "contradictions"—"and how!" one wants to add—and they were supremely important.

"The inconsistency," he concludes, "could not long endure, and a crucial question for the postwar South...was which would prevail, the broader vision or the defensive reaction." It is rather in the usual form for historians of the South to conclude their meditations so—as the South would not probably do both. The poets always ask, with Benét, that the "sick romance" be buried, while the pundits, like Mr. Ashmore, asks us to write RIP on the headstone. The obsequies go on, age to age; yet age to age the South goes on, unassimilable—if only her imagination and not her bank accounts or her factories elude the captor. May she not do so again? And what, for that matter, would regional historians do for work if she didn't?

From Virginia Quarterly Review,
Winter, 1968

Ignoring History

Emory Thomas, the University of Georgia historian, has an interesting theory about the shrinking readership of history. It is that professional historians have forgotten that "the first historians were story-tellers (who) probably sat in caves telling stories of the past that people listened to because they were interesting and because they offered the wisdom and inspiration of experience."

Having abandoned the narrative mission for technical disputes of only intramural interest, they have also lost their readers.

Actually, most of the best narrative history in English has been the work of amateurs. Lord Macaulay, for my money the most readable of historians, acquired his stupendously detailed knowledge of English history in his own study. Gibbon, his near rival at storytelling, abandoned Oxford after finding its faculty idle and somnolent, "steeped in port and prejudice" as he says in a famous passage of his autobiography and stupified by their "dull and deep potations." He studied Rome on his own. Winston

Churchill, who carried on the amateur tradition in this century, was a politician and soldier.

On our side of the Atlantic, too, many of the best narrative historians—Henry Adams, Prescott, McMaster in the last century; Bruce Catton, Douglas Southall Freeman and Alan Nevins in our own—came to the historical art from journalism.

No special point hangs thereby, for it would be risky to read such marvelously readable historians as Samuel Eliot Morison or C. Vann Woodward out of the company of storytellers, although they occupied academic chairs. But if, as Professor Thomas argues, Americans now look to novelists and journalists to satisfy their historical appetites it is nothing new.

The alarming possibility—and Mr. Thomas' piece reminds me that my yearly sermon on the subject is overdue—is that most of us will not read history of any kind, amateur or professional, and will shortly suffer from total amnesia about the past. I am a certifiable bore on the subject, as others are bores about other signs of the forthcoming end of civilization as we know it. To this foible my long-suffering family can attest—unwilling victims of impromptu bursts of historical pedantry to which I am especially prone during long family automobile trips.

During a recent drive southward, for instance, I thought to break the monotony with a quiz on Napoleon, surely a subject of universal interest. My children, though forced at various schools to plow through R. R. Palmer's *History of the Modern World*, could not or would not tell me where Napoleon was born, or of what French government of the Revolutionary period he was first a member. Undaunted, I was just getting to the Russian expedition when firmly admonished that I was also getting on everyone's nerves.

I like historical facts. They alone are not history, to be sure; but without them history is a flabby affair. And facts, the stuff of historical narrative, are almost always in short supply. I recently talked with a well-schooled young man who spoke with impressive authority about the diplomatic techniques and theories at Westphalia, but who could not, when asked, name the main provisions of the resulting treaty.

I have had to conclude, sadly, that narrative history, which unlike fancy theorizing must be built on a firm command of detail, is of limited interest to most Americans.

Why? My provisional theory, hardly original, is that the United States, in certain striking ways, has been exempt from the harsher penalties of history, which Gibbon called "a register of the crimes, follies and misfortunes of mankind." Most civili-

185

zations learn in a hard school to view present events, rather warily, as portending calamity; accordingly they scan the past for precedents and keys to understanding and avoidance.

But calamity has not been the common American experience. America afforded so much space, so much elbow room, so many resources for unpunished plunder, that the consequences of error have been mild—so far. Plagues, bombing, famine, mass displacement of populations, holocaust: these tragic instructors of mankind, even in our century, are happily lacking in what the national anthem complacently calls "the Heaven-rescued land, blessed with victory and peace."

Again, I cannot claim to have originated this theory. Variations on the theme of American exemption and innocence have been played by most of our major historians and novelists, from Henry James to Vann Woodward.

But if the theory is right, one supposes that historical consciousness, when it comes, will not result from admonition but will be a consequence of the familiar old calamities. It will be a high price to pay for insights that are more painlessly acquired at the library. But ignorance is always costly and mules, as we know, cannot be trained until you get their attention.

—*January 8, 1981*

An Old Town in Agony

When the big city newspaper reporters began to file stories out of smouldering Augusta, Ga., using words like "ghetto" and "establishment," one instantly sensed that they were strangers to an old river town we once knew and loved.

An old town, its decorum shattered by fire and pillage and bloodshed—indecently exposed—may be pictured by and for strangers in this bland sociological jargon. But for one who passed so many pleasant and adventurous boyhood summer days there, such terms merely mock the tangible, aching recall of colors, smells, sounds, spectacles.

For a small boy there was, above all, the secret and muddy Savannah, sliding seaward behind its levees, dotted here and there by lazily gliding barges or rippled on a Sunday afternoon by the mosquito buzzing of a speedboat. "Mozie," or Mr. Hood, dapper in his straw boater and cane, would take you down to the wharf to skip flat stones across the water.

Through the open windows in the still, sultry hush of Broad Street in the early morning the rattling wagons of the street vendors could be heard, and the shrill crying of their wares: "Heee-ah butterbeans! Niiice butterbeans! Heee-ah cawn! Heee-ah squash! Cucumbers!"

During the war, when according to the natives the old town was being "ruined," there were perilous walks to the uptown movie theaters. You would pass, one after the other, an array of tiny hole-in-the-wall bars, illegal, no doubt, but tolerated in a wicked old town. From their open doors, the fumes of cheap whiskey drifted richly to the sidewalk; and, more often than not, a derelict sprawled and snored undisturbed on the steamy pavement.

Augusta in those days was, I think, a place where experience was whole, where life's joys and desolations were not surgically separated as they often are today. There were no movies unless you passed, with a small thrill of fear, among the sidewalk drunks; no swimming without a bleak cross-town walk by the prison or the gloomy old cemetery at East Boundary. There was no fun on a hot midsummer afternoon without a dutiful call on some ancient great-aunt in a house from which, so it seemed to a small boy, all color had long since faded to a daunting gray.

One thing Augusta did not have in those days was "ghetto," unless one might have meant the white ghettos of the new suburbs on the Hill, or perhaps Camp Gordon, with its endless rows of barracks. The relationships of white to black were neither managed nor perceived in such stark or abrasive terms. To an Augustan of the 1940s, "ghetto" would have suggested Poland. No doubt there were unwritten rules about where one could live, but they were never mentioned, and of no concern to a 10-year-old boy. At any rate, they drew no lines; they checkerboarded the town into the usual Southern pattern of proximity without propinquity. For us—for my aunt and for my grandmother as long as she lived—one supreme and unalterable presence ruled the household. This was Mozie: ageless, tyrannical, irascible, mirthful, a gold tooth glinting from her mouth. Unfailingly at 7 a.m. her footsteps would ring, as they had for decades and still do now, the paved driveway. My first consciousness of the unwritten rules of segregation came one morning as I heard Mozie's footsteps outside the window and wondered why she never entered the front door in the first instance. To ask that question and others, as adolescence came on and with it the vague and

187

ineffectual guilt so familiar to Southern white boys, was to be firmly and kindly hushed. It was not a thing one discussed.

She ruled everyone, deferring only to my grandmother, Miss Stella, treating most grown men (except my father) with contempt and the women who had been her charges since infancy with a peremptory, mocking despotism. She thought nothing of commanding the removal of an unsuitable garment, new or not, as "trashy"; and usually the command would be obeyed. It was a mortifying day when this grand dame discovered me surreptitiously puffing a Kool cigarette behind the garage, subduing my terror with great hoots of laughter.

Yet for her, magnificent in her loyalty and friendship, we who loved her in so many ways wove a web of picayune custom that in ways invisible to us (and perhaps even to her) circumscribed her womanhood and humanity. It was, then, of her, of the kindest of aunts and of the pleasantest of old towns, that I thought this week as I read of the flames, the gunfire and the killings.

I thought of her sons, grandsons and great-grandsons, people we knew of but did not know, as I read about the six black youths shot (all in the back, the white coroner said). The vague stories about "ghettos" and "establishments," not to speak of the irrelevant prating of little Lester Maddox about "communism" and the Black Panther threat, seemed almost obscene. What do they mean, these silly and heartless words, to those of us who feel the agony of the old town as we might the agony of an old friend in mortal illness?

—May 16, 1970

188

IV. Literary Footnotes

Cotton-Patch Spenglers?

THE ARTIST, JOURNALIST, or historian who ponders the South for a living must at times be haunted, as I am, by the fear that the regional "differences" he traffics in are essentially obscurantist when you get down to it: elegantly so, it may be, but obscurantist all the same.

The Southern novelist may have schooled himself on Tolstoy, the Southern historian on the latest in scientific historiography, the regional political scientist or editorialist may be a master of computer science. Yet, rather to his astonishment, each relies on an asserted differentness that mystifies some, infuriates others, and occasionally gives aid and comfort to sworn political enemies. If this regionalist is Southern-born, as he almost invariably is, he feels the differences in his bones. His is a search for definition and explanation. Yet in the dark of night, he contemplates his profession in terror: Is it perhaps a sort of *trahison des clercs*? Is he dealing in tomfoolery, or raising ancient spirits better left sleeping? Is he a cotton-patch Spengler, a Lysenko of the magnolia groves?

Any student of the South who has known these agonies of self-doubt will find surcease from them in John Shelton Reed's *Enduring South*. Historians and journalists—the latter especially—have not hesitated to speak of a "mind of the South." But their portraits of this mind have rested, for the most part, on unsystematic observation, imaginative rendering of history, intuition, and sometimes sheer bluff. Mr. Reed, speaking from within the citadel of sociology (a discipline regarded by hardcore humanists with ambivalence, at best), has buttressed such imaginings and findings with facts and figures. With sophisticated opinion-sampling techniques, he demonstrates the persistence of a Southern "mind" (or set of mind) and it tallies, for better or worse, with what we had pictured all along. Nor does this regional mind seem a mere anachronism, headed for early extinction. To be sure, Mr. Reed focuses on this mind in limited aspects—as it shows itself in religion (or religiosity), in social

190

ideals and personal life-styles (which in the South remain strikingly parochial), in attitudes toward firearms in the home and the hickory stick in school. But such are crucial to cultural identity.

There is, to my mind at least, a pleasant difference between Mr. Reed's approach to the South and that of the usual regional sociologist. The professional susceptibility of the latter is, in my observation, to treat as "real" whatever regional differences are easily measurable, while dismissing as trifling differences more difficult to measure—like those which form the staple of Mr. Reed's book. He dwells, typically, on such hard data as per capita income, nutrition, the incidence of parasitic disease, urbanization—the nuts and bolts stuff of consumer capitalism—while brushing off as unobjective the historical or "belletristic" modes of perception. His mission, typically, is to wave good-bye to the South, to suggest that it is fading away, or at least being supplanted by one of those "New Souths" that come and go like French constitutions and theories of the decline of Rome. By and large, then, the social scientist has served the South over the years as a mirror serves a man with a physical deformity—suggesting the need for radical therapy. Yet the grossest deformity, ironically, may be his own: his suggestion, implicit in all this, that the imagination that produces a Colonel Sutpen or a Blanch DuBois is somehow less revelatory of the regional character than the computer that produces that composite of statistics. "the average Southerner."

I know, of course, that the typical sociologist I am depicting is himself a caricature; yet what too many social scientists who have studied the South have failed to see is that no sure correlation exists between condition and attitude. They deny the variety and indeterminacy of the human condition. That is why some of us who take a more than therapeutic view of Southern differences are driven back repeatedly to Cash, or Woodward, or Faulkner, whose lack of system is redeemed by modesty, insight and a sense of historical contingency.

No doubt therapy has been and continues to be in order for the South, in ways obvious to all of us (although one might suppose that Mr. Daniel Moynihan's devastating appraisal of the sociologist-as-therapist in *Maximum Feasible Misunderstanding* had sounded a warning). It may be that Mr. Reed's book has therapeutic implications, but it is valuable quite apart from them. For my part, I am at a loss to say whether the South would be better off if it traded its fundamentalist religion, say, for the commercial secularism that seems to be the prevailing "Amer-

191

ican" religion. In my view, at any rate, Mr. Reed's findings about the enduring South stand on their own ample, often amusing, terms—the more so, I should say, in view of the fashionable prevailing advice that all regionalists should go baptize themselves in the national mainstream.

In one of her best essays, the late Flannery O'Connor observed that "in the South the general conception of man is still, in the main, theological...I think it is safe to say that while the South is hardly Christ-centered, it is most certainly Christ-haunted. The Southerner, who isn't convinced of it, is very much afraid that he may have been formed in the image and likeness of God" (to which one must add, the fierce Baptist-Methodist God). For such an observation, Miss O'Connor was licensed by her genius as a storyteller, nothing else. It is pleasant, to me at least, to find that such fancies (as some would call them) may be given statistical foundation. (Not that statistics matter very deeply to the Southerner or his God.)

The same may be said of the perception readily observable in Southern novels at their best and worst: that Southerners are in some sense more prone to violent action than their fellow Americans. Mr. Reed deals modestly with this possibility. From opinion surveys, that is, it may be shown that the Southerner takes a more "permissive" view of firearms and corporal punishment, even when the sample is corrected for regional differences in income, education and rurality. But as Mr. Reed says, in qualification, the data linking these attitudes to "violence" in the larger sense are "embarrassingly tenuous." Never mind. Here again is a certifiable and persistent regional difference, although other Americans are increasingly going in for the pistol and the cudgel.

Without at all compromising the social scientist's exacting standards of inquiry, Mr. Reed renders his findings readable and even entertaining. I pause to note this since he professes a discipline not universally celebrated for the vigor, clarity, or grace of its prose; and all three qualities mark his own.

As for the persisting differences he notes, and whose persistence he probes in the concluding chapter, what shall we say of them? The larger questions are, for me, inspired by Mr. Reed's observation that the South has the "dubious distinction of being in the vanguard of a national trend—it was the most violent region in an increasingly violent nation." Perhaps conquered provinces devour their conquerors, as revolutions do their children. Conceivably Americans today are becoming more tribalistic (more localistic, to use Mr. Reed's term), more given to relaxation and religiosity (as Mr. Reich's "Consciousness III" and the Jesus music flooding the airwaves both suggest), and more tolerant of random violence. Thus trends in the nation at large may draw upon and reinforce what we take to be classic "Southern" attitudes. This is not the place, of course, to inquire what this development portends for all of us. But it is well worth pondering, as one of the many lines of thought provoked by this extraordinarily readable book.

From the Foreword to
The Enduring South, *by John Shelton Reed*
(Univ. of North Carolina Press, 1974, © 1972, D. C. Heath)

Mr. Styron's Nat Turner

When the Virginia-born author of the best-selling *Confessions of Nat Turner* first considered recreating the mind of a rebellious slave, the Negro revolt of our time was unheralded, Malcolm X a youth, Stokely Carmichael and H. Rap Brown unheard of.

If William Styron has written in these "Confessions" a work of literary art that also bears on the rebellious mood of some American Negroes now, its timeliness is an accident.

"Perhaps the reader will wish to draw a moral from this narrative," Mr. Styron writes in a cautionary note, "but it has been my own intention to try to recreate a man and his era and to produce a work that is less an 'historical novel' than a meditation on history."

In drawing this elusive distinction, I suppose Mr. Styron is saying: This novel is first an attempt to tell a story, and while the story of Nat Turner may pertain to our times it was not my intent to write a parable.

That is well and good. But Mr. Styron has nonetheless written a study in the psychology of rebellion that will be read—and examined—as such.

As a Styron enthusiast, I brought to *The Confessions of Nat Turner* a solid conviction that his precocious first novel, "Lie Down In Darkness," has few peers in American fiction. But I also brought to it the unshaken conviction that historical fiction—a "meditation on history," if you prefer—can never rival biography at its best as a medium of historical portraiture. Sometimes, as in Margaret Yourcanar's "Hadrian's Memoirs," or in Thorton Wilder's "The Ides of March," the novel supplements and enriches our understanding of historical personalities; but only that.

Of course, the case for a historical "meditation" on Nat Turner is stronger than usual. For despite good intentions, historians (most of them white) have made non-persons of American slaves, even the famous ones, and Turner is no exception. Primary accounts of his career are sketchy and, as Mr. Styron has said elsewhere, may be mastered in a long afternoon.

Nonetheless, a bias is a bias, and I couldn't avoid reading Mr. Styron's novel on two levels simultaneously—not only as a work of imaginative storytelling, but also as an attempt to render plausible the sensibility of a noted rebel slave. Willy-nilly, then, Mr. Styron's book raises a double problem for me: Do its characters, we ask, have not only literary but historical credibility?

Forgetting the historical background, Mr. Styron's Nat Turner, considered simply as a fictional hero, seems to me wholly credible—rounded, living, breathing, if a bit disordered in his mind. Some of his followers, on the other hand, have an occasional nuance of Stepin Fetchit—indicating the poverty of our literary tradition in respect of credible individual Negroes, bond or free. In any case, Nat Turner as a story is superb.

As a "meditation on history," Mr. Styron's novel seems to me to have flaws that are interesting to discuss precisely because, as a novel, it is so fine. The reviewers have been ecstatic, as they sould be, but when disturbed at all they seem disturbed that Mr. Styron had made himself Nat Turner, in the sense that Flaubert could say, "I am Madame Bovary." Styron, that is, endows Nat Turner, Southampton County Negro slave, with his own sensibility. Some critics find this presumptuous. They ask if a free contemporary white man may indeed feel himself into the anguished mind of a black man held as a chattel. Surely, the answer to such a query is that faced with bondage a white man would react to it as a sensitive black man did, so that the problem is not a racial one as such. Indeed, it is curious that some critics who would loudly decry the old racialist canard that Negroes are of inferior human sensibility should raise that point.

No, the real problem with Nat Turner, I think, is that his motivation is ambiguously established. If ambiguity will do in life, in art or history it leaves us unsatisfied. Mr. Styron's portrayal of Nat Turner's mind is essentially Freudian. He shows

194

not only how petty uncharities and betrayals wounded and disillusioned Turner, he also hints broadly and repeatedly that Turner's rebelliousness is compensation for thwarted lust. Turner himself killed only once during the bloodbath he instigated—a kindly and literate young woman named Margaret Whitehead. As Turner awaits the gallows, the divine voice having fallen silent, Styron has him muse ruefully over the Whitehead killing, and accompanies his rue with a sexual fantasy about her.

Such intimations are not, perhaps, without point. But what is the point? Turner's dammed-up sensuality is a major theme, woven through the metaphor and incident of the novel. My quarrel is not that Styron relates this to Turner's rebellion, but that he explores it hesitantly and inconclusively. Is he telling our post-Freudian age that Turner's wrath (and perhaps his religious fanaticism) are compensatory mechanisms? That if rebels had an orderly sex life they would be quiet? Styron, I think, toys with this theme without exploring it.

The second problem with his Nat Turner lies simply in the mechanics of the narrative. To probe Turner's mind so richly, Styron endows him with a dispassionate insight into his own fantasies that strikes me as precocious if not, for a man otherwise portrayed as a religious fanatic, unbelievable.

It is a bit unfair to mention it, really. For obviously if Styron had made Turner a one-dimensional fanatic—as simpleminded in believing himself called to slaughter and vengeance as he may have been—he would be dull to read about, perhaps with Eichmann another hollow monster. At any rate, Turner is the most dispassionate fanatic imaginable.

As a story, then, as a self-portrait, *The Confessions of Nat Turner* is rich. As a "meditation on history," a study of the intriguing interplay among fanaticism, religion and sex, I find the novel curiously unrealized. But those who begin with a bias are usually able to find evidence to sustain it; and I did. Mr. Styron has written a great tale. But of its historical verisimilitude, I have my doubts.

—November 27, 1967

The Reticences of Henry James

In good writing, we learn very early, a table is never just a table; it is a Chippendale table. Be *specific!* It is a golden rule that we plodders ignore at our peril; but it is one of many conventionalities of the craft that Henry James constantly defied.

You could build a whole theory of James' magic (or madness, as some feel) around the theme of unspecificity. Or so it struck me during a recent escapist binge of reading James: a predispostion which I luckily acquired years ago, before learning that he is supposed to be unreadable.

Henry James was what F. Scott Fitzgerald, in another connection, called a great "taker-outer" of a writer. To some tastes, though not to mine, he takes out too much and relies too much on suggestion and implication.

Consider some examples, at random: In *The Ambassadors*, the novel he liked best, James introduces the heir of a New England manufacturing fortune. While hinting that the source of his hero's wealth is vaguely embarrassing, he never tells us what the manufactured item is, only that it is some "vulgar little thing." In a famous tale, "The Death of The Lion," his subject is an author in the throes of devourment by hunters of literary lions. This author, we learn, has rejected the vogue for "larger latitudes" in storytelling that some of his fashionable colleagues are exploring. One is left to guess just what obscurely shocking territory these "larger latitudes" embrace.

In "The Aspern Papers," one of my favorites, a prurient scholar stalks the aged and dying friend of a famous poet in a damp old Venetian palace. He intrigues to put his hands on the poet's letters to her, thus to discover the secrets of their celebrated relationship. But the nature of that relationship, needless to say, is never actually specified and in the upshot the intrigue of this "publishing scoundrel" is discovered and the letters are—naturally—burned unread.

Henry James's stories overflow with unread letters, plotless books, nameless diseases, obscure disabilities, mysterious relationships, undeciphered designs, ominous obsessions, unplumbed depths, unmentionable vices, anonymous evils and hallucinatory ghosts.

"The Turn of the Screw," possibly James's most popular tale, is a thriller that leaves the reader to guess whether the spell of evil sensed by the children's anxious governess is real or imaginary; and "The Beast In The Jungle," his greatest fable, tells the story of a man obsessed with dread of his destiny—which turns out to be, in fact, the destiny of having no destiny.

As James's art matured—he died, aged 73, in 1916—he retreated all the more deeply into delicate, teasing, sometimes comic reticences. With the development of his difficult and opaque "late style," he drew a new screen around the solid textures of his world. His brother, the philosopher William James, admonished him in a letter to come more explicitly to the point.

"You know how opposed your whole 'third manner' of execution is to the literary ideals which animate my crude...breast...yours being to avoid naming it straight, but by dint of breathing and sighing all round and round it, to arouse in the reader...the illusion of a solid object...wholly out of impalpable materials, air, and the prismatic inferences of light, ingeniously focused by mirrors upon empty space. But you do it, that's the queerness!...The method seems perverse: Say it *out,* for God's sake..."

Henry James ignored the advice—all those wonderful tales he wrote about the loneliness and vulnerability of the storyteller echo his determination to do it his way. He did not "say it out" but persisted in the new style even at the peril of an absurdity that Max Beerbohm wonderfully parodied in "The Mote In The Middle Distance."

Yet the style, for all its obscurity, can be very evocative, especially when a vivid and unexpected picture suddenly flashes out of the mist. In his parable of journalism, "The Papers," a young London journalist speaks of the publicity-madness of the penny-paper era and how it brings subjects to him: "...They leap straight out of the water themselves, leap in their thousands and come flopping, open-mouthed and goggle-eyed to one's very door."

No doubt this eccentric and teasing unspecificity—together with the misconceptions and prejudice—keeps James too little read today. Ours is an age of explicitness, of telling all, and we have lost that sense of the excitement of the unseen, the implicit, the suggested, that the Victorians had. James belonged to an age of concealment when so much was clad that James characters can discuss the beauty of a female foot with all the avidity *Playboy* can muster for an acre or two of flesh.

But slowly, with the help of discriminating critics we are coming to realize that hesitant, sly, scrupulous, finicking, inexplicit old Henry James had a keen eye for the modern malaise. No modern storyteller has a more richly-furnished or subtly ob-

197

served world to show. But the solidity of the furnishings is another matter entirely. You must not imagine that Henry James's chairs are there to be sat upon, the books to be read, or the haunting spirits ever to be pinned down.

—*May 26, 1977*

Tennessee

My first and only brush with a Tennessee Williams play, except as a spectator, was as follows.

The student dramatic club at Oxford decided to put on "Summer and Smoke" and Southerners resident there were called in to coach the actors in the Southern drawl.

It seemed to work. All went swimmingly on opening night until the hero, a young doctor, shouts to his hovering mama (all Williams heroes, like the late playwright, seem to have had hovering mamas): "Do you-all 'spect me to spend the rest of mah life in a laBOrat'ry?"

There was muffled mirth among the Southern advisers, who knew that from New Orleans to Richmond, from Little Rock to Savannah, you will not find such a place, only "labba-tories."

Still it was and is easier for non-Southerners to get the drawl right than to catch the exact pitch of Williams' dramatic tone. He was one of us, warts and all, and we loved him for it. But that strange Southern blend of sadness, comedy and hysteria seems to have strained the emotional registers of outsiders.

If the Senate was, as they used to say, the South's revenge for losing the Civil War, Tennessee Williams' plays (and recent Southern literature generally) ran the Senate a close second. We found out quite early that you can tease the socks off the Yankees.

Whoever heard of so many bizarre places, with so many entertaining misfits? The inner music of "Night of the Iguana," or "Cat On A Hot Tin Roof," so clear to the native ear, was an everlasting puzzle to outlanders. They took Williams too seriously at one level and not seriously enough at another.

If you ventured far enough into the steamy, dangerous South, would you really cross a border into a country inhabited by Big

Daddies and Maggies, Blanche Duboises and Amanda Wing-fields—all counseled, at occasional intervals, by intoxicated Episcopal clergymen?

No, not exactly; there was no such alarming place. Indeed, Williams and the best of the other Southern writers—William Faulkner, Flannery O'Connor, Eudora Welty—succeeded too well, making their imaginary South more vivid that the "real" one.

It could be weird to the point of exasperation. After hearing the hair-raising tale of Col. Thomas Sutpen (in Faulkner's novel), a Canadian gasps: "So he just wanted a grandson. That was all he was after. Jesus, the South is fine, isn't it…It's better than Ben Hur."

By good bourgeois standards, the height of Tennessee Williams' great tease was the creation of Blanche Dubois, the collapsed belle of "A Streetcar Named Desire," perhaps the most memorable stage character of her sex since Lady Macbeth.

There was a lot of the South and Southern fantasy in Blanche, who says, "I don't want realism, I want magic." There is also a universal familiarity. Wherever a lonely woman is hurt by life and folly but sustained by grand imaginings, there you have Blanche Dubois. The reality may be assignations in a seedy hotel, but the sustaining magic is the lost home place Belle Reve ("beautiful dream"), crowded with "gentleman callers." One of them has even gone to Texas and struck oil and will someday return to carry Blanche off to the happy life to which her station entitles her. Unfortunately, the people from the asylum get there first.

In one sense, you could say that Blanche Dubois is grotesque, but in another very lifelike. Williams put a lot of himself into her, and into the family of "The Glass Menagerie," his first great success. Tom Wingfield, who works in the shoe warehouse for $65 a month but writes poetry on shoebox lids and dreams of the heroic life, is unmistakably Williams.

"Man," says he, "is by instinct a lover, a hunter, a fighter, and none of those instincts are given much play at the warehouse." His mother's response—Williams knew our Southern puritanism as well as our hedonism—is that instincts are for monkeys and pigs, not "Christian adults."

But she has a wonderful talent for missing the point. Most people have to settle for the shoe warehouse, or other places, where heroic instincts, poetry and magic get little play. That's where Tennessee Williams served so well—to enlarge the sense of life, to amuse, to tap buried emotions, to tell the truth that is bigger than "reality."

—March 4, 1983

James Dickey at Large

From the broad terrace a dozen or so early guests savored the early spring air, gazing down over a manicured lawn where some fleecy bird dog of obscure breed with a funny little whip of a tail stalked a robin. "From this distance, he almost looks like a sheep," someone said. "Perfect."

It was a fine setting for poetry—pastoral poetry, perhaps. It was a pastoral scene, comfortably suburban, but we were waiting there for James Dickey, whose poetry is not pastoral but usually violent—sharks hooked and fought bloodily in the surf; stewardesses falling from airplanes; nurses with blood on their uniforms; bruises and bandages and gyrating buckdancers.

Mr. Dickey, who teaches English at the University of South Carolina, is probably the country's best-known poet now, and perhaps the best as well. He has the reputation of a roistering figure on the college lecture circuit and indeed his approach can be sensed, as a gathering electric storm is sensed in the stirring of distant pine trees.

On this day he had been at large, as one might put it, since early morning, when he had refused a carefully-prepared breakfast of fresh croissants in favor of four cans of beer. Now, awaiting his arrival in this peaceful suburban back yard, one felt poised as if on the top doorstep of a storm cellar for the approaching cyclone.

Mr. Dickey, who stands about six-foot-six in his stocking feet, does not so much enter a gathering as burst upon it, teetering slightly from day-long libation, sweeping the black Stetson hat from his head in cavalier salute to all the pretty girls. He is especially a connoisseur of hairdos. "Honey! Wut booti-ful hai-ah! Did you do it yo-sef?" Then, with a sweep of the arm, he indicates another girl, entering just behind him: "Have you met mah ma-ad mistress?"

We had come to meet him in mingled curiosity and apprehension, too, having once written a mildly condescending magazine review of the novel, "Deliverance," that has lately earned him a fortune, and later the worst happened: He remembered. "You bastard!" he shouted, then laughed and began to talk about mutual friends and what could be done to promote their books.

At the dinner table, picking at his food, Mr. Dickey talks about football, which he played at Clemson, and the difference between coaches that badger their players (whom he dislikes) and the coaches that quietly stir up their players to win out of sheer expectation (whom he likes). He mimics William F. Buckley Jr., recalling his appearance on Mr. Buckley's program. "Firing Line" when he, Dickey, wanted to talk literature but Buckley wanted to discuss "the state of the national spirit." Next, he moves on to the banalitites of a Saturday television program, "The American Sportsman," and parodies the meager exchanges that occur over fallen moose or hooked salmon. ("It's a big one, isn't it?" "Sure is." "Golly what a fish." "It sure is.") All the while, he has been glancing at his watch. "Got to peak at 8 o'clock, haven't we?" Mr. Dickey asks of no one in particular.

The Dickey platform style is thoroughly entertaining theater, a merely heightened version of the dinner-table Dickey, with recitations of his poetry framed by deft, ribald commentaries. He has quickly won the audience, carefully depositing the black Stetson with its feathered hatband in a corner. Dickey's poems, which are even better in the hearing than in the reading—which is saying something—have reclaimed contemporary poetry from the obscurity and allusiveness of the modernist movement, though with no sacrifice of impact. They are earthy, vivid, dramatic, sensual, full of violent imagery. They deal with love-making in an auto junkyard; the death of Vince Lombardi (all Lombardi's great players are imagined rising in a vision of cast-off videotape and blue and yellow bruises to accuse him of not teaching them how to lose); the acrobatics of an Air Force buddy in the Pacific theater 30 years ago, who was beheaded by the Japanese ("And the headsman broke down in a blaze of tears, in that light/Of the thin, long human frame/Upside down in its own strange joy.")

Like all good poets, James Dickey falls in love with his best lines. They make him, as he recites them, draw his breath, stop and grin expectantly. "Parking lot of the dead," he intones in the poem about the assignation in a cast-off Pierce-Arrow. Pause. Grin. He ends the reading with a passage from "Deliverance," the scene in which three survivors of a canoeing misadventure shoot helplessly down a wild river to safety, and the prose takes on all the exciting cadences of Dickey's poetry.

We had not known quite what to expect, since Mr. Dickey is a poet pursued by a hundred gossipy anecdotes. But beneath the blustery jollity and the Claghorn there is the good-hearted innocence of the pure artist. By making news of himself, Dickey has made news of poetry again, as Robert Frost used to do. But it is a long way from the flinty New England-y presence of Robert Frost to the hijinks of this very knowing poet of North Georgia.

—*March 16, 1973*

Homage to John Stuart Mill

On the wise advice of the late Randall Jarrell, I read "at whim," and a whimsical excursion into Victorian literature recently brought me for the first time in 20 years to John Stuart Mill's *Autobiography*. Like the autobiographies of Benjamin Franklin and Henry Adams, it is a classic in which a supremely rational man seeks terms with his age.

What especially interested me is that Mill's pilgrimage, that of a Victorian liberal, foreshadowed so many of the dilemmas of our time.

Mill was the heir—in some ways the victim too—of a determined father, James Mill. The son's recollection that sticks with most of us is how he was force-fed on Greek and Latin at a precocious age. Greek poetry, too, was part of the younger Mill's diet; but it was not until a painful "mental crisis" struck him in the middle years that he felt a void in his education: It had been intellectual at the expense of the sensibilities.

From his father, disciple of Jeremy Bentham and a leading "utilitarian" thinker, John Stuart Mill imbibed all the prejudices characteristic of the generous and liberal mind. His father had subjected religion to the test of rationality and found it wanting; accordingly, he transmitted no "superstition" to his son. "I am thus," writes John Stuart Mill, "one of the very few examples, in this country, of one who has, not thrown off religious belief, but never had it." In the place of religion was left a striking and universal feature of the Victorian temper—a moral earnestness of such intensity that to encounter it is almost to feel a monster of flippancy.

The Mills believed—the father till his death, the son until

202

he found himself drifting into spiritual listlessness and turned to Wordworth and Coleridge for a belated education of the feelings—that the age needed analysis above all—analysis and more analysis. The drastic improvement of society (e.g., political reform, the disestablishment of the church, popular education, the emancipation of women, even the "improvement" of human beings) awaited only rational inquiry. Their model was science, their intellectual heroes the French "philosophers" who had put 18th Century France under the microscope. And above all the Mills believed—it was the fundamental of their creed—that the mind knows what it knows only by experience. From this followed an intemperate optimism, human nature and habit being malleable and improvable.

"We saw clearly," writes Mill, "that to render any…social transformation either possible or desirable, an equivalent change of character must take place in the uncultivated herd who now compose the laboring masses"—yes, Mill can exhibit a startling intellectual snobbery and priggishness—"…Education, habit, and the cultivation of the sentiments, will make a common man dig or weave for his country, as readily as fight for his country." This process, he acknowledged, would be slow: "But the hindrance is not in the essential constitution of human nature."

It is in all essentials an enduring creed, familiar to us after a century—analytic, secular, empirical, reformist, optimistic and in some degree presumptuous too.

What continues to be interesting about John Stuart Mill—what makes his *Autobiography* an enduring masterpiece—is the capacity for self-doubt that in due course brought him up against the limits of optimism. At a certain stage, his father's creed came to seem not so much false, not so much disappointing as a guide to political reform, as one-sided and incomplete. John Stuart Mill had an uncommon spirit of inquiry, a capacity for exploring and appreciating what he could not believe. Even when certain opinions seemed false, "the discovery of what it was that made them plausible would be a benefit to truth." This is the spirit of his masterly essay on Samuel T. Coleridge, surely the most generous appreciation of a conservative mind ever written by a liberal. It is also the spirit that pervades his famous essay, "On Liberty." Never has a man possessing so many final answers so strongly entertained the possibility that they might not be final, after all!

Any brief appreciation of Mill's autobiography leaves its riches unexhausted, but the point is simple. The timelessness of Mill illustrates, I think, the fallacy of "relevance," that breathless measure of value to which we attach such exaggerated importance. In reading Mill, we preview the intellectual thrashings of our age, our own constant re-invention of the wheel, intellectually speaking. In Mill's struggle with the legacy of English utilitarianism, all the dilemmas of liberalism are foreshadowed—the resistance of "human nature" to reform, the pitfalls of shallow optimism, the limits of the secular and analytic disposition, the neglect of the institution and feelings, even the snobbery and condescension. I do not plan to leave Mill's *Autobiography* unread for another 20 years.

—March 24, 1977

Heroic Fidelity

It is an irony that William Faulkner clearly did not foresee and might have deplored: he who said it was his ambition to be "as a private individual, abolished and voided from history, leaving it markless," has now been portrayed in one of the longest literary biographies in English, his private life exhaustively exposed in two hefty volumes that with index and notes total 2,232 pages.* The length and price would perhaps console him, since they may limit the audience to Faulkner devotees of some affluence.

Faulkner *might* deplore it, I say. One never knows in his case which of the many masks and poses echoed the bedrock of his complicated character. Was it, indeed, the fetishist of privacy? Was it the war hero with the gimpy leg who returned from his Canadian hitch in the RAF after the First War, claiming to have a metal plate in his head, though he didn't and hadn't in fact heard a shot fired in anger? Was it the puckish poseur who once asked companions in Charlottesville, Va., to drop him by the house to pick up his "Sears Roebuck" false teeth, or who once informed a nosy lady that in the film of *Sanctuary* he would "play the corncob"? Was it the Mississippi rustic, "farmer," and huntsman whom it took a full-scale family intrigue to produce in Stockholm to receive his Nobel Prize? The Charlottesville foxhunter of the later years? True, then, invasions of his privacy

Faulkner: A Biography
By Joseph Blotner (Random House 1974)

aroused William Faulkner to furious journalistic fulminations on the death of the "American dream," yet the privacy fetish may have been at least half a pose, like all the others. And when he befriended Joseph Blotner, then a young assistant professor of English at the University of Virginia, did he not recognize in this eager shepherd of a lion the ambitions of a Boswell?

The result, starkly imposing as the Firth of Forth bridge, is as formidable a job of literary detection and documentation as any since Boswell lurked at Dr. Sam Johnson's elbow in the coffee houses of eighteenth century London; and the reading of the one is akin to the painting of the other. It is also an appealing and sometimes moving portrait, one of the best since Boswell immortalized the Great Cham of Literature. For Blotner's zeal, fortitude, and thoroughness I for one am grateful. That would hardly need saying, ordinarily, but influential reviewers have committed the fallacy of begrudging the very scope of the work, apart from its content: as if the designer of a great battleship had been faulted for failing to launch a nutshell.

Whatever its length, the test of a biography, and maybe the only test that really counts, is whether the writer has done his duty to truth and form and has given credible and authentic shape to his subject. That Blotner has done, and as to detail almost faultlessly. In more than 1,800 pages of narrative, I counted two trivial errors: Lord Russell, the very English philosopher, becomes a "white-maned Welshman"; and since he was white-maned, if not Welsh, even this error is half true. Charles Wilson, Eisenhower's Defense Secretary, is identified as a former president of GE, not GM. Those more familiar than I with the minutiae of Faulkner's life and career may discover other slips of detail; they are nearly inevitable in a work of this scope. But I did not.

A further question about a monumental biography is whether it substantially reshapes the existing public image or reputation of the subject. Blotner's does not. From briefer studies, including distinguished sketches by Malcolm Cowley, James Meriwether, Cleanth Brooks, and Michael Millgate, we knew that Faulkner was a very private if not reclusive man who slaved at his writing table as dedicatedly as any American-born novelist since Henry James; that he was, in the best sense, intensely provincial; that his work, in part by reason of his own zeal for privacy, went unnoticed by the larger American reading public for perhaps the first two thirds of his career; that early popular critics, such as Henry Seidel Canby and Clifton Fadiman, dismissed him with maddening flippancies or pointless moralizing, to which he fortunately paid no mind.

We also knew that he enjoyed among family, friends, neighbors, agents, and editors a reputation for courtliness and generosity quite extraordinary. These characteristics are all confirmed, some in heart-rending detail. Blotner's principal contribution, then, is to take this almost spectral Faulkner, with its blurred lines and faint colors, and to daub in the highlights and shadows and cross-hatchings, the richer hues, so that at length a figure emerges into a man and a prototype into an artist.

Faulkner, as here depicted, was a writer cast by both heritage and ambition in an heroic mold, a character almost un-American in his self-possession and independence. He looked back to ancestors from the Scottish Highlands who after the lost cause of Culloden immigrated to America, bringing only their kilts and claymores. Whether this was fact or myth scarcely matters; this was Faulkner's heritage as he saw it: full of heroic fidelity and a bit wild. His paternal grandfather, Colonel William Falkner (his grandson was the first of the family to add the "u") was a Confederate cavalryman and a writer of minor note. On his career and his values as handed down in family lore, his poetry-writing grandson—"Count No'Count" whiling away the Oxford hours in tattered tweeds—patterned his own early ambitions. A magazine writer, one of the many who braved the screen that William Faulkner threw up around himself, was not alone in sensing "the airs of an ancient regime" in the secluded master of Rowan Oak. Blotner writes extensively about Faulkner's ancestry and immediate family. It is well along in volume one— page 246, to be exact—that he winds through the family tree down to Faulkner's first sale: a poem, to *The New Republic*.

Blotner, by the way, dispels any notion that Faulkner, the provincial by heritage, was a literary naïf or fauvist—another pose he sometimes struck. From the outset he was a deeply read, conscious, self-disciplined artist who incidentally drew upon the history, events, and people of North Mississippi because he knew them best. This land and people were his raw material, he explained to Malcolm Cowley, because "I...don't have time in one life to learn another one and write at the same time...Life is phenomenon but not a novelty, the same frantic steeplechase toward nothing everywhere and man stinks the same stink no matter where in time."

Countless details and episodes of peripheral importance might be mentioned, if space permitted: his affairs as tutor and would-be lover with several young women writers; his bouts with alcohol; his generosity to friends and family; his love of horses; his travels and friendships. I single out one of them—his Hollywood experience—because Blotner's patient discussion of Faulkner the moviemaker seems to me a significant addition to Faulkner lore. In the sideline of movie scriptwriting, as in any distraction from his serious work, Faulkner was ill at ease. It removed him from home and family for long spells, as he struggled for money to pay debts or to sustain some future siege upon a waiting novel. His imagination was unsuited to the social and artistic conventions of Hollywood in the Thirties and Forties; he was a Michelangelo among the set designers. In 1945, still struggling to make ends meet with a stint in Hollywood, he wrote a screenplay based on a minor novel by Stephen Longstreet. Longstreet, summoned to revise it, recalls that it was "wild, wonderful, mad. Utterly impossible to be made into the trite movie of the period. Bill had kept little but the names and some of the situations of my novel and had gone off on a Faulknerian tour of his own despairs, passions, and storytelling. Today it would be made as a New Wave film." For Faulkner, Hollywood was ultimately a curse and a blessing. He got into impossible contract scrapes; he took sudden unauthorized leaves; he dredged up banalities alien to his talent. Yet it was the movie sale of *Intruder in the Dust*, in 1948, that finally brought him release from financial insecurity.

Where this biography may be faulted a bit—lest I leave the impression that it is flawless—is in Blotner's resolute refusal to play critic, interpreter, or cosmic analyst of either the man or the writer, whether out of diffidence or some other motive I don't know. Better that it not be done that done badly, as criticism is in at least 90 per cent of highly touted "critical" biographies.

If you want to know where, over what stretches of time, from what early seedings, Faulkner's novels and stories grew— if your questions, in other words, are bibliographical—this book is a gold mine. One sees the great works, such as the Snopes trilogy, evolving over the years from germ to whole. If one wonders about the experimental form of early works like *The Sound and the Fury* or *As I Lay Dying*, it is helpful to know just when Faulkner's friend and early patron Phil Stone presented him with a copy of *Ulysses*; the date and gift are duly recorded.

If, however, your curiosities are critical and analytical—or if you want to know in some detail how Faulkner wrote and rewrote, how the creative chemistry worked—you must turn elsewhere. There is still a big job to be done here, notwithstanding Cleanth Brook's excellent critical study of the Yoknapatawpha novels of a decade ago. It will be done in time, no doubt. Blotner traces the origins of every novel and virtually every story with great care; he tells in what mood or necessity, whether of creative ease or in search of a slick magazine fee, it was done; but he has too seldom weighed, measured, and evaluated. And in this single major way the book, despite its appealing evocation of Faulkner the man and its invaluable chronicle of the work, may draw the attacks of those who believe critical analysis to be a central duty of the literary biographer. I am not certain; it often tends to be a bog of boredom, even in a good biography.

Blotner, at all events, has written a monumental study, massive and sedate and finally compelling, equal to the scope of his subject. Of it one may say that if it is not complete, critically speaking, it is certainly indispensable to the enjoyment and study of our finest American writer of prose fiction. As long as the work and memory of William Faulkner are valued, Blotner, his Boswell, must be reckoned with.

—July 5, 1974

A Village Explainer
in Washington

After reading Sherwood Anderson's *Winesburg, Ohio*, Gertrude Stein is said to have delivered the crushing verdict that Anderson "is a village explainer, which is okay if you like villages but if not not."

Perhaps Anderson, if he heard of the remark, felt duly crushed. But those who believe, as I do, that our best American fiction (including the very best, Faulkner's Yoknapatawpha cycle) has a lot to do with village-explaining will find that the comment tells more of Gertrude Stein than of Sherwood Anderson. A formidable critic and patron, Miss Stein failed as a storyteller. Her best novella, *Melanctha*, is read now as an experimental curiosity and that only in college classes. She was a cosmopolite; fiction is almost invariably provincial.

All this, I hasten to explain, is by way of preface to a belated tribute to Mr. Preston Jones, that village explainer from Dallas whose "Texas Trilogy" plays have been justly celebrated all summer by Washington theater critics. The latter naturally dwell for the most part on the theatrical merits of Mr. Jones' Bradleyville plays—merits to which, as an inveterate theater-sleeper, I can attest. I went to see "The Last Meeting of the Knights of the White Magnolia" the other night and it kept me wide awake. Having dozed through some of the great plays in the language, I can offer no higher tribute.

But what I want to consider here are not the special dramatic strengths of Mr. Jones' plays, but their qualities as literature, as pieces that aid us in self-recognition.

Mr. Jones' Bradleyville is a Texas town, a suitably dusty one I fancy. But like Faulkner's Jefferson, Miss., it is observed with an intimacy and fidelity that univeralize, bringing the shock of recognition. Its characters are three-dimensional; they carry resonances of personal history.

The mode of "The Last Meeting of the Knights of the White Magnolia" is gentle farce. We learn enough—though not too much: Mr. Jones is a writer of great economy—about the history of this "brotherhood" and its seedy remnant to understand that its great days are gone. It was one of those thriving white supremacy lodges in which the small-town South and Midwest once abounded; but now in the early 1960s time and change are sweeping over it. Its members have all but forgotten its origins and seem to find it mainly a refuge against their loneliness.

What I liked about Preston Jones' handling of these woebegone "knights" is the nice blend of gentleness and judgment. He quite skillfully intimates to us all that is limited and bigoted in their forlorn attempt to stop time without, however, destroying one's sympathy for their quest for human camaraderic.

This, of course, is where art often fails more didactic writers when they turn to "political" themes. Their worlds become harshly schematic; their characters become uncomplicatedly rotten. And if, moreover, the characters are Southern they often as not mirror that South of "violence and hatred" of which the historian David Donald was writing the other day—"the South where whites kept blacks in slavery for more than two centuries and then held them in segregated serfdom...the South that is thin in culture, suspicious in outlook, and bigoted in ideas."

That South exists—and not just in the Southern region of the U.S.—and it is certainly the South to which Mr. Jones' surviving knights of the White Magnolia belong. It is not their only world, however. As individuals they are too keenly and compassionately observed to be defined by this depressing and dehumanized scheme.

Old Colonel Kinkaid, the gentry's contribution to the lodge, wrapped in mists of senility and World War I military adventure, cannot conceal his esteem for the Negro doorkeeper of his ramshackle hotel. The cynical veneer of Red, the town barkeep, disguises a sharp eye for the social changes that are antiquating this world and rendering its silly rites more than a bit absurd. Asked why one of the more up-to-date Bradleyvillians refuses to join, Red says: "Because he thinks it's a bunch of B—S—," and one suspects that Red himself thinks the same thing.

These are the strengths of village explaining. It shuns the easy stereotyping of role and character that city life foists upon us. Preston Jones knows that in any given lodge of bigots there will be one member who is a pedant about kin and ancestry; another, like the Colonel, who is more passionately and unreasonably prejudiced against the whites in the next village than against the blacks in his own; a merchandizer of booze who has seen too much of what it coaxes from the stiffest people to take their pretenses at face value—or his own.

After seeing what Preston Jones does with the Bradleyville characters, one understands why in a town of transients like Washington the "Texas Trilogy" plays succeed.

These plays recall to us those rich and amusing complexities of places frozen in time and memory that we have, to our loss, left behind.

—*September 2, 1976*

The "Washington novel"

If there were medals for the prevention of cruelty to readers, I would vote to decorate the publishers who rejected Senator James Abourezk's novel about how the Senate works.

I have nothing against Senator Abourezk, I hasten to say. All sorts of potential Tolstoys, including the senator, may be ingloriously muted by rejection slips all the time, though I doubt it. Witness the political novels that actually slip past the Madison Avenue watchdogs. They suggest that a Washington novel must be gosh-awful to be refused the dignity of print.

It was Tolstoy who observed that happy families are all alike but every unhappy family is unhappy in its own way. The reverse seems to hold of Washington novels. Few are good, and every bad one is bad in the usual ways. The plot is a tissue of bizarre improbabilities; the characters are wooden—carved from a bad grade of pine at that; and documentable history is melded with the feeblest invention, often paranoid or cynical or both.

Why is the "Washington novel" so bad, even when written by writers of demonstrated talent? I think it has to do with a basic difference between politicians and artists.

Politics (like the satellite trade of journalism, whose practitioners also find political fiction a temptation) often attracts keen intellects but seldom keen imaginations. Imagination is a handicap in politics. A politician necessarily believes that a mere measure—good energy bill or higher wheat prices—serves some vision of the good society. He believes in improvement, certainly of society and implicitly of human destiny. The imaginative writer is likely to take a less hopeful view of politics—tragic, comic or ironic—and to believe that human nature and destiny are constant and, being constant, are unaffected by measures that absorb the energies and passions of politicians.

There is a subclass—the good bad political novel, as one might say—the novel whose characterizations are knowing and colorful, whose plot is faithful to the observed traits of the political animal, and which is, if not a work of imaginative art, at least an engaging extension of journalism.

The good bad political novel will at least get its documentation right. Unlike a ludicrous Washington novel reviewed across town the other day, it will place the Oval Office in the White House West Wing, get the north-south elevation of Connecticut Avenue right, and spell Sam Ervin's name correctly.

But matters of detail are beside the basic point about political fiction. It is a demanding form. The novel originally brought "news" (*nouvelles*) to the reader. Defoe, who founded the English novel, was a reporter. His *Journal of the Plague Year*, apparently factual, was all invention and artifice; yet the invention was so plausible that the reader felt that he was learning something.

To say no more, the demands of successful novelizing are dramatically greater, now that we are saturated with news. A novel about how the Senate "works," let's say, which Senator Abourezk aspired to publish, must be informative indeed to en-

211

gage our interest as intensely as a good article or memoir. On the other hand, political fiction whose claim on the reader's attention is primarily imaginative must be as good in that way as the best fiction. The Washington novel typically fails both tests: As documentation, as "news" about the world of public affairs, it is stale or gratuitously inaccurate or banal; as imagination, as insight into the "old truths of the human heart in conflict with itself" which William Faulkner identified as the enduring subject of storytelling, it is usually soap opera.

It is conventional to add, at this point, that there is at least one really good American political novel: Robert Penn Warren's *All The King's Men*, a novel "about" Huey P. Long. Is it, however, really "about" Long or Louisiana politics? You will learn far more about both from T. Harry Williams' huge but absorbing biography of the Kingfish. No, *All The King's Men* succeeds as a novel because Mr. Penn Warren was artist enough to build his story not on Louisiana politics *per se* but on the discoveries, illuminations, revelations (largely about himself) that come to the observer-narrator, Jack Burden, a young historian who has apprenticed himself to the life of action. It is a novel about a young man's heart "in conflict with itself" that happens to be set in politics.

All The King's Men is a rule-proving exception because it is not an orthodox political novel. It is a novel about interesting characters who happen to be in politics, as they might be farmers or lawyers. The distinction is too much ignored by those who try to write political novels. But that doesn't seem to trouble the publishers who crank up their presses at the very mention of a scribbling senator.

—October 13, 1977

Manhattan Bumpkin

The late Francis Butler Simkins, historian of the South and no fool, was convinced that there is a New York City conspiracy against Southern writers. He used to make a charming but unpersuasive case for the theory, but it was actually a mild paranoia.

I couldn't help recalling the Simkins theory when I read

Anatole Broyard's smug review of Peter Taylor's new short-story collection, *In The Miro District*, in the New York Times Book Review.

You don't expect contrived sympathy from book reviewers; you do expect that a reviewer will understand the book. I would feel the same if Mr. Taylor came from Michigan, not Tennessee, and Mr. Broyard had been writing in, say, the Atlanta *Journal* instead of the New York *Times*.

Peter Taylor may be the best short-story writer in America at the moment, but he has been described by a sympathetic critic, Jonathan Yardley, as "a principal contender for the peculiar distinction of being the most thoroughly undiscovered major writer in American literature"—a victim, Mr. Yardley believes, of the disappearance of mass-circulation audiences for the short story.

And, I would add, of obtuse reviewers.

Mr. Broyard comes on with an air of authority, dropping literary names and speaking of "Southern syndromes," "the unquiet ghosts of the changing South," of "conventional" versus "universal" Southern fiction. I think he's bluffing.

It is risky to be dogmatic about what a story "means," but Peter Taylor is never murky. Let's look at "The Captain's Son" and what Mr. Broyard says about it: a reading not without a certain specious brilliance.

The story, to simplify, is about an old Nashville-Memphis feud, spanning the generations, which began with an act of political ingratitude. The rivalry goes on, only ostensibly healed, when the son of one party to it marries the granddaughter of the other. It now takes a marvelously subtle and comic form: a struggle over what we would call "life-styles." The Nashvillians frown on Memphis people as lotus-eaters happy in their ostentatious, unseemly idleness (these are the great Depression years), living high on their unearned incomes. When the Captain's son, Tolliver Campbell of Memphis, marries Lila, of Nashville, and moves in with her family there ensues a mighty struggle of wills. Lila's family is bent on putting Tolliver to gainful employment; he, in turn, becomes bent on corrupting Lila in the Memphis fashion, mainly with grog. (The story reminds me of the terribly willful Mrs. Gereth in Henry James' *The Spoils of Poynton*, who burns her exquisitely-furnished house to the ground rather than have it entailed to a Philistine daughter-in law.)

"The Captain's Son" is no more "regional" than the James novella. It is a story of similar theme, differentiated by setting, a story about human willfulness and the urge to dominate and domesticate human differences and tastes. Mr. Broyard sees only

213

the regional bric-a-brac, finds Tolliver Campbell a "passive carrier of his culture...of genteel Memphis mores" and searches vainly for "the inscrutable imperatives that dominate Tolliver's life."

What does all that mean? I think it means Mr. Broyard doesn't understand the story.

Notwithstanding his bogus air of authority, Mr. Broyard misses the rich comedy of the story and can hardly see the play for the props. He is not the first critic to misunderstand Mr. Taylor through vain searching for the individualized *angst* of modern fiction.

You can't read Peter Taylor accurately unless you see that he is entertained by the conflicts of a settled society. Mr. Broyard is offended by a pattern of life unfamiliar to him. He finds Peter Taylor's fictional world "as uninteresting as a society column in the local newspaper," with its "meaningless, silly local eccentricities, like the bizarre rituals of certain Masonic lodges."

When a reviewer can write a sentence like that, he has no nose for fiction, which always springs from the intimate, the particular, the local. Any settled society may strike an unsympathizing outsider as "silly" and "eccentric," but it is "uninteresting" or "meaningless" only to those whose horizons are constricted by West Side myopia and psychoanalysis. The hollowness of Mr. Broyard's critical canons would be obvious if he had dared write of Faulkner or Balzac as he does of Peter Taylor.

By his odd standards, what is "sillier" than the ambitions of Colonel Sutpen, or more "eccentric" than the intrigues of Cousin Bette? No, Mr. Broyard finds the oddities and quirks of Mr. Taylor's Tennesseans beneath the sympathetic attention of a busy New York critic ("...there is in his manner a complacent, and sometimes irritating, assumption that you are more than willing to hear him out"). They are accordingly beyond his understanding.

It may not be regional prejudice, but if it isn't what would you call it?

—April 14, 1977

Mr. Blatty's Pop Demons

My friend Dorothea Wright, a superb movie reviewer, takes the broadminded view that we all ought to see movies, however trashy or absurd, that make it big at the box office—this, she argues, to get a handle on trends in popular taste. In this ecumenical spirit, I recently saw "The Exorcist," then spent several hours reading the novel by William Peter Blatty.

Here is a novel that went through 13 printings in hardback, is now in its 20th paperback printing, and which a New York Times reviewer calls "terrifying" and "as superior to most books of its kind as an Einstein equation is to an accountant's column of figures."

Maybe that qualifying phrase, "most books of its kind," is the catch-22 of this encomium; for if "The Exorcist" terrified the Times reviewer he or she is easily terrified and one wonders what effects Grimm's fairy tales or "The Hunting of the Snark" would have. My own reaction was more like that of the Life Magazine reviewer, who confessed that he had "consumed" the novel "as if it were a bottomless bag of popcorn." It is popcorn all right; but even the Life reviewer had the impudence to be reminded of Poe and Mary Shelley.

Still, Dorothea is right. Those who pretend to some interest in the quality of American fiction and the state of public taste ought to read one of these literary consumer goods occasionally. They have all the built-in obsolescence of a Detroit automobile; and we ought to ask ourselves how a tale told with such incompetence could sell out a score of editions while the masters of demonic obsession, from Dostoyevski to James, from Thomas Mann to Flannery O'Connor, gather dust on the shelves.

It is the perennial question—as baffling as the high school student who sits with an Irving Wallace potboiler concealed behind his literature book while the class discusses "King Lear."

Some years ago, Dwight Macdonald wrote a sassy essay in which he described something called "midcult," of which, I dare say, "The Exorcist" would be a classic example. A midcult novel is one that deals pretentiously but superficially with a potentially serious subject—in this case demonic possession and the nature of evil—and thereby feebly apes high culture. These condescending distinctions have always bothered me; for I believe, with the late Randall Jarrell, that the world of sensibility, far from being the esoteric playground of the happy few, is actually a democracy, accessible to anyone of reasonable intelligence and feeling with the will to train and use them.

Mr. Blatty, we read, is the holder of a master's degree in English literature from the George Washington University. It is not a glowing recommendation for the G. W. English department. You might assume that a master of English literature would exhibit at least a nodding acquaintance with the best treatments of diabolism and possession in our literature. He would have pondered the supernatural elements in Shakespeare's "Hamlet" or "Macbeth"; he would know Henry James's "The Turn of the Screw"; he might even be familiar with the most ambitious attempt by a 20th Century novelist to deal with diabolic possession: Thomas Mann's "Dr. Faustus."

But if Mr. Blatty has read or considered these works, they have left not a trace of influence on "The Exorcist." One can pass over, in amused silence, the opening premonition of the aging priest-archeologist who ultimately performs the exorcism. (That premonition, we read, "clung to his back like chill wet leaves," a bizarre sensation indeed).

A more serious defect is the poverty of imaginative technique at every crucial juncture of the novel. Every time we come to the edge of some real issue—for instance, that between an overactive imagination and objective reality—Blatty takes refuge in psychiatric jargon.

As for Mr. Blatty's demons, who are so unsporting as to attack a child of 12, and who manage to bump off two priests before fleeing the premises, they are recognizable by their fetid breath, their iciness, and their wicked capacity for making the child babble in foul language and urinate on her mother's best carpet.

To a good, clean-living boy like Mr. Blatty, these bodily afflictions may seem quite sinister and shocking; but they are surely pop-demons invented by a Madison Avenue advertising agency intent on selling mouthwashes, with some help from the Watch and Ward Society. There is simply no sense that the real monsters and terrors of our age are the spiritual ones that produced Auschwitz, My Lai and other bestial events.

Even old John Milton, in his ornate way, understood far more than Blatty about the nature of diabolism. He equipped his Satan and lesser demons with a pride, a guilefulness, an amiable skin-deep attractiveness, that could be imagined corrupting the innocent. They are not repellent mechanical devils who jump, as whim prompts them, from one skin to another.

It would be a happy world if the reality of evil had produced nothing worse than wet spots on the living room rug, or green vomit, and not gas-jet shower rooms. It is too bad that Mr. Blatty has conned millions of readers into a kind of dime-store Hallowe'en view of the demonic, where possession comes and goes as capriciously as a virus and reflects no permanent stain on our mixed natures.

It is also no wonder that he has accomplished this trick with resources so meager that it would bring a blush to the cheek of any reader of Edgar Allen Poe. Poe at least knew where to look for real demons.

—February 8, 1974

Sherlock and Dixie

"Students of criminology will remember the analogous incidents at Godno, in Little Russia, in the year '66, and of course there are the Anderson murders in North Carolina, but this case has some features which are entirely its own."

No, that isn't an excerpt from the recent FBI report placing Charlotte's murder rate first in the nation. It is a comment by Sherlock Holmes on the famous mystery of "The Hound of the Baskervilles."

A recent excursion, the first in many years, into the annals of Dr. Doyle's famous detective persuades me of the keenness of Edmund Wilson's feeling: while most mystery stories are a bore, the Sherlock Holmes stories possess a fascination independent of the subject of sleuthing, simply as stories. A part of that fascination for a student of Southern lore is that whenever the fabulous detective tackles an American mystery, often as not Dixie provides the backdrop.

Readers of "The Hound of the Baskervilles" won't find "the Anderson murders in North Carolina" in any history of the state, but the Southern reader of "The Five Orange Pips" will, of course, know all too well of the Ku Klux Klan, with which it deals.

As Holmes' collaborator and chronicler, Dr. Watson, tells the story, a young man appears at Baker Street one September day in 1887. He is the nephew and heir of a onetime Florida planter. The young man provides this brief on his uncle: "Uncle Elias emigrated to America when he was a young man and became a planter in Florida, where he was reported to have done

217

very well. At the time of the war he fought in Jackson's army, and afterwards under Hood, where he rose to be a colonel. When Lee laid down his arms my uncle returned to his plantation, where he remained for three or four years. About 1869 or 1870 he came back to Europe and took a small estate in Sussex." His uncle, the account continues, left Florida out of "aversion to Negroes and...dislike of the Republican policy in extending the franchise to them. He was a singular man, fierce and quick-tempered, very foul-mouthed when he was angry, and of a most retiring disposition."

Uncle Elias is a marked man, and in token of his fate has received by mail an envelope marked with the letters "KKK" and containing five dried orange pips. With his usual deductive powers, exercised, as Sherlock Holmes fans will recall in nocturnal trances aided by a mound of pipe tobacco, Holmes discovers the significance of the mysterious initials as well as the portent of the dried orange seeds. And by a careful examination of sailing-ship schedules to and from Savannah, Ga., Holmes also persuades himself of the identity of the murderers, from whom, alas, he is too late to save Uncle Elias.

Like all Holmes stories, "The Five Orange Pips" is a pudding of historical and quasi-historical detail, to which the great sleuth may apply his supernatural deductive powers.

It is interesting to speculate on the origins of this story, for we know that Holmes's creator, Dr. Doyle, worked as a ship's surgeon for a time and may well have visited Southern ports. It is obvious as well that Doyle knew the rudiments of Klan history, since in just the years Uncle Elias fled Florida the original Klan was losing its grip on "respectable" people in the South. Gen. Nathan Bedford Forrest, its first imperial wizard, had quit and at President Grant's request was urging others to do likewise.

The business of the orange seeds, however, appears to be invention. Authorities on Klan history find no parallel to the encyclopedia passage quoted by Holmes to Watson: "Its outrages were usually preceded by a warning sent to the marked man in some fantastic but generally recognized shape—a sprig of oak leaves in some parts, melon seeds or orange pips in others."

In the late "Memoirs" of Sherlock Holmes, Watson tells us of another episode with Southern antecedents. A distraught young husband, recently married to a widow from Atlanta, enlists Holmes's aid to plumb her strange nocturnal prowlings and to explain the "Yellow Face" (the name of the tale) that appears occasionally in the upper window of a nearby house. The story ends with a shocker. It transpires that the wife's former mar-

218

riage had been to "a man strikingly handsome and intelligent-looking, but bearing unmistakable signs upon his features of African descent."

The hideous "yellow face" is simply a mask worn by the widow's daughter by the previous mixed marriage, who "dark or fair...is my own dear little girlie and her mother's pet." The secret out, it all ends happily enough with the acceptance of the little girl by her astonished stepfather. "I am not a very good man, Effie," he declares, "but I think that I am better one than you have given me credit for being."

Thus unfolds another tale suggesting that along with his innumerable other interests—ranging from opium to spiritualism—the fascinating creator of Sherlock Holmes had informed himself beyond the ordinary on Southern life and taboos in the decades after the Civil War. How he came to do so is a problem which—naturally, Watson—I shall leave to a better detective than I.

—August 1, 1966

Allen Tate and the "Locked-out Ego"

An accurate appraisal of Allen Tate's role in national letters and in the so-called "Southern Renaissance" of the 1920s was hard to come by while he lived, and will be no easier after his death.

He usually went against the grain—a classicist among romantics, a sectionalist among nationalists, an esthete (in no pejorative sense) in a political age, and a man who sighed, among the smokestacks, for the South's agrarian past.

Final appraisal will rest in more expert hands than mine. But it happens that through the good offices of my friends Peter and Eleanor Taylor, I saw something of Mr. Tate in the late Sixties, and some vivid impressions linger.

He had returned to North Carolina, where he'd once taught, and sent word that he liked a piece I had written on the Nashville "Agrarians" and would welcome a talk.

It was late afternoon when we sat down in the little bungalow he was renting for the academic year. He soon produced a bottle of bourbon. He talked brilliantly—memories of Ernest Hemingway and Ford Maddox Ford in Paris, literary politics, his role in the controversial Bollingen Prize to Pound's "Pisan Cantos," criticism, playwrights, modern art, Lyndon Johnson, Vietnam ("a barbaric war") and—of course—the South. I soon laid my notebook aside, fearful of missing something: a mistake, as it proved.

When my lengthy account of our pleasant but foggy conversation appeared two days later, he rang early in the morning.

"A fine piece," he said, "but oh, my dear Mr. Yoder, I've made a dreadful error." My grip on the telephone moistened. If there was an error it must be mine. And error there was. "I did not mean to say that *Flannery O'Connor* wrote in 'baby talk'—I meant to say *Carson McCullers*."

There was no irritation in the soft voice. Mr. Tate was worried only about what Flannery O'Connor's *mother* might think. And he insisted, good naturedly, that *he* had confused the two names: which was most unlikely.

A few days later, at a party, he pointedly rattled the ice in his glass: "Some people," he whispered, "lead lives of quiet intoxication." He had the knack of the genuinely great, to be altogether disarming.

No recent American man of letters was less intoxicated, quietly or otherwise, than Allen Tate. His intelligence shed a dry light. Not even Southern nostalgia intoxicated him, although poems like "Ode To The Confederate Dead," or his fine novel *The Fathers*, or his essay in *I'll Take My Stand*, the "agrarian manifesto," gave that impression when superficially read.

"Ode To The Confederate Dead," a magnificent poem and a decade in the writing, was and is for me one of the touchstones of recent American literature. Like most "modern" poems, it is tautly compressed and ambiguous; and it can be read, at one level, as a full-throated celebration of the Lost Cause. But Mr. Tate himself dispelled that notion in his fascinating essay on the poem, "Narcissus as Narcissus."

He had, he explained, intended a far more fundamental theme than regional nostalgia—no less than "the failure of the human personality to function objectively in nature and society...the remarkable self-consciousness of our age...the locked-in ego."

The locked-in ego? The explanation seems puzzling, but his novel, *The Fathers*, illuminates it as do the many references in

220

his poetry to "the living dead" or the "animated dead," that is, people who just go through the motions of life without living it.

Major Buchan, hero of *The Fathers*, is one of the living— one of those admirably civilized people whose actions spring from a sense of unity and order. He has it all together, as we say. But his son-in-law, George Posey, has no such integrity and is always doing the impulsive, unaccountable thing. All the Poseys, in fact, are afflicted by chaotic egos; they make up their world as they go along. Posey's mother, a recluse absorbed in hypochondria, dies (appropriately?) of fright in the opening weeks of the Civil War. One baroque uncle, a dilettante, scribbles away in his attic on a florid (and, needless to say, unpublishable) "history" of mankind's comeback from the ice age.

The egotistical Poseys are cousins to the unidentified narrator of "Ode To The Confederate Dead," who experiences the same disabling doubts and questions as he meditates on heroism and death in a wind-blown war cemetery at twilight.

This contrast—between the life of action in a civilized order and the over-refined life of no fixed definition: a form of life versus a form of death—was, I think, also the key to Tate's agrarianism. The memory he invoked was Southern; that was his own tradition. But geography was incidental.

"Of course I still believe in it," he once said, speaking of what he wrote in the Agrarian manifesto. "But I never thought it would make any kind of political difference. I was interested in a revival of humanism."

"Humanism," I now take him to have meant, in which action and reflection would be at one: the unified sensibility; civilization; the life eternal.

He understood, because he shared, the doubts of "Ode To The Confederate Dead." But that did not lessen his conviction that the modern world had lost something its ancestors had enjoyed: "a formal ebullience of the human spirit in an entire society, not private, romantic illusion." His writing was, I think, a search for clues to this lost unity of sensibility, not only in novels and poetry but in biographies of men of action like Stonewall Jackson and Jefferson Davis. He did not find it, nor could he lay it out programmatically. It could only be evoked, if at all, in the symbolism of art. As with all great lives in letters, it was the form and the beauty of the search that mattered—permanence in a world of contrivance.

—February 15, 1979

Flannery O'Connor's World

When I think of the late Flannery O'Connor, whose collected stories have just been published, I recall Randall Jarrell's graceful observation that a certain poet's work silences comment—that you want to walk through her gallery in a hush, "pointing." In Flannery O'Connor's case one must add, "...and trembling."

If you understand the broad streak of tawdry gentility that remains central to the Southern character, you may suppose why in her later years, crippled and dying of lupus, she hobbled painfully from platform to platform disputing those who called her stories grotesque, gothic or freakish.

It was a gallant try. But probably as vain as if Sophocles had stumped rural Greece, insisting that in "Oedipus Rex" his real subject was not incest or violence but the horror of human pride. Her work speaks for itself in its own terms or not at all.

"Whenever I'm asked why Southern writers particularly have a penchant for writing about freaks," she once said, "I say it is because we are still able to recognize one. To be able to recognize a freak, you have to have some basic conception of the whole man, and in the South the general conception of man is still, in the main, theological...I think it is safe to say that while the South is hardly Christ-centered, it is most certainly Christ-haunted. The southerner, who isn't convinced of it, is very much afraid that he may have been formed in the image and likeness of God."

Again: "I hate to think that in 20 years Southern writers too may be writing about men in gray-flannel suits and may have lost their ability to see that these gentlemen are even greater freaks than what we are writing about now."

Of course, she meant moral freaks—people who have lost their moorings to the divine order of things. In a kind of artistic cunning, she peopled her stories with physical freaks—outlandish bumpkins and fat people, club-footed boys, blind men, decrepit and senile elders—as if to throw the unwary reader off the scent.

Her reputation for grotesquerie undoubtedly began with the publication of her first novel, *Wise Blood,* in 1952—an uncertain and groping work. *Wise Blood* has the authentic touch in places, but unleavened unfluences bulge in its texture and event. Indeed, this tale of the "Christ-haunted" freak Haze Mote is often

222

closer to Erskine Caldwell and *God's Little Acre* than to the supreme tragedienne of "Everything that Rises Must Converge," her last book of stories.

Flannery O'Connor was many persons—a Georgia girl of Savannah and Milledgeville with a drawl so thick that outlanders were baffled by it; a Roman Catholic of a bleakly Jansenist strain; a southerner; a diseased and dying young woman; a lover and farmer of peafowl and guinea-hens; and perhaps the best writer of tragic short stories in English of her age.

All these qualities merge consummately, in a majestic integrity, in the collection, "Everything That Rises Must Converge," published after her death at 39.

In their hermetic settings, their constantly recurrent situations (often the clash of young and old), their deadly observation, their bizarre comedy, these stories are a self-contained education in human folly. Compare these stories with the formless sadism that sometimes passes for realism, and you see quickly enough what separates tragedy from the merely sordid—an ultimate feeling not of waste but of cleansing through pity and fear.

Her constant target throughout is a trashy and secular emancipation (through sentimentality or shallow learning or whatnot) from the darker, earthier side of things. She no sooner establishes the setting and mood with a few deft strokes and peoples it with characters than you see with a terrible clarity where the thing must come out, as in all masters.

You see that the grandfather in "A View of the Woods" loves his granddaughter not wisely but too well, that the flaw in the love is a grasping urge for self-perpetuation, that it invites a terrible penalty.

In "The Lame Shall Enter First," her greatest story, you see that the liberal-minded reformer, Sheppard, in his blindness to the diabolical in a boyish nature, will suffer like Lear. No tragic stage, even with Hamlet or Macbeth at their bloodiest, was ever so littered with corpses as the conclusions of Flannery O'Connor stories. Death is her ever-ready deus ex-machina, the only force powerful and conclusive enough to mend such distortions. Dark it is; but never sordid, never gratuitous.

Just what Miss O'Connor meant to say to us about the modern world or the South, or about the human condition in them, is to me more elusive than some find it. She is too much of an artist to preach. With his exaltation of romance and chivalry, Faulkner, dark as he often is, seems hopeful by comparison. Her world is clearly "theological," just as she says, a world governed

223

by divine laws, too dimly perceived, the violation of which brings judgment—a world awaiting some terrible redemption.

It is a tough secularity that can pass through her writings and emerge as it entered.

—*December 9, 1971*

G. W. Cable: A Voice of Conscience

"Confrontation" is all the rage today, and in this climate of racial politics George W. Cable, storyteller and "Southern heretic" may be doomed to resume the antiquarian interest he had before Edmund Wilson and others revived him a decade ago.*

Cable was an incurable moralist, a civilized man, and so long as the civil rights issue was cast as an issue of conscience and not of clashing hostilities he had something to tell us. Professor Louis Rubin does not, I think, stretch matters when he writes that "what Cable was saying and thinking in the 1880s and 1890s, almost entirely alone among white Americans, would one day be what millions...many of them southerners, would say and think." For a while, anyway.

If yet another contemporary study of Cable needs defending it is not on his merit as a novelist. His most enthusiastic refurbishers—Rubin among them—concede that while his fiction is interesting it is flawed and that his tales, while foreshadowing the Southern realism of our time, are of largely historical interest. His first novel, and his best, a colorful melodrama about Louisiana Creoles called *The Grandissimes*, is a period piece. It delved into the forbidden realms of race and miscegenation. But no reader of *Absalom! Absalom!* could today be awed by its daring.

Rubin does supply here a new and interesting examination of the strains under which Cable worked—chiefly the reticences of the Genteel Tradition. Fortunately there was also a tradition of local color, the making of Whig gentlemen who had painted their social inferiors in a ribald vein not restrained by false constraints—local color being thought sub-literary. It was ready for

---

George W. Cable: The Life and Times of a Southern Heretic, by Louis D. Rubin, Jr. (Pegasus, 1970)

a serious realist like Cable, and in describing the New Orleans scene he strained if he did not finally snap the shackles of gentility.

What is genuinely original about Cable is his view of the race issue. He could not accept the prevailing post-Reconstruction orthodoxy. The longer he strove to understand the nation's racial problem the sharper his dissidence grew, alarming the lurking apologists of the Southern way of life, threatening his own art with an enfeebling preachiness. But even as he wrote, the nation was busily resigning the Negro's fate to the South. Cable's notable tract, "The Freedman's Case in Equity," appeared in the *Century Magazine* in 1885, two years after the Supreme Court had declared the first civil rights act unconstitutional. Influential organs of national opinion—*The New York Times*, the *Nation*—stifled big yawns over the Negro question. Everyone was bored with crusaders. Jim Crow's strange career was in the making. Eight years before, there had occurred the great sellout of 1877, when the party of Lincoln purchased the presidency at the price of leaving the freedmen entirely to the mercies of Southern state governments.

Cable's views on race, although prophetic of the cost of this cynical business, are not without their angularities—and would lack interest if they were. Despite his storyteller's fascination with the wicked sensuality of New Orleans, Cable was himself a Calvinist—a Presbyterian Sunday school-teaching kind of Calvinist. He had lost a job on the New Orleans *Picayune* for refusing to attend and report on the theater. Years later he would with his unyielding sabbatarianism irritate his lecture-platform companion Mark Twain. As a Confederate cavalryman he had always knelt and prayed every night by the campfire.

The declining fortunes of the freedman worried Cable's conscience. The freedman's was a case in *equity*—in simple rightness. Cable did not believe in social equality; in fact, in his first venture into public controversy over race, he had argued that the New Orleans schools need not be segregated because racial differences would assure social apartness. Cable merely felt, as he put it, that the U.S. could afford to allow no class or race to impose on another "a civil status from which no merit of intelligence, virtue or possession can earn an extrication. We have a country large enough for all the *unsociality* anyone may want, but not for *incivility*, either by or without the warrant of law."

The central point has never been more succinctly stated. Yet the southerners were defensive, the northerners heedless. If there existed, as Cable supposed, a "silent South" waiting to rally to a call of conscience it kept its silence. Meanwhile the decrepit Creole historian Gayarré pilloried Cable in the New Orleans press as a man who wanted to "africanize the South." And the celebrated Georgia editor Henry Grady, speaking in a year following 211 lynchings, pulled 100 per cent wool over everyone's eyes. "Nowhere on earth is there kindlier feeling, closer sympathy or less friction between two classes of society than between the whites and blacks of the South today," he said.

Cable would not yield. In 1885 he moved north, less to escape critical arrows than to have his family close by during his lecture tours, but it confirmed the suspicion of his detractors that he was a yankee at heart.

Rubin has written an interesting, serviceable study of an admirable man. But just what place we are to assign to this classic Southern moralist today I am not sure. The clash of white power against black, the cry of "you do your thing, honky, and let us do ours" would have deeply disconcerted him. He seems the honky-liberal par excellence, the figure easy for everyone with an eye for fashion to hate. The dust so recently brushed from his noble brow is, I fear, already gathering there again.

—February 8, 1970

The Battle of the Bibles

Chad Walsh writes with far more civility and good sense about the New English Bible than the usual combatant in the Battle of the Bibles, managing in his generous concessions to the King James Version to disarm all but the most recalcitrant "agnostic aesthetes" who relish the latter's archaicisms merely because they are there.

Walsh assures us, for instance, that the NEB "is not intended primarily for use in public worship" and does not "dare usurpation" of the King James Version at the root of our language. Yet he does suggest, as most of its celebrants do, that it will make Scriptures "more comprehensible to the average reader." He joins less guarded—and less learned—touts of the NEB in this claim: for instance, Louis Cassels, religion columnist of the Associated Press, who calls the NEB "infinitely easier for contemporary readers to understand."

Despite these claims, and not for a moment denying the

226

utility of clarity, especially in the purely narrative portions of the Bible, I suggest that the net effect of the NEB is a loss of clarity, not to mention beauty and force. I would not contest the usual charge that the King James sounds quaint to an age whose Shakespeare, Bacon and Milton are dimly recalled; but the difference seems to me to go beyond quaintness to the very basis of what language is all about.

Sinch Walsh has cited the 23rd Psalm for comparative purposes, awarding the NEB a "polished eloquence" I find elusive, let us pause over it. In the NEB "I shall not want" becomes "I shall want nothing"; "still waters" (an image of consummate clarity) becomes "the waters of peace" (which are apt to be murky); "valley of the shadow of death" becomes "a valley dark as death"; "thou anointest my head with oil" becomes "thou hast richly bathed my head with oil"; "mercy" becomes "love unfailing," and "I shall dwell in the house of the Lord forever" becomes, in the NEB, "my whole life long." Knowing no Hebrew I cannot say whether the new translation is more faithful, but in every instance it surrenders focus and depth to false exactitude. What are "waters of peace"? Is the ancient ritual of anointment the same as "bathing a head richly with oil"? Why destroy the image of death as a shadow by reducing it to unspecific "darkness"?

Cassels, less modestly, cites the NEB version of Psalm 90, Verse 10, as a rendering that "manages to hold its own with the King James in literary beauty while achieving a notable gain in clarity." Let us see.

KJ: "The days of our years are three-score years and ten; and if by reason of strength they be fourscore years, yet is their strength labor and sorrow; for it is soon cut off, and we fly away."

NEB: "Seventy years is the span of our life, eighty if our strength holds; the hurrying years are labor and sorrow. So quickly they pass and are forgotten."

In its majestic sonority, the King James gives us a serious statement about the brevity of life and the limit of human striving. By contrast, I find the NEB uncertain in mood and evasive in diction. I am reminded somewhat of the parody circulated some years ago in which the late President Eisenhower was imagined rewriting the Gettysburg Address in press conferencese, beginning, "About 87 years ago, I think it was..." Hearing the NEB version of Psalm 90 read aloud (as, pace Chad Walsh, it surely will be from trendy Protestant lecterns) I will think of the Whiffenpoof Song, of the tables down at Morey's and how each generation "will pass and be forgotten with the rest."

Of course, any new Englishing of the Bible for a long time

227

has been hailed as a model of clarity. To cite a particularly unfair example, when one Rudolphus Dickinson brought forth his *New and Corrected Version of the New Testament* (Boston, 1833) he deplored the "quaint monotony and affected solemnity...the frequently rude and occasionally barbarous attire" of the King James, promising instead "a sweetly flowing diction" suitable for "accomplished and refined persons." Our ear, debased as it may be, suffices for a last laugh on Dickinson. Thus: "When Elizabeth heard the salutation of Mary, the embryo was joyfully agitated" (Luke 1:41) and "Festus declared with a loud voice, Paul, you are insane! Multiplied research drives you to distraction." (Acts 26:24).

The translators of the New English Bible are not so arrogant as Dickinson, yet they challenge the King James for our ear and we are entitled to ask whether our ear can afford more "clarity" at the expense of depth. I share Lionel Trilling's fear that "people will eventually be unable to say 'we fell in love and married,' let alone understand the language of Romeo and Juliet, but will...say, 'Their libidinal impulses being, reciprocal, they integrated their individual erotic drives...'" "Many young people," Trilling says, "carry no model in their minds by comparison with which they could stamp that sort of thing as barbarism."

No model—that is the key point. That one or another Biblical translation should or could be a "model" does, I know, infuriate the scientific linguists with their quantitative standards, not to speak of the busy inventors of those barbarous newspeaks Trilling has more specifically in mind. I think we "agnostic aesthetes" would be at ease with a translation bidding to supplant the King James Version if it were a truly "modern" landmark of the language. But the NEB seems to me to be neither. The chosen medium of poetry and prose is derivative—an attenuated version of the best of the past. (Walsh's "donnish urbanity" describes it very well.)

There are, of course, writers whose use of the language forms the medium of our age, a very unstable medium, among whom one might mention at random a Hemingway, a Salinger, a Roth, a Mailer, an Updike. It is they, not the translators of Bibles (or even the "specialist" literary consultants of the translators), who formulate the taste of our age—which unlike that of the King James translators is not elitist, not confined to the educated, not stabilized and not shielded for vulgar intrusion. To my mind, the best translators of our age are people like Christopher Logue and William Arrowsmith, working the Greek and Latin clas-

228

sics, and producing what is slangy, pungent and informal. But this resource seems for some reason barred to Biblical translators; and it may be, as I suspect, that we lack the resources to translate the Bible in any contemporary medium at once convincing, pungent, poetic and grave—a medium whose dignity lies in its authenticity. And that, I suggest, is another reason for holding fast to the best we have: the King James Version, incontestably.

—July 19, 1970

Big Brother's Failure

All over George Orwell's fantasyland of Oceania—which, happily, we still know as Britain and North America—people are bracing for the coming New Year's Eve.

They know that they will crawl blearily from bed Jan. 1 into 1984—the most famous (and ominous) fictional date in history.

From January on, moreover, we shall be symposiumed and seminared within an inch of our lives on such unlikely themes as, "Does Ronald Reagan Practice Big Brotherism?" If you thought "The Day After" was oversold, wait until you make it through the alarmist prattle of 1984.

It is, of course, largely nonsense—not Orwell's brilliant novel; merely the proposition that we were or are in danger of becoming like Oceania. Someone has said, catchily, that Orwell's novel "failed as prophecy because it succeeded as a warning." That, too, is nonsense.

Where its warning might have been appropriate (the Soviet Union, Maoist China), "1984" was unavailable and unread. Where it was widely read and admired, in the United States and Western Europe, no such "warning" was needed, because there existed neither the historical basis nor the predisposition for totalitarian statism.

In any event, none of Orwell's imaginary nightmare materialized—at least not literally. The world, though as tense as ever, is not divided into three perpetually warring superstates. Nor is a totalitarian party in charge of Airstrip One (better known as Great Britain). Nor are people in that most private of countries under 24-hour surveillance by two-way telescreens. Nor is there in Whitehall a Ministry of Love, in whose sinister chambers people like Orwell's Winston Smith are tortured and brainwashed.

No, "Oceania" is no more with us than Lilliput.

Why, then, the fuss? It is, I believe, explained by the book's two striking virtues.

The first is its uncannily accurate insight into the psychology of statist terror. If Orwell's imaginings have not been fully acted out, even in the frenzy of Mao's great Cultural Revolution in 1966 China, there has been no more persuasive imaginative picture of the techniques of induced mass-mindedness.

When he was writing this book in the late 1940s, dying of tuberculosis and deeply dejected, Orwell had before him the examples of Stalinist Russia and Nazi Germany. Even with these models, however, it needed extraordinary imagination to add to the familiar devices of torture a disturbing truth: When people are deprived of the small, vital intimacies (love, friendship, loyalty) they may transfer (displace, as the psychiatrists say) these thwarted affections to some messianic political figure. It is not by hostility or brutality alone that Big Brother wins.

The second success of "1984" is to demonstrate, plausibly, how fragile are the reference points of memory and document by which we anchor ourselves in the swirl of time.

By the devices of "doublethink" (eliminating the sense of contradiction), by the "memory holes" down which telltale evidence disappears when it no longer fits the latest authorized version of events, by the "vaporization" of persons into "unpersons"—by such techniques human consciousness in "1984" is constantly remade. It is kneaded and molded like clay, as changing circumstance requires. And all for the sake of keeping "the inner party" in power. For as Orwell knew, tyranny is always its own justification.

Orwellian words and phrases (including the adjective "Orwellian") have entered the language. They are ingenious approximations of manipulative techniques that are, indeed, in use today; and not merely in statist nations.

In the coming months you will hear more than you care to of what a near miss it all has been, how we dodged the grip of Big Brother by the skin of our teeth. Try to overlook it. It never was a real danger in this neck of the planet.

For that we may thank not only a fortunate history (and those who made it fortunate) but also the factor of human resilience. Winston Smith, Orwell's hero, briefly gropes at that factor before relapsing into despair and submissiveness. In the

real world, that spirit, while it may be bowed and even per-
verted by the techniques of terror and psychological manipulation, cannot be snuffed out.

Even in the worst of tyrannies, even today, the nightmare
of total human conditioning remains but an ominous fantasy.
And Orwells' brilliance notwithstanding, it never was otherwise.

—December 8, 1983

Solzhenitsyn:
The "Dark Side" of the Prophet

Our natural impulse—probably as vain as natural—is
to try to fit the characters of great writers to the smooth contours
of "normality." But most of them, especially if Russian, remain
square pegs in our round holes.

Tolstoy did, and so does Alexandr Solzhenitsyn. When the
Kremlin expelled him five years ago, we expected him to fit a
pattern, with tame opinions to match. But as he disclosed his
contempt for our lax, accommodating, democratic habits—especially in the 1977 Harvard commencement address—reaction
set in. Here was a cranky guest who even scorned the lodgings
and values of his host. In the May *Harper's*, there is the first
overtly hostile piece—the first to go beyond criticism of Solzhenitsyn's ideas to an attack on his character. George Feifer
pictures a "mystical authoritarian...hopelessly prone to bombast and error," treacherous to friends, editors and patrons.

How good Mr. Feifer's information is I cannot say. But it is
a dangerous notion that Solzhenitsyn's searching prophecies can
be ignored because he has a "dark side." Solzhenitsyn demands
a hearing, although a critical one. And a good place to start is
his current *Foreign Affairs* article, "Misconceptions About Russia Are a Threat to America."

The article shows, in some detail, that insensitivity to democratic custom that we have come to expect of Solzhenitsyn. And
his impassioned Russian bias leads him to some debatable historical judgments. He suggests, for instance, that the Russians
armies reeling before Hitler's attack in June 1941 saw a chance
to "cast off the scourge of communism"—which came to naught

231

because the U.S. used Lend-Lease "to buy the murderous Stalin's help."

But in the summer of 1941 there was no time to calculate the odds that Hitler's attack on Russia offered an opportunity to stifle communism. That most ardent anti-Bolshevik interventionist of two decades earlier, Winston Churchill, would surely have seized the opportunity if it had existed. It seemed more urgent to forge an alliance to defeat Hitler.

But this is detail. The point is that Solzhenitsyn is outraged that some Westerners identify Russia, the principal *victim* of communism, as its natural *host*. He excoriates historians (e.g., Richard Pipes and George F. Kennan) who take the view that communism is in some sense a culminating expression of Russian autocracy.

"In recent years," he writes, "American scholarship has been noticeably dominated by a most facile, one-dimensional approach, which (explains) the unique events of the 20th century...not as something peculiar to communism, not as a phenomenon new to human history, but as if they derived from primordial Russian national characteristics established in some distant century."

Westerners who lack Solzhenitsyn's impassioned Russian patriotism do tend to see old Czarism writ large in the new communism—reincarnations of Ivan the Terrible and Peter the Great in Lenin and Stalin. Solzhenitsyn protests, not without force: "One could just as easily find two or three kings no whit less cruel in the histories of England, France or Spain, or indeed of any country, and yet no one thinks of reducing the complexity of historical meaning to such figures alone. And in any case, no two monarchs can determine the history of a 1,000-year-old nation."

Of course, Henry VIII had his Thomas More, and Mary Tudor her Cranmer and Ridley, whose martyrdoms affected the tradition of Western freedom far more than any resister of czarist autocracy. It is the Russian tragedy that its martyrdoms have been historically ineffective.

Solzhenitsyn argues nonetheless that an ultimate rehabilitation of the Russian spirit blighted by six decades of Soviet rule is the world's best hope, since communism in his view will not mellow. The West must recognize, he writes, "that communism is irredeemable, that there exist no 'better' variants...that it is incapable of growing 'kinder,' that it cannot survive as an ideology without using terror, and that, consequently, to coexist with communism on the same planet is impossible. Either it will spread, cancer-like, to destroy mankind, or else mankind will have to rid itself of communism (and then face lengthy treatment for secondary tumors)."

Is this the "messianism" with which Solzhenitsyn is sometimes charged? There was a time, a few years ago, when the suggestion that the Russians might ultimately redeem themselves from communism would have been dismissed as hopeless romanticism. It is less easily dismissed today, and for that change of perspective Solzhenitsyn is primarily responsible.

His witness continues to nettle us. He refuses to trim his historical vision to suit conventional expectations. He forces us to face fundamental and uncomfortable questions about our spiritual and political destiny.

—April 17, 1980

The Enduring Genius of Mencken

Sept. 12, 1980, will be the 100th birthday of H. L. Mencken and his home city of Baltimore is gearing up for the centennial year.

He is hardly a forgotten man, to be sure. Old-timers still cherish Henry Louis Mencken for airing out the stuffy '20s; but homage is due from all who savor bracing prose.

There is a lively traffic in Mencken studies today. Mr. Theo Lippman Jr. of *The Baltimore Sun* even informs us that there has been "a recent study of Mencken's thought." His *thought?*

"Thought," in the heavy sense, was never H. L. Mencken's long suit, as he would be the first to say. His rare ventures into "thought"—for example, in his *Treatise on the Gods*, which solemnly swallows whole a shallow anthropological hodgepodge—are uncharacteristically leaden stuff. His forte was not the solemn discourse; it was the breezy, sassy newspaper piece, pegged to a passing event and written on the wing.

Like many incurable Menckenians, I remain indebted to Alistair Cooke. His *Vintage Mencken*—still, I think, the best introductory collection of Mencken's journalism—hit me head-on at a highly impressionable age.

233

For a would-be journalist in search of models, the dicovery of Mencken's bombast was an intoxicating but perilous event. Not only did the style serve the most satisfying irreverence. His targets—philistinism, revivalist religion, Calvinistic politics, Prohibition, Babbitry, plutocracy, the genteel tradition in literature, etc.—were attractive ones; his merciless way with them had its appeal. But it was the manner itself that entranced—Mencken's uncanny agility at stringing words together in explosive, brilliant and funny juxtaposition:

"If I had my way, no man *guilty of golf* would be eligible to any office of trust or profit under the United States, and all female athletes would be shipped to *the white slave corrals of the Argentine.*"

"[George Washington] was not pious. He drank whiskey when he felt chilly, and kept a jug of it handy. He knew far more profanity than scripture, and used it more."

"Until [Lincoln] emerged from Illinois they always put the women, children and clergy to bed when he got a *few gourds of corn aboard*, and it is a matter of unescapable record that his career in the state legislature was indistinguishable from that of a *Tammany Nietzsche.*"

"[William Jennings Bryan] was the most sedulous fly-catcher in American history...His quarry...was not *Musca domestica* but *Homo neandertalensis*. For 40 years he tracked it *with coo and bellow*, up and down the rustic backways of the Republic. Wherever the flambeaux of Chautauqua smoked and guttered, and *the bilge and idealism* ran in the veins, and Baptist pastors *dammed the brooks with the sanctified*, and men gathered who were weary and heavy laden, and their wives who were *full of Peruna and as fecund as the shad*...there the indefatigable Jennings set up his traps and spread his bait."

I have italicized some random words and phrases that strike me as the unique Mencken seasoning—his sage and garlic, salt and pepper. These "gourds of corn," these backwoods women "full of Peruna and fecund as the shad," pastors "damming the brooks with the sanctified," men "guilty of golf." Here are rhetorical signatures you will not find elsewhere.

In his introduction to the *Vintage Mencken*, Alistair Cooke observes that the Mencken style, audacious and sparkling, developed gradually as Mencken read and absorbed Shaw, Nietzsche and Lord Macaulay. It was not visible in his early reporting. It is, like all memorable styles, an artifice, the result of hard work.

But it is naive to suppose that style is ever detachable from the spirit of the man. Mencken on paper is full of mocking ferocity. He sounds like a man-eater, but his friends say that he was a paper man-eater, kindly and meek as a kitten in person. The theatrical cockiness of his opinions was precisely that—theatrical. It was a role, a mask. And "Dear Sir (or Madam): You may be right," was a standard reply to critics.

H. L. Mencken's secret, I think, was a sense of the play-element in all things. Life to him was divine comedy, inviting jovial detachment and laughter. That his work has lasted proves that one route to immortality is a sense of mischief, although if you set out to be mischievous in the grand style, as he did, it helps to be a genius, as he was.

Mencken never lacks imitators, but the ersatz stuff is awfully perishable. Shallow iconoclasm is plentiful in the journalism of any age; but it represents a strained and partial view of the world and a little goes a long way.

Mencken's own iconoclasm never palls. He got away with murder every day. But his readers loved it, and still do.

—September 13, 1979

The Greening of the South

"We receive the illusion of having power over nature, and lose the sense of nature as something mysterious and contingent." A quotation from the latest handbook of ecotactics? The prologue of an Earth Day manifesto? The text of a theologian boosting Saint Francis as the patron of the environmental movement?

In fact, it is the Fugitive poet and critic John Crowe Ransom, writing in his introduction to the Agrarian manifesto *I'll Take My Stand* (1930). The date and authorship of this strikingly contemporary ecological sentiment are worth noting, for the Nashville Agrarians who underwent so much liberal bully-ragging forty years ago for their attack on the myth of industrial progress may be candidates for a revival.

At least the possibility occurs to one; it occurred to me quite suddenly, the other day, when a neighboring journalist, quite a literate and sensible one, pronounced the customary dismissal: "Theirs was no voice of prophecy," he wrote of the Nashville

235

Agrarians of forty years ago, "but an echo of something nostalgic and vaguely foolish."

Indeed? Indeed so—forty years ago. When the twelve Nashville Southerners dug their heels into the cotton patch, crying "whoa" to industrial progress in the South, they exposed themselves to attack on any number of such lines. And they were attacked.

It went without saying that the captains of southern industry, insofar as they could be alarmed by books, thought that the Agrarians had taken leave of their senses; let them stick to poetry. In fact, as everyone knew, almost all of them were men of the academy, centered around Vanderbilt University, the beneficiaries of good salaries and expensive classical educations. Some of them—Ransom himself, Robert Penn Warren, Allen Tate, Andrew Lytle—were poets.

There was, as hard-headed men saw it, something la-de-da in their crabbed pages. Their vision of a life close to nature had little attraction, one might suppose, to the yeoman farmer they extolled, to whom the industrial leviathan meant extra cash income from the local textile mill. The Agrarians seemed to envision the squire with a julep (or more authentically a bourbon-and-branch) in one hand and a well-thumbed copy of Horace in the other, his feet comfortably propped on the veranda rail, while inferiors in a well-defined social hierarchy grunted and sweated in the sun. Dreamers of such dreams—academic Miniver Cheevys—were accused of knowing little economics, less sociology, and nothing at all of public health: even of begrudging indoor plumbing. "Are they unaware of pellagra and hookworm, two flowers of Southern agrarianism?" demanded Gerald Johnson indignantly. His Baltimore colleague Mencken observed that if the Agrarians relied on Tennessee farmers for economic sustenance, "they would be clad in linsey-woolsey and fed on side-meat, and the only books they read would be excessively orthodox." Jonathan Daniels, touring the South in 1938, summed up the liberal South's indictment after an evening of communing in Nashville with Donald Davidson, their fiercest spirit: " a retreat in force to the Old South...the spinning wheel but not the nakedness of Gandhi...velvet and lace, roses and the sword... the denial of bathtubs to the southern rural population."

It is true that Wilbur J. Cash rendered a more discerning judgment a decade later. He conceded that the Vanderbilt Agrarians had encouraged "smugness and sentimentality in many quarters," but he hailed them even so for "puncturing

236

the smugness of Progress, in directing attention to the evils of laissez-faire industrialism."

When I first read the Agrarian manifesto fifteen or twenty years ago, it struck me much as it evidently had Johnson, Mencken, and Daniels—antiquarian and nostalgic in tone, neofeudal in its economic and social views, a bit above-it-all. To a student of eighteen or twenty, what is antiquarian and nostalgic may be fine for literature but seems contemptible in politics. All of us probably missed, as we would not in this environment-conscious age, the key point of what the Agrarians tried to say— the leitmotif of the twelve essays: that humanness is one; that unless work and outlook are organically knit together, the result may be alienation, rootlessness, boredom. Today its animating vision of a way of life more closely harmonized with the natural order seems less fanciful. Certainly its critique of industrialism is far more bracing than any the cold war years permitted, when skepticism of the industrial mystique could be identified as un-American if not un-Southern. In its way, *I'll Take My Stand* foreshadows a good many recent assaults on what Professor Galbraith has called "the industrial discipline," not only *The New Industrial State* but even *The Greening of America*.

Ransom, writing in 1930, went so far as to suggest darkly that "the blind drift of our industrial development" would finally yield "much the same economic system as that imposed by violence on Russia in 1917." Alarmist, perhaps; Ransom may have underrated the restraints of a free polity. Yet the two superstates have embraced remarkably similar visions of the good society, featuring massive industrial power, huge arms establishments, and yielding identical problems of land spoilage, dirty air and water, and few beyond the material human satisfactions.

In any case, the Agrarians of Nashville addressed their wrath to the fallacies and illusions of industrialism; they aimed at altering attitudes—attitudes well worth altering—but the trouble was, forty years ago, that they appealed in the main only to parlor rustics.

No longer. If I understand what Dr. Commoner and the other ecologists are saying, a mere counter-technology, another rabbit pulled from the engineers' hat, will not arrest environmental degeneracy. Our abuses spring naturally from abusive attitudes—the very attitudes resoundingly damned from Nashville in 1930—and they must be readjusted to the rhythms and resources of nature. If, as some of the essayists were at pains to note, that did not spell the doom of the machine age, it at least pointed to an economic order severely chastened by human needs. As Ransom wrote:

> Our vast industrial machine, with its far-flung organs of mass production, is like a Prussianized state which is organized strictly for war and can never consent to peace...But after a certain point this struggle is vain...Nature wears out man before man can wear out nature...The concept of Progress is the concept of man's increasing command...over the forces of nature; a concept which enhances too readily our conceit, and brutalizes our life. I believe there is possible no deep sense of beauty, no heroism of conduct, and no sublimity of religion, which is not informed by the humble sense of man's precarious position in the universe.

Reread today, when smog and eutrophication are front-page news, there remains much in the revolt of the twelve Southerners that is patronizing, even fatuous, and quirkily regional. Thus James Gould Fletcher could register the Southern tory's quaint skepticism of public education, and could relegate Negroes to vocational schools that "produce," in his words, "far healthier and happier specimens...than all the institutions for 'higher learning' we can ever give them." Andrew Lytle, in an otherwise enchanting résumé of the yeoman farmer's life ("The Hind Tit") can rhapsodize over the superiority of the churn, the well and the springhouse to the refrigerator—hind tit, indeed.

In general attitude, all the same, the Agrarians called for that truce with the natural order we are seeking today—a truce we must find, so we are told, if we are not to be extinguished by our own ingenuity. I think a lot of environmentalists will find that these twelve Southern literary tories were speaking their language, though no doubt the discovery will horrify them.

—*July 4, 1971*

Thomas Wolfe:
Of Time and the Artist

I recently undertook an act of homage and piety—I re-read all of Thomas Wolfe's *Look Homeward, Angel* for the first time since high school years. What prompted this was the sudden realization that this great novel of American boyhood is 50 years old this autumn, having first appeared in the year of the Great Crash.

Do I speak of homage and piety? You must understand the special place of this book and its author in North Carolina. Some of us from the Piedmont or the Eastern coastal plain might regret that Thomas Wolfe gave thousands the false impression that the Old North State is entirely mountainous, but no matter. He put Old Catawba, as he called it, on the literary maps; for Carolinians of a certain heritage, he was always *the* writer, as Aristotle was for Greeks *the* philosopher.

For a time in my teenage years Wolfe became a sort of obsession—not just the wonderful tale of Eugene Gant but the writer himself, his struggles to achieve his literary destiny and his association with the state and with the university at Chapel Hill, which he called Pulpit Hill and of which he memorably wrote:

"There was still a good flavor of the wilderness about the place—one felt its remoteness, its isolated charm. It seemed to Eugene like a provincial outpost of great Rome: *the wilderness crept up to it like a beast.*"

Some of us followed Thomas Wolfe to that place in a state of Wolfean intoxication: mesmerized not only by his powers of narrative and characterization, but by the Joycean and Homeric mannerisms of his rather overripe rhetoric.

I shall not forget—it was one of those traumatic events that loom large at the age of 17—the astonished indignation with which an English instructor at Chapel Hill scored the Wolfean apostrophe to the Mojave Desert which I handed in as a freshman theme: *Embarrassing! Really! No! D-plus*. It was a chastening experience.

But such was the spell that Thomas Wolfe cast. So I hardly knew what to expect when I began reading *Look Homeward, Angel* again. Intermittent excursions had left me fearing that it really might be a book for adolescents, too fruity for even the most pious adult reader: that in its cloying intensity it might deserve the verdicts of hostile critics like Alfred Kazin and Bernard DeVoto. Thomas Wolfe had dared greatly, it was true, but the pertinence of Scott Fitzgerald's observation had to be granted: "He who has such infinite power of suggestion and delicacy has no right to glut people on whole meals of caviar."

There *is* a glut of caviar in *Look Homeward, Angel.* Its bookshelf companions are not the chiseled tales of Flaubert or James but the sprawling canvases of Dickens, Sterne, Joyce, and Faulkner at his more exuberant. It tells no story, strictly speaking, but for the story of the precocious and romantic mountain boy, Eugene Gant.

Yet Wolfe could elevate mundane life to a mythic level; and my, how he could draw character. *Look Homeward, Angel* is not only the story of a boy of almost neurasthenic sensitivity; it is the chronicle of a family. Who forgets the Gants? I could not, although at 15 or so I found them hard to believe in—the penny-pinching mother, Eliza, with her real estate schemes; the rip-snorting stonemason-father, Oliver Gant, with his roaring drunks and his self-pitying Lear-like bombast. And all their brawling, sad, disorderly, vital brood.

Wolfe's Altamont (Asheville) reminds you of a Breughel landscape in which gaping yokels, revolving between mischief and indolence, sense death and decay hovering over their rural festivities. Indeed Wolfe writes of Eugene Gant, looking down on Altamont: "He saw it as might...Peter Breughel, in one of his swarming pictures."

The Gants are arty, querulous, turbulent dreamers, always on the brink of tragedy and madness, living narrow lives of almost unearthly intensity. A few, for instance the noble Ben, Eugene's closest older brother, are touched with mysticism. Ben Gant's head is usually cocked, as if addressing some guardian angel. His death of pneumonia, followed by the appearance of his ghost, is one of many episodes in which Wolfe's soaring prose suddenly becomes chastened. It has few rivals in American fiction.

Thomas Wolfe was a controversial case for fastidious critics. They said he was undisciplined, that his novels had to be "processed" and given coherence by the great Scribner's editor, Max Perkins. This whisper drove Wolfe before his early death (in September 1938), to change editors, characters, even styles.

But even if they were right about certain matters of detail they were misled by fastidiousness. Wolfe, when he died, was still toiling to equip himself with the armory of the great masters. Already he was, as Perkins and many of his fellow writers recognized, one of the great originals. After half a century, *Look*

Homeward, Angel, flaws and all, wears well. It has an unmistakable air of permanence.

—November 15, 1979

Master of the Literary Tease

Even an ardent reader of William Faulkner may react to his most sensational novel, *Sanctuary*, as Winston Churchill did to Calcutta. After visiting that dismal city as a young British Army subaltern, Churchill wrote that he was glad to have been there once because he would never have to go again. Similarly, one reading of *Sanctuary*, the story of the impotent gangster, Popeye, and Temple Drake, the college coed whom he rapes with a corncob and abducts to a Memphis brothel, will do for a lifetime.

But *Sanctuary* is back in the news, and for all my resolution I could not resist rereading it.

What has put this disturbing piece of fiction in the news is Mr. Noel Polk's edition of the original text—from which Faulkner rewrote *Sanctuary* for publication in 1930. It offers some important clues to one of the great American literary scams.

It was William Faulkner's mysterious impulse, presumably for delight as well as concealment, to plant misconceptions about his life and work. Not even much later, when he was posing for sophomores at Virginia or West Point as a simple Mississippi farmer who had stumbled into writing, did Faulkner contrive a more entertaining fraud than in his introduction to a cut-rate 1932 edition of *Sanctuary*. Among the powers of any great writer are those of the ventriloquist, adopting made-up voices to go with his masks. Here we have the voice of the *faux-naif*.

"To me," he wrote, "it [the book] is a cheap idea, because it was deliberately conceived to make money." He had not lived among literary folk, he tells us, and didn't know that they wrote for money. He went "a little soft" after the publication of his first two novels and "began to think of books in terms of possible money." So he "speculated what a person in Mississippi would believe to be current trends, chose what I thought was the right answer and invented the most horrific tale I could imagine and wrote it in about three weeks." His editor rejected it, saying that

241

publication would land them both in jail, so William Faulkner claims he just forgot about the manuscript and went to work shoveling coal in a steam plant. When his editor (or publisher) abruptly changed his mind and sent him galley proofs, "I saw that it was so terrible that there were but two things to do: tear it up or rewrite it." He did the latter, he claims, hoping to sell perhaps 10,000 copies.

This was in fact malarkey. Mr. Polk's edition of this "cheap idea...conceived to make money" demonstrates that (a) the first version of *Sanctuary* was an inventive, interesting, even brilliant piece of work which (b) couldn't have been written in three weeks and (c) had nothing beyond its setting to do with "current trends" in Mississippi.

While this literary myth may now be of mainly antiquarian interest, it suggests how our romantic view of the life of writing predisposes us to accept almost any far-fetched deception a writer issues with a straight face. Faulkner, a master of the tease, had only one serious rival in that respect among major American writers—the poet T. S. Eliot, a deeply amused man who posed as ponderous, especially in his famous "footnotes" to "The Waste Land." But the tease Faulkner pulled off in the introduction to the Modern Library edition of *Sanctuary* was his most extravagant by far.

Sanctuary is, indeed, a "horrific tale"—that was almost the only true thing Faulkner said about it. It is also a great novel, filled with memorable characterization and incident. No one who reads it forgets Popeye, the man of "stamped tin" and rubberlike eyes, or Gowan Stevens, the drunken ass of a college boy who abandons his girl friend to Popeye's tender mercies, or any of the others.

In my view, Mr. Polk's only debatable act as an editor is to denigrate the novel's hero (if it can be said to have one), the lawyer Horace Benbow. Benbow is one of those figures—the flawed but sentient and responsible man who is fascinated, repelled and finally defeated by casual brutality—into whom, one suspects, Faulkner poured something of himself.

Benbow, defending a man falsely accused of one of Popeye's murders, tries to avert injustice, obstructed the while by his sister, Narcissa, who like Temple and many others in the story is a slave to respectability. He fails; his client is lynched: burned outside the jailhouse. Benbow is not so strong as some Faulkner heroes (Isaac McCaslin, for instance), but he is not the self-indulgent and unrealistic dreamer Mr. Polk takes him for.

So we know now that Faulkner's account of the origins of

Sanctuary was woven of whole cloth. But we still don't know why this consummate artist who saw so deeply into our nature enjoyed posing, as he did when he set up the mythology of the "cheap" *Sanctuary*, as a naive money-grubber who hardly knew which end was up. But he always insisted that his work should speak for itself. And in this book it speaks with the force of genius.

—March 12, 1981

Hamlet's Problem and Ours

A self-interview about Shakespeare on his 415th birthday? What are your qualifications?

Only that I'm human and able to read; otherwise meager. I studied Shakespeare at Chapel Hill under Prof. Peter Phialas, a splendid teacher. But that was 23 years ago and I was too callow to know how far out of my depth I was—like a novice swimmer in mid-ocean who thinks he's treading four feet of water.

This, then, is a whim?

Not entirely. One December night about a year and a half ago I reread "The Merchant of Venice" for the first time in years. That began a process of reacquaintance. And there are the BBC productions on PBS.

Which are?

A mixed bag. "Richard II" was the best of the first series, superb, some of the others good. I switched off "Romeo and Juliet."

Why?

It was a ghastly production. Besides, there's a strange incongruity in R&J—that lyrical language joined with astrological fatalism. I think of the best story I know about "Romeo and Juliet." On a U.S. Navy ship in the Pacific the crew watched a film version. Afterwards, a hardened sailor sat stunned, shaking his head. "Shakespeare," he was muttering, "you son of a bitch." That's always been my reaction too.

What did you mean when you said you were too callow for Shakespeare 23 years ago?

I was one of the greenest people ever exposed to great drama, a true barbarian. Most of us at 20 are untouched by the thorns, the pities, the graces of life. Shakespeare is wasted on us then. We "understand" it in a certain way, but it doesn't reach the

243

marrow—reading it tends to be an exercise in cleverness. I tended to be distracted by the metaphor—G. Wilson Knight was an awful influence at that age. I remember writing a term paper, "The Image of Breakage in 'Coriolanus,'" but I'm not sure I understood the play at all.

Think how limited our experience is at best. George Steiner, discussing Shakespeare's language, says that "Elizabethan England was still in close, natural contact with rural life. ...A man knew whence his bread came and how it was baked; how his boots were shod and his cloth woven...The names of things retained the subtle liveliness of that which we have held in hand." Besides, how many of us, at age 20, can conceive of the ambition of Macbeth, the metaphysical worries of Hamlet, the calamitous passions of Othello or Cleopatra? It is too heroic to be believed.

And now?

Now, in middle age, you begin to see the richness and *accuracy* of the characterizations and the justice of their consequences.

Can you be more specific? If you had to be marooned with only one play, which would it be?

"Hamlet," hands down. It has everything—except a master key. But that's part of the fun. Did you ever read John Dover Wilson's book, *What Happens in Hamlet?* It is one of our great detective stories. And the discussion never ends. William Gibson, one of our best playwrights, has a new book, *Shakespeare's Game*, studying the Shakespeare plays as laboratory cases in dramatic technique. Of the jumbled progression of "Hamlet," he asks, "Can we not lend a hand to this poor writer?" and relocates "one great chunk" of Shakespeare's words. It makes more sense of the play. But a hundred scholars are probably at their typewriters to reprimand Mr. Gibson for taking these liberties.

If "Hamlet" is such a puzzle, what is Hamlet's problem?

Hamlet is a very young, very shocked, very troubled hero—prodigiously disgusted by the rottenness of the court, shocked by the flouting of natural loyalties, fearful that his father's ghost may be an illusion, seeking certainties in a world suddenly emptied of them.

That's deep water, all right. Speaking of which, do you ever wonder how Shakespeare became Shakespeare?

I am not a Baconian, if that's what you mean. Prodigy usually finds its way. Shakespeare found a high tradition waiting, it was one of those consummate intersections of man and moment, like Newton or Einstein, one still influential world dying, another approaching but undefined. Our society is unstable and

244

untraditional and our dominant spirit is one of exclusivity. We are temperamental heirs of the puritans, who bashed out the stained glass, broke up the pipe organs and closed the theaters. That kind of politicized high seriousness finds the catholicity and curiosity, the inclusivity, of Shakespeare uncongenial. You must be a bit simple-minded to be a passionate partisan; he never was. As John Dover Wilson says, "Shakespeare never committed himself deeply to a cause or a point of view, whatever his affection or admiration for those who held it might be, because life itself in its infinite variety is far more interesting than any opinion, doctrine or point of view about it."

You make reading Shakespeare sound dangerous, even subversive.

It is. After more than four centuries he makes all else seem superficial. Follow any tangent from the day's news—any extravagance or perversity, any passion, any heroic enterprise, any character flaw—and you will find Shakespeare there before you, hounding the matter right to the core. It is intimidating, but in its way very liberating too. He makes us human.

—May 3, 1979

Phillips Russell

In a memorable portrait of William Strunk, his writing teacher at Cornell, E. B. White tells us that Strunk felt so strongly about his precepts of English style that he was given to triple admonitions: "Be brief. Be brief. Be brief," he would say.

Any master teacher teaches by reiteration, and especially teachers of writing. I don't recall that Phillips Russell of Chapel Hill repeated his maxims in triplicate; but all had the fixity and simplicity of tried wisdom: "Be specific. Be specific. Be specific," was perhaps his most famous. By this he meant that you don't call a water oak a tree, though for God's sake don't call it a lonely sentinel either.

I have been thinking about my days at Mr. Russell's feet in Chapel Hill, since at this commencement season both that institution (he was in the class of '03) and another have had the discrimination to confer honorary doctorates of letters upon him.

245

They formalized a rank that his students long ago recognized in gratitude.

In my day, the university catalog described Mr. Russell's course as "creative writing," although in a typical gesture of independence he had moved it years before from the English Department to the department of journalism. His complaint was simple: It was that an earlier cadre of English professors, his quondam colleagues, considered that nothing of consequence had happened to the written language since Tennyson. But I think he also sought the plainer spirit of journalism, believing that good writing, "creative" or otherwise, was a matter of hard labor, not waiting for the muse to strike. I never heard him mention it, but I am sure Mr. Russell subscribed to the clever remark attributed to Thomas Mann: A writer is someone who finds it hard to do what others do easily.

His precepts were plain and challenging; and like Strunk he pounded them home by repetition:

"If you're going to write about a bear," he would say, "bring on the bear." He would then tell the story of how he was reading "Goldy-locks and the Three Bears" to his small daughter and how she, annoyed at the preliminary stage-setting, exclaimed: "I thought this was a story about a bear. Bring on the bear!"

Or he would say: "If you put a gun in a story, someone should fire it to some purpose before the story ends."

Or: "If you want to interest somebody in a story from the outset, don't write: 'He went to the window and looked out,' Write: 'He went to the window and looked out—but drew back.'"

Another bedrock Russell principle was that the human mind will willingly follow and absorb only three points at once—a rule to be violated by Shakespeare (five acts) or Milton (12 books), perhaps, but not by his students. "Structure, structure, structure," he might have intoned. Good writing, like a good bridge, rests on sound architecture and engineering.

Not that he ignored diction. There was, as I have said, the constant injunction, "Be specific." There were also basic drills. One was to write an essay using only one-syllable words—only in that way could you discover how the heart of a strong sentence is the interaction of simple verbs and nouns, unencumbered by adjectives and adverbs. The other was to study and imitate two forms of Oriental writing—the Confucian analect (or apogthegm) and the Japanese haiku (or picture-poem). Where a thought or a picture must be vividly relayed in a spare sentence or two the essential role of a crisp verb in the active voice comes clear.

The Russell doctrines of writing sprang from the attentive observation of books and people, which is to say from Phillips Russell's own character. Before returning to teach at Chapel Hill he had worked as a journalist in London and Philadelphia; he had trekked the wilds of the Yucatan and written a book about it; he had worked as a publicity agent for figures as diverse as Jack Dempsey and Rudolf Valentino, and had written an assortment of biographies—notably one that had first unearthed the obscure Parisian gallantries of Benjamin Franklin and had nearly become a best-seller of the 1920s.

Like all great teaching, his was a distillation of great character. Today in "retirement" he wears his 87 years as gracefully as he wore 72 in the upstairs classroom in Bynum Hall. He tells me that his next book will be called "Great Teachers and What They Taught." In fairness, he ought to include a chapter about himself.

—June 9, 1971

Acknowledgments

ALL THE PIECES in this collection, with the exceptions listed below, appeared in the *Greensboro Daily News* (before June, 1975) or the *Washington Star* (between June 1975 and August 1981), or *The Washington Post* and other newspapers (after August 1981). "W. J. Cash After A Quarter of a Century" and "Eckhardt of Texas" appeared in *Harper's Magazine;* "Louisiana's Kingfish" in *Saturday Review;* "Jonathan Daniels Remembered" in *The Washington Journalism Review;* "Francis W. Dawson Revisited" in *South Carolina Journals and Journalists,* edited by James B. Meriwether, Columbia, S. C., 1975; "An Irrepressible Conflict," "The Importance of Being Earnest," "G. W. Cable: A Voice of Conscience," and "Battle of the Bibles" in Book World, the book supplement of *The Washington Post;* "The Dixiefication of Dixie" in *Dixie Dateline,* Edited by John B. Boles, Rice University Studies, Houston, Tex., 1983; "The South Goes On," in *Virginia Quarterly Review;* "Cotton-Patch Spenglers," in *The Enduring South,* By John Shelton Reed, Chapel Hill, 1974; "Heroic Fidelity" in *National Review.*